THE STATE OF FOOD AND AGRICULTURE 1997

FAO Agriculture Series No. 30

ISSN 0081-4539

THE STATE OF FOOD AND AGRICULTURE 1997

FOOD AND AGRICULTURE ORGANIZATION OF THE UNITED NATIONS
Rome, 1997

The statistical material in this publication has been prepared from the information available to FAO up to July 1997.

David Lubin Memorial Library
Cataloguing in Publication Data

FAO, Rome (Italy)
The state of food and agriculture 1997.
ISBN 92-5-104005-2

(FAO Agriculture Series, no. 30)
ISSN 0081-4539

1. Agriculture   2. Food production
3. Food security   4. Agro-industrial complexes

I. Title   II. Series

FAO code: 70   AGRIS: E16 E21

Printed in Italy

Foreword

Although the year 1996 was rich in momentous developments, the World Food Summit surely was among the major events of the year. The historic importance of the Summit should not be understated. Never before had leaders of the world gathered in such large numbers to work together for such a deserving cause.

The Summit has conveyed one fundamental message: although hundreds of millions of people around the world are still suffering from hunger and malnutrition, world food security is an achievable goal. Indeed, participants of the Summit committed themselves to halve the number of malnourished by the year 2015 at the latest. There is no doubt that securing food for all is an immense task. It is equally true, however, that no other endeavour can be compared in urgency with the achievement of world food security. This is so on moral grounds – freedom from hunger is a right of everyone, as was repeatedly emphasized at the Summit – but also because ensuring world food security is of critical interest to all, being a precondition for world peace and security.

We are confident that the Summit's message has been heard. This optimism is derived from the fact that an impressive number of countries and parties, represented at the highest levels of technical competence and responsibility, worked together to make this meeting a success; heads of state and government unanimously endorsed the Rome Declaration and the World Food Summit Plan of Action, a realistic and necessary guide for defining and implementing food-related policies at the national and international levels; and many countries have already initiated activities aimed at translating the principles contained in the Plan of Action into specific policy action.

The State of Food and Agriculture this year reports that numerous concrete initiatives have recently been taken or strengthened to address the various dimensions of food security, including through formulating and coordinating the implementation of integrated food security programmes. We also welcome the fact that, after earlier positive signs, many poor countries have seen their prospects for food security further improve because of their success in creating a policy environment conducive to sustained economic and agricultural growth. Although economic and food security problems remain serious in Africa, the improvement made in much of the region over the past two years is most heartening in this respect. Furthermore, a number of countries in Latin America and the Caribbean and Asia and the Pacific appear to have entered a phase of solidly based growth, sustained in many cases by a good performance of the agricultural sector. The fact that many economies that are crucially dependent on commodity exports have shown resilience to the weakening prices of several of these commodities since 1994-95 has been a significant and encouraging feature of the past year.

Despite these positive developments we cannot ignore the fact that, for many parts of the world, the current situation and future prospects are less than bright. The global economic environment demonstrates many positive features and favourable trends, but it also shows uncertainties and latent risks, including that of perpetuating or even accentuating inequities. The concept of globalization could become a threat for many economies and large segments of society that are facing increasing risks of marginalization. Many delegations at the World Food Summit raised the point that privatization, free market and foreign direct investment cannot obviate the need for development aid; yet such aid, including for agricultural development, continues to shrink. Many countries continue to be ensnared by debt and therefore face major obstacles to creating a basis for sustainable growth or an environment that attracts foreign capital. Many others find it impossible to gain competitiveness to the extent and at the speed required by the rising tide of free trade. In these circumstances, it is hardly surprising that income and food security gaps among countries have tended to widen in recent years, as indicated in this publication.

This year's special chapter of *The State of Food and Agriculture* focuses on the agroprocessing industry and its symbiotic links with economic and agricultural and rural development. The problem of food security is also related in a significant measure to the efficient processing and distribution of agricultural products. Agroprocessing industries represent in many countries an important component of overall economic activity and trade, as well as being a sizeable source of employment and income and, thus, access to food. The special chapter explores the rapidly changing conditions for agroprocessing development in the face of factors such as liberalizing world markets, technological innovation, changing patterns of consumption and the increasing importance of international capital activities in agro-industry. It focuses on the implications of these trends and issues for the developing countries and explores the policy lines that might optimize agro-industry's contribution to sustainable economic and agricultural development.

Jacques Diouf
DIRECTOR-GENERAL

Contents

PART III
THE AGROPROCESSING INDUSTRY AND ECONOMIC DEVELOPMENT

ANNEX TABLE

EXHIBITS

BOXES

TABLES

FIGURES

Acknowledgements

The State of Food and Agriculture 1997 was prepared by a team from the Agriculture and Economic Development Analysis Division, led by F.L. Zegarra and comprising J. Skoet, L. Glassco and S. Teodosijevic. Secretarial support was provided by S. Di Lorenzo and P. Di Santo. Statistical and research support was provided by G. Arena and P.L. Iacoacci.

Contributions and background papers for the World review were prepared by M. Palmieri (Forestry: production and trade), FAO Fisheries Department (Fisheries: catch, disposition and trade), L. Naiken and P. Narain (External assistance to agriculture), D. Vanzetti (Global climate change abatement policies: implications for developing countries), R. Stringer and L. Drewery (Raising women's productivity in agriculture) and S.M. Braatz (Forests in a global context). The sections on food shortages and emergencies, the cereal market situation, food aid and international agricultural prices were prepared by the staff of the Commodities and Trade Division units supervised by J. Greenfield, P. Fortucci, W. Lamadé, A. Rashid and H. Ryan.

Contributions and background papers for the Regional review were prepared by P. Bonnard (Angola and Mozambique), D.H. Brooks (Asia and the Pacific), L. Glassco (Bangladesh), S. Hafeez (Near East and North Africa), J. Budavari (Central and Eastern Europe) and W. Liefert (Russian Federation).

The special chapter, Agroprocessing industry and economic development, was prepared by J. Skoet with contributions from P. Scandizzo, M. Spinedi and P. De Castro.

The State of Food and Agriculture 1997 was edited by R. Tucker. The graphics were prepared by G. Maxwell, the layout by M. Criscuolo with G. Ancona and S. Fava, cover and illustrations by O. Bolbol.

Glossary

ACPC
Association of Coffee Producing
Countries
APRA
American Popular Revolutionary
Alliance (Peru)
AsDB
Asian Development Bank
ASEAN
Association of Southeast Asian
Nations

BADC
Bangladesh Agricultural
Development Corporation

CAC
Codex Alimentarius Commission
CAP
Common Agricultural Policy
CEFTA
Central European Free Trade
Agreement
CGIAR
Consultative Group on International
Agricultural Research
CIS
Commonwealth of Independent
States
COMESA
Common Market for East and
Southern Africa
CPI
Consumer price index
CSD
Commission on Sustainable
Development (UN)

DAC
Development Assistance Committee
DES
Dietary energy supply

ECLAC
Economic Commission for Latin
America and the Caribbean
EHDAEs
Economies highly dependent on
agricultural exports
ERSAP
Economic Reform and Structural
Adjustment Programme (Egypt)
ESAF
Enhanced structural adjustment
facility
EU
European Union

FAC
Food Aid Convention
FDI
Foreign direct investment
FRELIMO
Frente para a Libertação de
Moçambique

GCC
Gulf Cooperation Council
GCMs
General circulation models
GDP
Gross domestic product
GNP
Gross national product

HIPCs
Heavily indebted poor countries
HYVs
High-yielding varieties

IBRD
International Bank for Reconstruction
and Development
ICAC
International Cotton Advisory
Committee

IDA
International Development Association

IEFR
International Emergency Food Reserve

IFAD
International Fund for Agricultural Development

IFPRI
International Food Policy Research Institute

IMF
International Monetary Fund

IRRI
International Rice Research Institute

ISA
International Sugar Agreement

ISIC
International Standard Industrial Classification of All Economic Activities (UN)

LIFDCs
Low-income food-deficit countries

MERCOSUR
Southern Common Market

MMA
Minimum market access

MP
Muriate of potash

MPLA
Movimento Popular de Libertação de Angola

MVA
Manufacturing value added

NGO
Non-governmental organization

NIEs
Newly industrializing economies

OECD
Organisation for Economic Co-operation and Development

OPEC
Organization of the Petroleum Exporting Countries

PRE
Economic Rehabilitation Programme (Mozambique)

PRESA
Programa de Reactivación Agropecuaria y Seguridad Alimentaria (Peru)

PRONAA
Programa Nacional de Ayuda a la Alimentación (Peru)

PSE
Producer subsidy equivalent

RENAMO
Resistência Nacional Moçambicana

SAARC
South Asian Association for Regional Cooperation

SADC
Southern African Development Community

SARD
Sustainable Agriculture and Rural Development

TSP
Triple superphosphate

UNCED
United Nations Conference on Environment and Development

UNCTAD
United Nations Conference on Trade and Development

UNDP
United Nations Development Programme

UNEP
United Nations Environment Programme

UNIDO
United Nations Industrial
Development Organization
UNITA
União Nacional para a
Independência Total de Angola

WAEMU
West African Economic and Monetary
Union

WFP
World Food Programme
WHO
World Health Organization
WTO
World Trade Organization

Explanatory note

Symbols
The following symbols are used:

- = none or negligible (in tables)
... = not available (in tables)
$ = US dollars

Dates and units
The following forms are used to denote years or groups of years:
1996/97 = a crop, marketing or fiscal year running from one calendar year to the next
1996-97 = the average for the two calendar years

Unless otherwise indicated, the metric system is used in this publication.
"Billion" = 1 000 million.

Statistics
Figures in statistical tables may not add up because of rounding. Annual changes and rates of change have been calculated from unrounded figures.

Production indices
The FAO indices of agricultural production show the relative level of the aggregate volume of agricultural production for each year in comparison with the base period 1989-91. They are based on the sum of price-weighted quantities of different agricultural commodities after the quantities used as seed and feed (similarly weighted) have been deducted. The resulting aggregate therefore represents disposable production for any use except seed and feed.

All indices, whether at the country, regional or world level, are calculated by the Laspeyres formula. Production quantities of each commodity are weighted by 1989-91 average international commodity prices and summed for each year. To obtain the index, the aggregate for a given year is divided by the average aggregate for the base period 1989-91.

Trade indices
The indices of trade in agricultural products are also based on the base period 1989-91. They include all the commodities and countries shown in the *FAO Trade Yearbook*. Indices of total food products include those edible products generally classified as "food".

All indices represent changes in current values of exports (free on board [f.o.b.]) and imports (cost, insurance, freight [c.i.f.]), expressed in US dollars. When countries report imports valued at f.o.b., these are adjusted to approximate c.i.f. values.

Volumes and unit value indices represent the changes in the price-weighted sum of quantities and of the quantity-weighted unit values of products traded between countries. The weights are, respectively, the price and quantity averages of 1989-91, which is the base reference period used for all the index number series currently computed by FAO. The Laspeyres formula is used to construct the index numbers.

Geographical designations
The Annex Table shows the regions and groupings in which countries are classified for statistical purposes.

Developing countries include those in sub-Saharan Africa, Latin America and the Caribbean, the Near East and North Africa[1] and Asia and the Pacific.[2] The countries in transition are classified as developed countries.[3]

Country and city designations used in this publication are those current during the period in which the data were prepared.

---

[1] The Near East and North Africa includes: Afghanistan, Algeria, Bahrain, Cyprus, Egypt, Iran, Iraq, Jordan, Kuwait, Lebanon, Libyan Arab Jamahiriya, Morocco, Oman, Qatar, Saudi Arabia, the Sudan, Syrian Arab Republic, Tunisia, Turkey, United Arab Emirates and Yemen.

[2] Asia and the Pacific also includes the former Asian centrally planned economies: Cambodia, China, Democratic People's Republic of Korea, Mongolia and Viet Nam.

[3] The "countries in transition" include:Albania, Bosnia and Herzegovina, Bulgaria, Croatia, Czech Republic, Hungary, The Former Yugoslav Republic of Macedonia, Poland, Romania, Slovakia, Slovenia, Yugoslavia and the newly independent republics, Armenia, Azerbaijan, Belarus, Estonia, Georgia, Kazakstan, Kyrgyzstan, Latvia, Lithuania, Republic of Moldova, Russian Federation, Tajikistan, Turkmenistan, Ukraine and Uzbekistan.

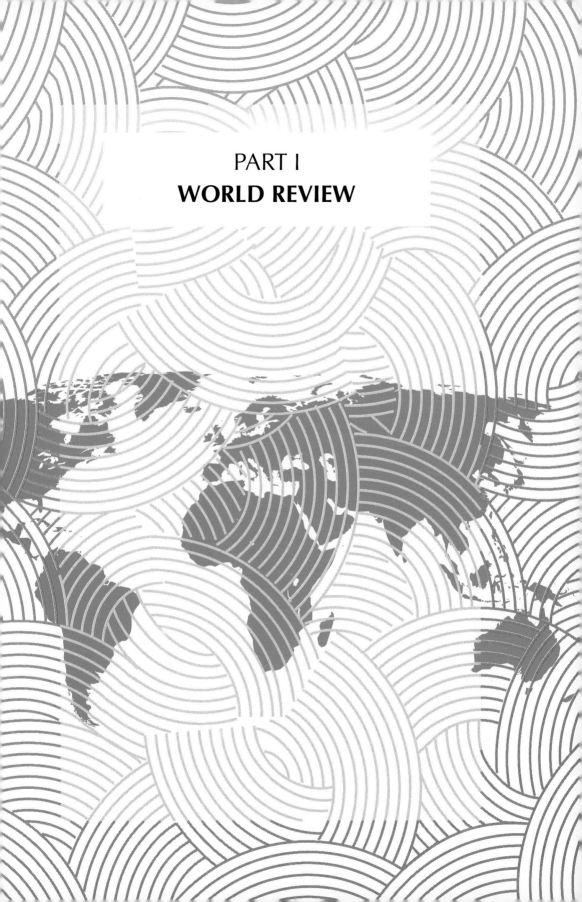

PART I
WORLD REVIEW

WORLD REVIEW

RECENT DEVELOPMENTS IN WORLD FOOD SECURITY

The Sixth World Food Survey,[1] issued shortly before the World Food Summit, concluded that while significant progress has been achieved in global food security during the past decades, 20 percent of the population in the developing countries still had inadequate access to food in 1990-92 compared with 35 percent two decades earlier. The absolute number of people with inadequate access to food had declined only slightly from 920 million in 1969-71 to 840 million in 1990-92. As was forcefully pointed out during the World Food Summit, the latter is an unacceptably high figure and implies that about one out of five people in the developing world was facing food inadequacy in 1990-92. This is what motivated the World Food Summit's commitment to halve, by 2015 at the latest, the present number of undernourished people. The set of objectives and actions for this purpose were enunciated in the World Food Summit Plan of Action.

Assessing more recent developments in food security presents a number of difficulties, given data limitations for a large number of countries. The interpretation of short-term changes in indicators underlying food security should also be subject to caution, as such changes may reflect, for the countries concerned, transient factors that have limited significance in food security trends. Nevertheless, recent data do present a number of distinct patterns that enable tentative conclusions to be drawn.

Table 1 presents selected indicators relating to food availability, stability and access in developing countries. The countries are grouped according to average levels of dietary energy supply (DES) in 1993-95 (column 4). A close relationship between the various indicators is evident: in particular, the higher the average per caput income (column 11), the lower the level of relative food inadequacy[2] (column 6) and the higher the ability to finance food imports (columns 13 to 16).

---

[1] FAO. 1996. *The Sixth World Food Survey*. Rome.
[2] The methodology for assessing food inadequacy in a given country is explained in *The Sixth World Food Survey*, Appendix 3. This methodology replaces the Aggregate Household Food Security Index, previously developed for the Committee on Food Security assessment reports.

TABLE 1

Selected indicators relating to food security in developing countries, by DES group

1	2	3	4	5	6	7	8	9	10	11	12	13	14	15	16
Country classes by DES levels in 1993-95	Number of countries	DES (kcal per caput/day)			Percentage of under-nourished population, 1990-92 average	Food production per caput (% annual changes)				Real GDP per caput (1987 US$)		Share of food imports in total exports		Share of food imports in total imports	
		1989-91 average	1993-95 average	Percentage change 1989-91 to1993-95		1994	1995	1996	1991-96 average	1993-95	Average annual change, 1990-94 (%)	1989-91 (%)	1993-95 (%)	1989-91 (%)	1993-95 (%)
<2 000	20	1 941	1 853	-4.5	52	-1.3	-1.4	3.1	0.0	343	-4.2	40	55	20	25
2 001-2 300	21	2 213	2 158	-2.5	34	0.3	-2.2	0.3	-0.6	603	0.5	36	44	15	16
2 301-2 500	22	2 406	2 397	-0.4	23	-0.1	2.2	-0.3	0.0	1 573	-0.5	24	26	12	14
2 501-2 800	18	2 548	2 653	4.1	18	1.5	1.8	-0.1	1.2	1 740	2.9	12	13	11	11
2 801-3 000	8	2 787	2 888	3.6	9	-0.1	0.5	1.3	1.0	4 000	1.4	15	16	13	13
>3 000	14	3 135	3 234	3.2	6	0.1	2.0	8.1	4.3	4 736	2.5	19	19	11	11

Note: This review focuses on experiences at the country level. Therefore, all country group averages are simple arithmetic averages, in which all the countries are given equal weight. Population-weighted averages were inappropriate for the purposes of this review, since a few countries dominate each of the country groups in terms of population. It may be noted, nevertheless, that the percentages of undernourished population in the different groups, as shown in column 6, are very close to population-weighted averages.
Sources: FAO and World Bank data.

As regards recent trends, the following main features can be observed:

• For most indicators relating to food security, the overall pattern seems to be one of a growing gap between the countries with relatively high levels of average food intake and those with relatively low levels. Indeed, average levels of DES declined between 1989-91 and 1993-95 in the countries where such levels were already initially very low but rose significantly in a majority of countries where the DES was already relatively high. Whereas the average per caput DES of the 20 countries with the lowest levels in 1989-91 was 1 941 kcal per caput/day, it had declined to a mere 1 853 in 1993-95, indicating more widespread and deeper food insecurity in the latter period. Nevertheless, on a positive note, countries that recorded higher DES levels included some of the most populous countries in each region: Argentina, Brazil, Colombia and Mexico in Latin America and the Caribbean; Nigeria in Africa; China, India and Indonesia in Asia; and Egypt, the Islamic Republic of Iran, Morocco, the Syrian Arab Republic and Turkey in the Near East.

• Whereas only 14 countries had a per caput DES of less than 2 000 kcal in 1989-91, the number of such countries increased to 20 in 1993-95, which is further evidence of a worsening situation at the lower end of the food security scale. Moreover, at least two of the countries with a DES of less than 2 000 kcal in 1993-95 (Mongolia and Togo) had a DES of more than 2 200 kcal in 1989-91. Despite limited progress in a few countries, only one, Rwanda, had graduated from the <2 000 category. However, more recent data for this country would probably have shown a marked deterioration of the situation as a consequence of civil strife and poor production and trade performances.

• Underlining the close correlation between domestic supply performances and food intake levels, the largest gains in per caput food production during 1991-96 again took place in countries with already high levels of DES. Food production increased at particularly robust rates in countries with a DES of more than 3 000 kcal per caput/day (those in North Africa, except the Libyan Arab Jamahiriya, being among the highest), and moderately in those with a DES between 2 500 and 3 000 (although China, Ghana and Myanmar achieved major gains in per caput food production). By contrast, no progress, and even some deterioration, was recorded in the countries with a DES of less than 2 000. Among the 20 countries in the latter group, only Ethiopia, and to a lesser extent Angola,

Cambodia, Chad, Malawi, Zambia and Zimbabwe, achieved
significant gains in per caput food production during 1991-96.

• The strongest gains in per caput GDP accrued to countries where
DES levels were above 2 500 kcal. In the group of countries with a
DES of more than 3 000 kcal, strong gains in per caput income
between 1990-92 and 1993-95 were recorded, particularly in
Argentina, the Republic of Korea and the Syrian Arab Republic.
Asian countries in the 2 500 to 3 000 DES bracket, such as China,
Indonesia, Malaysia, Thailand and Viet Nam, also recorded strong
growth in per caput income. Other examples of rapidly expanding
economies with relatively high levels of DES included those of
Chile, Panama and Uruguay. In stark contrast, countries with the
lowest levels of DES actually saw declines in per caput GDP. Such
declines were dramatic in Haiti, Angola, Mongolia and Sierra Leone,
but all other countries in the <2 000 DES group, except
Mozambique and Cambodia, experienced falling or stagnating per
caput incomes. Tentative data for Afghanistan point to a particularly
disquieting situation, as its average food consumption level was the
lowest of all (1 456 kcal per caput/day in 1993-95, 24 percent less
than in 1989-91). Furthermore, Afghanistan's per caput food
production fell significantly during 1991-95 and collapsed in 1996,
owing to a combination of civil strife, resultant large-scale
population displacements and a shortage of inputs because foreign
exchange reserves were diverted to import food for current
consumption.

• A similarly unfortunate turn of events is suggested by indicators of
the financial weight of food imports (the indicators being the ratios
of food imports to total imports and food imports to total exports).
Not only do food imports represent a large share of total trade in
countries with a low DES (more than 50 percent of the value of total
exports in those with a DES of less than 2 000 kcal per caput/day in
recent years), but the relative weight of such imports appears to be
growing. By contrast, the ratios remained relatively constant in the
countries with higher levels of DES. For several countries in the
<2 300 groups, including Mozambique, Haiti, Comoros, Rwanda,
the Gambia and Sierra Leone (and a few others in higher DES
classes), the value of food imports exceeded that of total export
earnings. An extreme case was that of Iraq, where the trade
sanctions following the years of conflict brought the food imports-
total exports ratio from 57 percent in 1989-91 to 189 percent in
1993-95. While in some cases these situations implied the
availability of other sources of import financing, such as tourism and
remittances, in most cases they were explained by grave

shortcomings in the export sector and a strong dependence on food aid or various forms of concessional financing.

• Of the 20 countries with a per caput DES of less than 2 000 kcal per caput/day in 1993-95, 16 are in Africa (three – Afghanistan, Cambodia and Mongolia – are in Asia, and one – Haiti – in Latin America and the Caribbean). In 10 of the 16 African countries, the precarious food intake situation in 1989-91 further deteriorated in 1993-95. The steepest declines in DES (of 7 percent or more) in Africa in the <2 000 kcal category were to be found in Togo, the United Republic of Tanzania, Liberia, Somalia, the Democratic Republic of the Congo and Zimbabwe. Such gravely deteriorating situations resulted from a variety of factors, including adverse climatic conditions and problems of transition as economies shifted from strong government control to a liberalized environment. However, the worst deteriorations were often associated with civil strife and political instability. In particular, the civil war in Somalia, combined with natural disasters, resulted in a dismal food security situation that has tended to worsen in recent years. With a per caput DES of only 1 727 kcal already in 1989-91, the country faced further declines in food production (by 1.7 percent per annum in the 1991-96 period), large population displacements associated with the civil strife and the destruction of economic infrastructure. The worsening food security situation in Liberia is also mostly a result of civil strife, while the breakdown of economic and administrative infrastructure was at the root of a marked deterioration of food security conditions in the Democratic Republic of the Congo

• Despite the apparent growing polarization between countries at the high and low ends of the income and food security scales since the early 1990s, the most recent years have seen a number of encouraging developments. The good news came mainly from the region of Africa. As reviewed below, sub-Saharan Africa as a whole saw its crop and livestock production expand significantly in 1995 and more markedly in 1996, with a majority of countries sharing in the expansion. Further, the economic upturn that took place in sub-Saharan Africa in 1994-95 broadened in 1996, bringing the region's GDP growth rate in the latter year to about 5 percent, the highest in two decades.

WORLD REVIEW
I. Current agricultural situation – facts and figures

1. CROP AND LIVESTOCK PRODUCTION IN 1996

• Estimates of crop and livestock production in 1996 indicate growth at the global level of 2.6 percent, close to the rate of 2.4 percent recorded in 1995. However, while the expansion in 1995 reflected strong output expansion in developing countries and a contraction in developed countries, the estimated increase in 1996 was more balanced between the two country groups. For the developing countries as a whole, the 2.9 percent growth in crop and livestock production in 1996 represented a significant slowdown relative to the preceding years (5.2 percent in 1995, 5 percent in 1994 and 4 percent in 1993). For the developed countries, the increase of 2.4 percent in 1996 represents a recovery after the 1.9 percent decline of the previous year.

• The expansion in output in the developed countries mainly reflected a recovery in North America from the sharp weather-induced drop the previous year. In the United States, crop and livestock production in 1996 increased by an estimated 5.5 percent, largely recovering from the 6.1 percent fall in 1995. In particular, crop production rebounded by an estimated 12.1 percent after the 15.3 percent drop recorded in 1995 but still remained short (by about 5 percent) of the record production level of 1994. Crop and livestock production also expanded in Canada by a robust 3.1 percent, continuing the upward trend of the previous years. In the European Union (EU), production grew by 3.1 percent after three years of declining output. Increases of 4.5 and 2.7 percent were recorded in Australia and New Zealand, while production in Japan fell by 1.9 percent.

• After the halt in the downward trend in crop and livestock production experienced in 1995, production in the transition countries fell further in 1996, although at a more moderate rate of an estimated 1.9 percent. The decline was concentrated mainly in the Eastern European transition countries (-4.6 percent after the 6.1 percent increase in 1995). Substantial production shortfalls were recorded, in particular in Bulgaria, Romania, the Federal Republic of Yugoslavia and Poland. Within the area of the former USSR as a

Exhibit 1

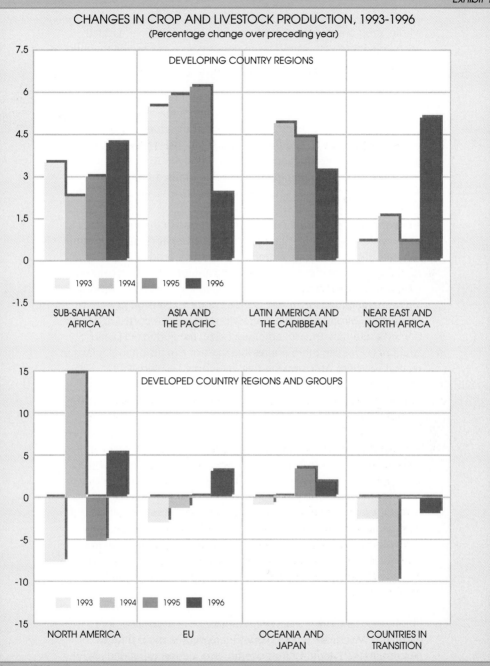

CHANGES IN CROP AND LIVESTOCK PRODUCTION, 1993-1996
(Percentage change over preceding year)

DEVELOPING COUNTRY REGIONS

1993 1994 1995 1996

SUB-SAHARAN AFRICA | ASIA AND THE PACIFIC | LATIN AMERICA AND THE CARIBBEAN | NEAR EAST AND NORTH AFRICA

DEVELOPED COUNTRY REGIONS AND GROUPS

1993 1994 1995 1996

NORTH AMERICA | EU | OCEANIA AND JAPAN | COUNTRIES IN TRANSITION

Source: FAO

whole, crop and livestock production in 1996 remained virtually unchanged, but with variations in performance among the republics. In particular, production is estimated to have expanded by 3.8 percent in the Russian Federation and by 1.5 percent in Kazakstan. In both cases this represents the first year of increasing total agricultural production since the beginning of the reform process. In Ukraine, on the other hand, production fell by a further 1.1 percent, continuing the downward trend although at a slower pace than the preceding years. Production increased slightly in Armenia and Kyrgyzstan but continued to expand at a sustained rate in Azerbaijan.

• Among the developing country regions, one of the most encouraging features in 1996 was the positive performance in sub-Saharan Africa, where total crop and livestock production is estimated to have increased by 4.2 percent, up from 3 percent in 1995 and 2.3 percent in 1994. The vast majority of countries in the region participated to varying degrees in the expansion in production. Strong percentage growth rates were reported in Angola (+9), Mauritania (+9), Mozambique (+16), the Sudan (+11) and Ethiopia (+7). Even more impressive rates of expansion took place in several southern African countries, including Lesotho (+22), Swaziland (+11), Zambia (+18) Botswana (+16), Malawi (+7) and Zimbabwe (+42), as improved weather conditions enabled recovery from the disastrous shortfalls the previous year.

• In Asia and the Pacific, production growth slowed dramatically in 1996 to an estimated 2.4 percent, from rates of about 6 percent in each of the three previous years. The slowdown primarily reflected less buoyant performances of the sector in China where, at 3.4 percent, crops and livestock expanded at the lowest rate since 1989. In India, production growth also fell to a mere 0.5 percent, well below the rates of the preceding years. Poor performances were experienced in the Philippines, where crop and livestock production virtually stagnated, and in Pakistan where production actually declined after several years of sustained expansion. On the other hand, generally favourable performances were recorded in Indonesia, Cambodia, Malaysia, Thailand, Viet Nam and, in particular, Myanmar, where output increased by more than 9 percent. In the Pacific Islands overall, production expanded slightly, reflecting modest expansions in Papua New Guinea and Solomon Islands and broadly unchanged production levels in Samoa.

• In Latin America and the Caribbean, growth of crop and livestock production slowed down somewhat in 1996 to an estimated 3.2

percent, compared with the 4.4 percent recorded in 1995 and the 4.9 percent in 1994. The rate of production growth, however, remained above the rate of population growth for the region, ensuring gains in per caput agricultural production for the third consecutive year and confirming the trend towards recovery of the sector at the regional level after a prolonged stagnation in per caput production through the 1980s and 1990s. Among the major countries in the region, the preliminary estimates point to declines in production in 1996 only in Colombia and Venezuela. Increases in production, both absolutely and in per caput terms, are estimated to have occurred in Brazil, Mexico, Argentina, Peru, Chile and Ecuador. The Caribbean subregion recorded a small increase in production: Bahamas, Cuba and Haiti achieved production increases – in the case of Haiti, this represented only a partial recovery from the shortfall in 1995 – while Trinidad and Tobago experienced a fall in production for the second consecutive year, although less pronounced than in 1995.

• In the Near East and North Africa, crop and livestock production rebounded after mediocre performances the preceding years, increasing by 5.1 percent for the region as a whole. The overall high rate of expansion can be largely attributed to vastly improved agricultural conditions in Maghreb countries, more particularly Morocco and Tunisia, where production expanded by around 50 percent, more than offsetting the severe drought-induced shortfall in 1995. Very strong production growth (12 percent) was also recorded in Algeria, following the 15 percent increase in 1995. Strong rates of expansion were also recorded in the Syrian Arab Republic (8 percent), continuing the strong upward trend of the previous two years, and in Jordan (9 percent). In the Islamic Republic of Iran and Turkey, production in 1996 grew at relatively modest rates of 1.9 percent and 1.2 percent, respectively, while production remained stagnant in Egypt after the robust 7.4 percent increase recorded in 1995. In Iraq, crop and livestock production continued the decline of the previous two years, contracting by a further estimated 3.6 percent.

2. FOOD SHORTAGES AND EMERGENCIES

• No fewer than 29 countries worldwide were facing acute food shortages requiring exceptional and/or emergency food assistance at mid-1997. More than half of these countries were in Africa.

• In sub-Saharan Africa, despite a recovery in production in several parts of the region in 1996, large-scale emergency assistance continues to be needed for millions of people affected by natural or human-caused disasters.

• In East Africa, in spite of a satisfactory cereal output for the main season in 1996, large numbers of people were suffering severe food shortages owing to the failure of the secondary season crop. Emergency food assistance was needed in eastern and northeastern parts of Kenya, in pastoralist southern regions of Ethiopia, in northern parts of the United Republic of Tanzania, eastern Uganda and in Somalia. There was also a need for emergency assistance in Eritrea, where grain production in 1996 was 29 percent below average. In Burundi, despite the recent partial relaxation of the economic embargo, the food supply situation remained tight for most products. In Rwanda, the huge number of returning refugees and the considerable deterioration of the security situation in areas bordering the Democratic Republic of the Congo (former Zaire) aggravated the already precarious food supply situation in the country. In the Sudan, despite an overall satisfactory food supply position, several areas of Darfur and Kordofan states, where cereal harvests were reduced for the second consecutive year, needed to be closely monitored and contingency plans worked out for provision of food assistance. In addition, food aid was required in the states affected by prolonged civil war.

• In West Africa, despite average to above-average 1996 harvests in the main producer countries, food supply difficulties were reported in several areas of Chad, Mauritania and the Niger, owing to localized poor harvests and income constraints. The 1997 rainy season started on time and even early in the western Sahel. Following several years of civil strife in Liberia, the food supply situation remained precarious, while in Sierra Leone the situation had deteriorated significantly following the recent upheaval. Food assistance continued to be required in both countries.

• In central Africa, the food situation continued to be tight in the eastern part of the Democratic Republic of the Congo. Famine conditions faced the tens of thousands of Rwandan refugees in the region whose repatriation back to Rwanda was under way with the help of relief agencies. Civil disturbances in the Congo were affecting the food supply situation in Brazzaville and that of refugees coming from the Democratic Republic of the Congo.

• In southern Africa, the 1997 cereal harvest was expected to be lower than the previous crop year but close to average levels. However, substantial food assistance will be needed in Angola and Lesotho where production was seriously affected by below-normal rainfall and reduced planting. In Mozambique, despite an overall 11 percent increase in coarse grain output, immediate food assistance was required for approximately 172 000 people, particularly those in central regions, who lost their crops as a result of floods.

• Elsewhere in the world, agricultural activities throughout Afghanistan continued to be hindered by shortages of agricultural inputs, damage to the irrigation system and insecurity. Displaced and destitute people will continue to need food assistance for some time to come. In Iraq, production of the 1997 winter crops was estimated to be the lowest since 1991 owing to a reported low rainfall in all parts of the country, a shortage of inputs and pest infestations. The food situation is expected to improve as a result of the implementation of the oil-for-food deal, but more food and agricultural assistance is still needed.

• In the Democratic People's Republic of Korea, the food situation continued to deteriorate and the outlook for 1997 appears grim. Following severe floods over two consecutive years, domestic supplies of rice and maize were depleted and large-scale food imports (including assistance) were urgently needed to avert human suffering. In Mongolia, cereal production (mainly wheat) declined for the fifth consecutive year in 1996 as a consequence of insufficient rainfall and continuing problems in the sector, caused by economic transition and market reforms. Dwindling domestic cereal supplies and the limited capacity of the country to import sufficient quantities of grain resulted in a further deterioration of the country's food security situation.

• In Laos, low and irregular rainfall in June and July 1996 delayed the transplanting of paddy, affecting crop growth, while typhoons caused widespread flooding in major rice-producing areas in the lowlands of central and southern regions. Emergency food assistance was needed to meet the needs of 420 000 of the most vulnerable people affected by floods. In Sri Lanka, rainfall during the 1996/97 maha season was low and erratic. As a result, the area cultivated was as low as in the drought-affected year of 1995. Part of the population in the north was not able to practise normal farming because of civil strife and drought conditions.

• In Haiti, despite an improved food supply situation in most parts of the country, serious food problems were being experienced in the North-West Department where almost 70 percent of the crops were lost because of a long severe dry spell which seriously affected about 120 000 people. Food assistance was required for an estimated 350 000 people in the whole country.

• In Bosnia and Herzegovina, although the food supply situation has improved with the cessation of hostilities and the progressive normalization of economic and trade activities, low purchasing power remains a constraint to food access. The food aid requirement was estimated to be 119 000 tonnes in 1997/98. In Armenia and Georgia, the food supply situation continued to improve with increased crop yields resulting from good spring rains, an increased use of fertilizer and the improved availability of fuel. However, emergency food assistance was needed for vulnerable populations. In Azerbaijan, some recovery in food production was expected in 1997 but a large number of vulnerable people were in need of targeted food assistance. In Tajikistan, the food situation continued to be precarious, and more than 600 000 people were in need of relief assistance.

Exhibit 2

COUNTRIES EXPERIENCING FOOD SUPPLY SHORTFALLS*
AND REQUIRING EXCEPTIONAL ASSISTANCE

Source: FAO, Global Information and Early Warning System, July 1997   * In current marketing year

3. WORLD CEREAL SUPPLY SITUATION AND OUTLOOK

• World cereal production in 1996 is estimated to have been 1 873 million tonnes (including rice in milled terms), about 8.5 percent above 1995 and above the trend. A larger coarse grain crop, particularly in the United States, accounted for the bulk of the increase, although outputs of wheat and rice also rose significantly. World wheat output increased by 8 percent following bumper harvests in the major exporting countries and good crops also among the developing countries. Rice output rose by about 2 percent to a record level in 1996.

• Global cereal stocks from crops harvested in 1997 are forecast to increase to 281 million tonnes, 9 percent above their reduced opening volume. The combined cereal carryover stocks held by major exporters are expected to increase for the first time in three years, approaching about 36 percent of the world total, compared with 28 percent at the beginning of the season. Globally, the ratio of end-of-season stocks to expected utilization in 1997/98 is just over 15 percent, an improvement from 14 percent in the previous season but still well below the 17 to 18 percent range that FAO considers to be the minimum necessary to safeguard world food security.

• Prospects for 1997 cereal crops point to another above-trend output of 1 881 million tonnes (including rice in milled terms). Wheat output is forecast to be 593 million tonnes, marginally up from the previous year and above-trend for the second year in succession. Output is forecast to rise in most of Asia, Europe and the Commonwealth of Independent States (CIS) and to remain similar to last year's in North America, but will slip back somewhat in South America, North Africa and, in particular, Australia after a record crop last year. World coarse grain output in 1997 is forecast to remain similar to the above-trend crop in 1996 of about 911 million tonnes. The bulk of the increase is expected in North and South America but also in the CIS, where production is expected to recover from the reduced crop last year. As regards rice, assuming growing conditions remain as good as they were the previous year, paddy output could be around 562 million tonnes (377 million tonnes in milled terms), almost unchanged from the previous year.

• If current forecasts materialize, cereal output will be sufficient to meet expected consumption requirements in 1997/98 and should allow for a further modest replenishment of cereal stocks for the second consecutive year after the sharp drawdown in 1995/96. Nevertheless, the forecast global stock-to-utilization ratio may only

Exhibit 3

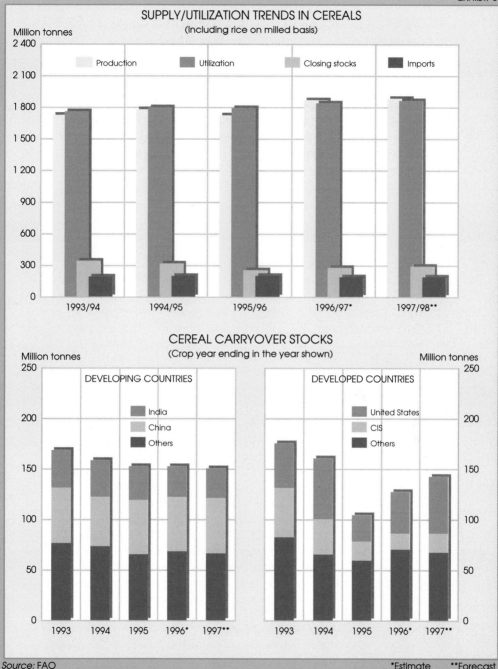

SUPPLY/UTILIZATION TRENDS IN CEREALS
(Including rice on milled basis)

Million tonnes

Production Utilization Closing stocks Imports

CEREAL CARRYOVER STOCKS
(Crop year ending in the year shown)

Million tonnes

DEVELOPING COUNTRIES

India
China
Others

Million tonnes

DEVELOPED COUNTRIES

United States
CIS
Others

Source: FAO

*Estimate **Forecast

reach 16 percent and thus would remain below the minimum level considered safe by FAO. The global cereal market would be particularly tight for wheat, with ending stocks in 1997/98 expected to remain low. By contrast, coarse grain carryovers are projected to continue to expand significantly, particularly among the major exporters. This outcome, however, would very much depend on coarse grain price developments next season, as a fall in prices could trigger more intensive feed use and thus cause utilization to rise faster than currently anticipated, with an ensuing downward adjustment in stocks.

4. EXTERNAL ASSISTANCE TO AGRICULTURE

• Total commitments made by bilateral and multilateral donors to agriculture (broadly defined) amounted to $10 312 million in 1995, just short of the $10 345 million reached in 1994. In real terms, however, this constituted an 8.6 percent decline which indicates the continuation of an overall declining trend in external assistance to agriculture. Indeed, when measured in 1990 prices, total assistance fell by 21.2 percent from $12 113 million in 1991 to $9 549 million in 1995. The share of external assistance to agriculture in total development financing has declined from 13 percent in 1990 to about 10 percent in recent years.

• Contrary to 1994, which saw a decline in bilateral and an increase in multilateral commitments, the total decline in 1995 was primarily the result of a decrease in multilateral contributions. In particular, commitments by the International Fund for Agricultural Development (IFAD) fell by 36 percent and those by the Asian and African Development Banks by as much as 60 percent in real terms. However, the level of commitment, in real terms, from the World Bank remained roughly the same. Commitments by the International Bank for Reconstruction and Development (IBRD) expanded from $2 016 million to $2 281 million, representing about 4 percent in real terms, while those by the International Development Association (IDA) also increased from $1 472 million to $1 545 million, but declined by nearly 4 percent in real terms. The aggregate commitments from the United Nations Development Fund (UNDP), FAO and the Consultative Group on International Agricultural Research (CGIAR) went up to $656 million from $647 million; however, in real terms this represented a decrease. After a sharp drop in assistance in 1994, multilateral assistance from the Organization of the Petroleum Exporting Countries (OPEC) rose significantly from $45 million to $161 million.

• Total bilateral commitments increased from $3 792 million in 1994 to $4 515 in 1995, corresponding to an increase in real terms of 9.2 percent. Half of total bilateral commitments in 1995 came from Japan, the major contributor to bilateral assistance among the Development Assistance Committee (DAC) members. Japan's commitment was 48 percent higher than the previous year. Among DAC members, Germany was the second highest donor in 1995, followed by the Netherlands, the United States and France.

• While the share of concessional commitments in total commitments to agriculture remained broadly constant at close to

73 percent from 1994 to 1995, the amount in grants increased from $4 461 million to $5 044 million. Virtually all (95 to 97 percent) bilateral assistance is channelled through grants. The grant element in multilateral commitments has increased slightly, from around 10 percent in 1991 to 12 percent in 1995.

• For 1996, information is available only for lending to the agricultural sector from IBRD and IDA. According to the *World Bank Annual Report 1996*, $2 577 million were lent in 1996 for the development of agriculture, down from $2 752 million in 1995. This fall was noted in both IBRD and IDA assistance.

• In terms of the areas of channelled assistance, commitments towards environmental development increased substantially, from $139 million in 1994 to $1 465 million in 1995, as did commitments for rural development, rising from $875 million in 1994 to $1 678 million in 1995. On the other hand, commitments towards fisheries, forestry and land and water development declined significantly between 1994 and 1995.

• With regard to the regional distribution of assistance flows, while the major share of commitments went towards Africa and Asia, they fell from the 1994 level. Latin America and countries in transition, on the other hand, registered increases in external assistance in 1995. In fact, the share of total external assistance to agriculture in countries in transition has increased steadily over the past five years from 1.4 percent of overall assistance in 1991 to 5 percent in 1995. In per caput terms (with respect to rural population and agricultural population), however, availability of assistance was highest for Latin America, followed by Africa and Asia.

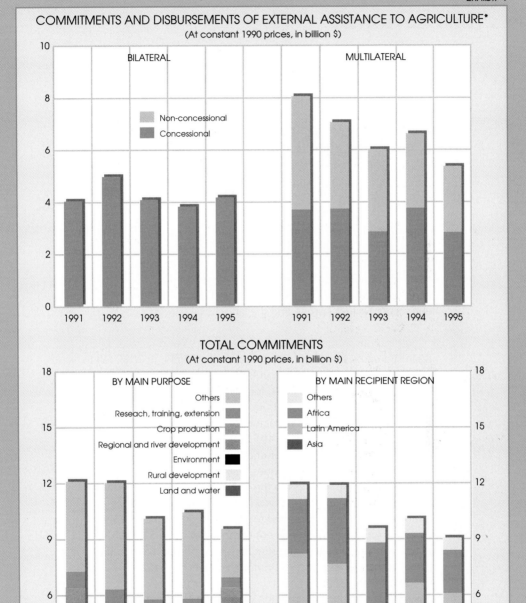

Exhibit 4

COMMITMENTS AND DISBURSEMENTS OF EXTERNAL ASSISTANCE TO AGRICULTURE*
(At constant 1990 prices, in billion $)

BILATERAL   MULTILATERAL

Non-concessional
Concessional

TOTAL COMMITMENTS
(At constant 1990 prices, in billion $)

BY MAIN PURPOSE

Others
Reseach, training, extension
Crop production
Regional and river development
Environment
Rural development
Land and water

BY MAIN RECIPIENT REGION

Others
Africa
Latin America
Asia

Source: FAO and OECD

* Broad definition

5. FOOD AID FLOWS

• As of July 1997, total cereal food aid shipments under programme, project and emergency food aid in 1996/97 (July/June) were estimated to have reached 7.5 million tonnes, which is about the same as in 1995/96 and more than 2 million tonnes above the minimum commitments of 5.35 million tonnes agreed under the 1995 Food Aid Convention (FAC). Aggregate cereal shipments to low-income food-deficit countries (LIFDCs) in 1996/97 were likely to have reached 5.9 million tonnes, almost the same as in 1995/96. Of this total, some 2.5 million tonnes were destined for LIFDCs in sub-Saharan Africa.

• Global food aid shipments in non-cereal food commodities fell in 1995 (January-December) to about 1.2 million tonnes, about 460 000 tonnes, or 28 percent less than in 1994. Reduced shipments of pulses and vegetable oils accounted for most of this decrease. The bulk of the decline occurred mostly in Africa and countries of Eastern Europe and the CIS.

• Contributions to the International Emergency Food Reserve (IEFR), administrated by the World Food Programme (WFP), in 1996 fell to 849 000 tonnes of cereals from 908 000 tonnes in 1995. Similarly, contributions were also reduced for non-cereal shipments, from 238 000 tonnes in 1995 to 198 000 tonnes. In addition, contributions to the 1996 Protracted Refugee Operations, also directed by WFP, amounted to 495 000 tonnes of cereals and 85 000 tonnes of other food commodities, compared with 535 000 tonnes and 58 000 tonnes, respectively, in 1995. As of 31 December 1996, pledges to the regular resources of WFP, which account for 98 percent of total food aid deliveries through multilateral channels, amounted to $840 million for the 1995-96 biennium, representing 56 percent of the target of $1.5 billion. Of the total amount pledged, an estimated $576 million were in the form of commodities and $264 million in cash.

• As regards the future orientation of the food aid programme of the United States, the world's largest donor, initial proposals released in February 1997 for the 1998 fiscal year (October/September) suggest a cut in funds for the Food-for-Peace programme, known as PL-480, by $117 million to $990 million. The full amount of the reduction is expected to be made in Title I, the concessional sales programme, which is targeted at $123 million compared with $240 million initially appropriated for fiscal year 1997.

Exhibit 5

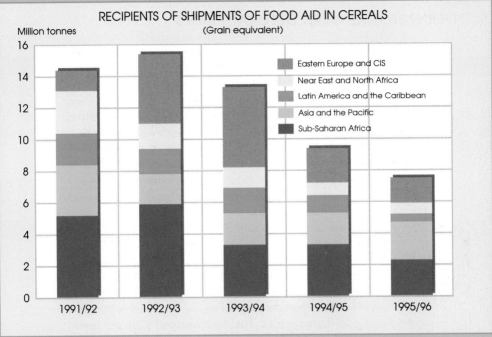

RECIPIENTS OF SHIPMENTS OF FOOD AID IN CEREALS
(Grain equivalent)

Million tonnes

Legend:
- Eastern Europe and CIS
- Near East and North Africa
- Latin America and the Caribbean
- Asia and the Pacific
- Sub-Saharan Africa

Years: 1991/92, 1992/93, 1993/94, 1994/95, 1995/96

Source: FAO

Note: Years refer to the 12-month period July/June

6. INTERNATIONAL AGRICULTURAL PRICES

• By July 1997, international wheat and maize prices had dropped by 32 and 48 percent, respectively, from their average in July 1996, largely as a result of generally improved production, including in major importing countries. Looking ahead to the 1997/98 marketing season, in the absence of any significant increase in import demand, wheat prices are projected to remain under pressure and become more volatile in the second half of the season owing to the relatively small size of stocks, a development which would replicate the situation in the 1996/97 season. Next season's maize prices may also face downward pressure as demand in the international market for maize is forecast to grow slowly while supplies remain ample among the major exporters, in particular the United States.

• World rice prices in the first six months of 1997 were relatively weak compared with the high prices that prevailed in the same period in 1996. The decline in prices was a result of the overall slackening of world import demand following two years of bumper trade. Among the higher grades, Thai 100 averaged $336 per tonne in June 1997 compared with $363 in June 1996, while the lower-quality, fully broken rice, such as Thai A1 Super, was about $17 per tonne lower than in June 1996.

• The decline in the prices of oils and fats accelerated during the 1995/96 marketing season, with the monthly average FAO price of edible and soap fats and oils falling by nearly 10 percent when compared with the previous season. However, prices remained quite high in historical terms. Refurbished stocks and a good new oilseeds crop were the main contributors to this decline, despite the continued increase in the prices of lauric oils (coconut and palm kernel) throughout the season, caused by tight supplies. The decline in oil prices has slowed down considerably since the beginning of the 1996/97 season, to a level about 4 percent below the same period last season. Moreover, since early 1997, the prices of soft oils have strengthened somewhat, reflecting a recovery in demand in certain markets. This upward trend is likely to be maintained until the end of the current season, although not enough to register a significant increase over the entire season when compared with 1995/96.

• A unique feature of the past two seasons has been the fact that the movements in international prices of oilcakes and oilmeals have exhibited a tendency opposite to that observed for oils and fats. Thus, the fall in global output, coupled with the upward shift in the

Exhibit 6

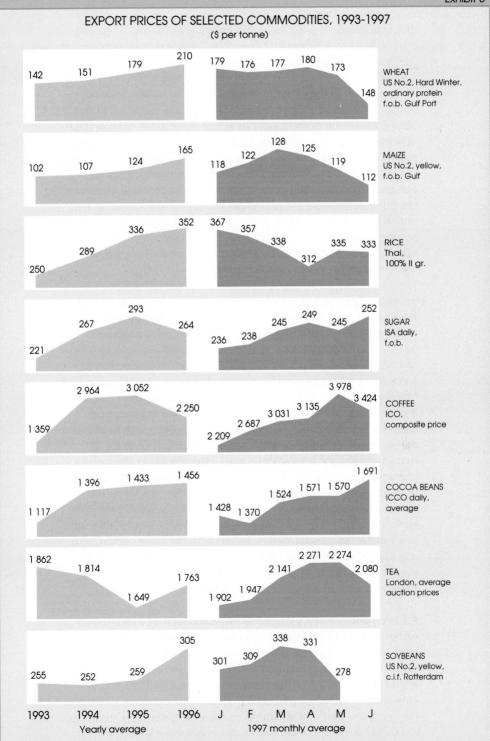

EXPORT PRICES OF SELECTED COMMODITIES, 1993-1997
($ per tonne)

WHEAT
US No.2, Hard Winter,
ordinary protein
f.o.b. Gulf Port

MAIZE
US No.2, yellow,
f.o.b. Gulf

RICE
Thai,
100% II gr.

SUGAR
ISA daily,
f.o.b.

COFFEE
ICO,
composite price

COCOA BEANS
ICCO daily,
average

TEA
London, average
auction prices

SOYBEANS
US No.2, yellow,
c.i.f. Rotterdam

1993   1994   1995   1996   J   F   M   A   M   J
Yearly average   1997 monthly average

Source: FAO

global demand for oilcakes and oilmeals, was the primary cause which triggered a substantial drawdown of stocks during the 1995/96 season and resulted in a sharp rise in prices of these commodities of about 38 percent compared with 1994/95.
The rapid rise in the monthly average prices of meals, however, appears to have subsided appreciably since the beginning of this season as a result of the supply response observed in most of the countries producing meal-rich oilseeds. Between October 1996 and May 1997, meal prices rose by 14 percent compared with the same period for 1995/96. Although the demand for livestock products in fast-growing developing economies is likely to continue increasing, the pressure on meal prices is expected to ease somewhat, at least until the end of the season, as a result of the soybean harvest in the Southern Hemisphere. Nevertheless, it is unlikely that these developments will eventually lead to a decline in meal prices for the entire 1996/97 season when compared with 1995/96.

• Following good harvests and rising stocks, world sugar prices have been under downward pressure since the beginning of 1995, when the International Sugar Agreement (ISA) price peaked at 13.3 US cents per pound. The price fell markedly to a two-year low of 10.5 US cents per pound in April 1996 and, following some recovery in the middle of the year, weakened again in October and November when a larger than expected surplus began to emerge. It is believed, however, that the decline in world market prices during 1995-96 would have been even greater but for two factors: the supply of high-quality white sugar, particularly from the EC, remained tight and a substantial part of the surplus in India was channelled to re-build stocks rather than being exported. World sugar production for 1996/97 is estimated to be 122.5 million tonnes (raw value), slightly below the record 122.9 million tonnes set in 1995/96. However, production for 1996/97 would still result in a surplus, as consumption is not expected to grow significantly and therefore continues to exert pressure on prices in 1997. The average ISA price in July 1997 was 11.08 US cents per pound, compared with 12.81 US cents per pound 12 months earlier.

• Coffee prices continued their downward trend in 1996 despite earlier efforts by producers to maintain firm market prices by instituting an export retention scheme. In July 1995, the Association of Coffee Producing Countries (ACPC) agreed to restrict their exports of green beans to 3.6 million tonnes between mid-1995 and mid-1996, approximately 8 percent less than in the previous 12 months. However, the goal – to lift futures prices in the New York exchange to 180 US cents per pound – was, not achieved, although prices could have slipped further without the retention scheme. As the ACPC strives to bring supply levels more into line with consumption, prices should gradually firm during 1997. In addition, expectations of a shortfall in Brazil owing to frost damage contributed to the strengthening of prices in early 1997. Although prices subsequently eased somewhat, by mid-year quotations were still more than 50 percent above the 1996 average level.

• World cocoa prices remained relatively firm in 1996, with the ICCO daily price closing at 68 US cents per pound in the third quarter, 5 US cents per pound higher than in the corresponding period of 1995, and substantially higher than in the early 1990s when they averaged 52 US cents per pound. By July 1997, the price peaked at 77.10 US cents per pound, bringing the average for the first seven months of 1997 to 70.34 US cents per pound. Thus, cocoa prices have been on a continuous upward trend since the new International Cocoa Agreement of 1993. World cocoa consumption, as measured by grindings of cocoa beans, rose in 1995/96 by 6 percent to 2.7 million tonnes, the highest annual growth rate in ten years. All major consuming countries recorded increases, notably the Netherlands and the United States. Prospects are for lower rates of growth in 1996/97, however, as a reaction to the higher prices.

• World market prices of tea firmed considerably in 1996, averaging $1.76 per kg and 8 percent higher than in 1995 for all teas in London, mainly owing to increased demand in the Russian Federation. Prices continued to rise in the first five months of 1997, reaching $2 271 per tonne in April and $2 274 per tonne in May and reflecting production shortfalls, particularly in Kenya and Sri Lanka. Some corrections occurred in June and July 1997 when prices fell to $2 080 and $1 943 per tonne, respectively. Although expected to remain relatively high during the remainder of the year, world prices beyond 1997 could again be vulnerable to downward pressure given the slow growth in demand in importing countries and the strong supply potential in major exporting countries.

• World cotton prices, as indicated by the Cotlook 'A' Index for July 1997 were only 1.5 US cents per pound above the 1996 average of 80.5 US cents per pound, considerably lower than the peak levels of over 110 cents per pound in early 1995. The International Cotton Advisory Committee (ICAC) expects that, with modest prices, production in 1996/97 will contract by more than 1 million to 19.1 million tonnes. Consumption is expected to increase by about 500 000 tonnes to more than 19 million tonnes. Since world production and consumption are almost equal, stocks at the end of the 1996/97 season (on 31 July 1997) are expected to be almost unchanged, at 9 million tonnes. Global trade is expected to contract from 6 million tonnes in 1995/6 to 5.8 million tonnes in 1996/97. China continues to play a key role in the world cotton trade. ICAC estimates that, despite a marked fall in production and a small increase in consumption in 1996/97, imports by China will contract as stocks are drawn down. This weaker demand in world markets is one of the factors contributing to the relatively weak prices in 1996/97. For 1997/98, further increases in both production and consumption are forecast.

7. FISHERIES: CATCH, DISPOSITION AND TRADE

• Fish supplies have expanded rapidly in recent years, reaching 110.5 million tonnes in 1994 and an estimated new peak of 112.9 million tonnes in 1995, the latest year for which complete data are available. The increase was due mainly to continued rapid growth in aquaculture production, particularly in China, and a rapid expansion of highly fluctuating harvestable stocks of pelagic species off the west coast of South America. As a result, both fishmeal production and fish supplies for human consumption have reached record levels.

• Aggregate fishery production in developing countries continued expanding in 1995, although at a slower rate (2.6 percent) than in the preceding years. The cumulative increase in developing country production in the five-year period from 1990 to 1995 amounted to 39 percent, while developed country production contracted by an estimated 18 percent over the same period. Overall, the developing country share in total fishery production increased from 58 percent in 1990 to 70 percent in 1995.

• In 1995 total landings by capture fisheries are estimated to have remained at about 92 million tonnes, the same level as in 1994. Provisional production figures for marine and inland aquaculture show an estimated increase from 18.4 million tonnes in 1994 to 20.9 million tonnes in 1995.

• The rapid growth in aquaculture production is the result of increased expansion of carp species, primarily in Asia. Five Asian countries (China, India, Japan, the Republic of Korea and the Philippines) accounted for 80 percent of the volume of aquaculture produce in 1995. In 1994, carps accounted for almost half of the total volume of cultured aquatic products (aquatic plants excluded). Even though cultured fish and shellfish contribute significantly to total national fishery production, aquaculture in most countries is dominated by only a few species.

• Of the preliminary figure of 112.9 million tonnes of total fishery production in 1995, it is estimated that about 31.8 million tonnes were used for reduction. The amount of fish available for direct human consumption in 1995 was estimated to be 81.1 million tonnes, 5.3 million tonnes more than in 1994, representing a greater increase than the estimated population growth rate in the same year. Therefore, the average annual per caput availability of food fish increased to 14.3 kg.

• The value of international fish trade continues to increase. In 1985, the value of international fish exports was $17 billion; in 1990, it was $35.7 billion; and by 1994 it had reached $47.4 billion. The increased volume of international trade in fishery products in 1994 was associated with higher trade in low-value commodities such as fishmeal, with the result that the value of exports increased less than the volume. Preliminary figures for 1995 indicated an increase in the value of trade, reaching $51.7 billion, owing to higher prices.

• Developed countries accounted for about 85 percent of the total value of fish imports in 1995. Japan continued to be the world's largest importer of fishery products, accounting for about 30 percent of the global total. In 1995, fish imports by all three major world importers (Japan, the EU and the United States) increased.

• For many developing nations, fish trade represents a significant source of foreign exchange. The increase in net receipts of foreign exchange by developing countries – calculated by deducting their import from their export value – is impressive. As such, net receipts rose from $5.1 billion in 1985 to $16.0 billion in 1994, and further to $18.4 billion in 1995.

Exhibit 7

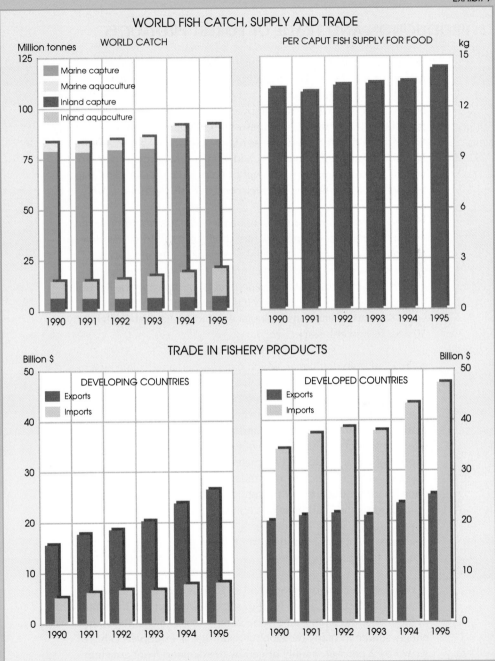

WORLD FISH CATCH, SUPPLY AND TRADE

WORLD CATCH

Million tonnes

- Marine capture
- Marine aquaculture
- Inland capture
- Inland aquaculture

PER CAPUT FISH SUPPLY FOR FOOD

kg

TRADE IN FISHERY PRODUCTS

Billion $

DEVELOPING COUNTRIES

- Exports
- Imports

Billion $

DEVELOPED COUNTRIES

- Exports
- Imports

Source: FAO

8. PRODUCTION AND TRADE OF FOREST PRODUCTS

• The year 1996 witnessed the interruption of a longstanding ascending trend in world production of paper and paperboard. World paper production had in fact grown steadily, but by the beginning of 1996 there was an oversupply of pulp and paper products in major markets as a result of a weakened paper demand and increased industrial capacity. Many pulp and paper mills in North America and Scandinavia had to take downtime in order to reduce an exceptionally high level of pulp and paper stocks. Output and operating rates of the industry consequently declined rapidly.

• The 1996 drop in production of paper and paperboard occurred only in the main developed country producers, while production is estimated to have grown by about 8 percent in the developing countries. As in the past, Asian countries enjoyed the strongest growth. In fact, production of paper and paperboard in the Republic of Korea was up by an estimated 9 percent from the previous year. Large capacity expansions took place in Indonesia and Thailand (by 30 and 15 percent, respectively).

• Prices of pulp and paper, which had reached an all-time high in October 1995, continued to fall sharply for a good part of 1996. In the last part of 1996, however, prices tended to stabilize at a low level as some signs of recovery began to appear in major paper markets. The strong fall in pulp and paper prices had a negative effect on the total value of trade of forest products. The total value of exports of forest products is estimated to have decreased by approximately 14 percent, and trade in wood pulp and paper and paperboard products by 22 percent. Imports of round coniferous pulpwood by the Scandinavian countries, for example, which had grown strongly in the last few years, were reported to have decreased by about 2.5 million m³, reflecting the diminished fibre needs of their pulp industries.

• World production of roundwood in 1996 is estimated to have remained at last year's low level of some 3.4 billion m³. Production of fuelwood, the main roundwood component and the dominant energy source in many developing countries, is estimated to have grown by 2 percent, mainly driven by the demand from growing rural populations of developing countries. Production of industrial roundwood, on the other hand, is estimated to have decreased by 2 percent. The developed countries experienced a sharp drop in pulpwood removals, which went down by 6 percent, as a reflection of weak pulpwood demand by the pulp industries in Europe. In both

Exhibit 8A

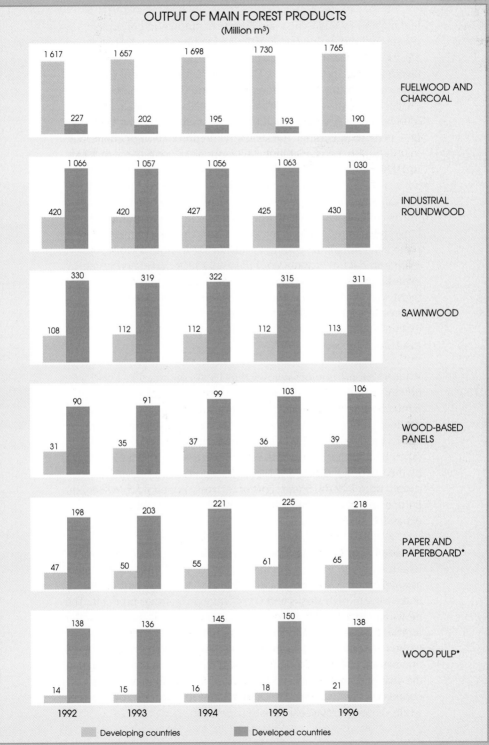

OUTPUT OF MAIN FOREST PRODUCTS
(Million m³)

FUELWOOD AND CHARCOAL

1 617 · 227 · 1 657 · 202 · 1 698 · 195 · 1 730 · 193 · 1 765 · 190

INDUSTRIAL ROUNDWOOD

420 · 1 066 · 420 · 1 057 · 427 · 1 056 · 425 · 1 063 · 430 · 1 030

SAWNWOOD

108 · 330 · 112 · 319 · 112 · 322 · 112 · 315 · 113 · 311

WOOD-BASED PANELS

31 · 90 · 35 · 91 · 37 · 99 · 36 · 103 · 39 · 106

PAPER AND PAPERBOARD*

47 · 198 · 50 · 203 · 55 · 221 · 61 · 225 · 65 · 218

WOOD PULP*

14 · 138 · 15 · 136 · 16 · 145 · 18 · 150 · 21 · 138

1992 · 1993 · 1994 · 1995 · 1996

Developing countries   Developed countries

Source: FAO

* Million tonnes

Finland and Sweden, the main European pulpwood consumers, consumption of pulpwood is estimated to have fallen by nearly 15 percent. Markets for pulpwood, on the other hand, were more favourable in North America. World production of coniferous logs followed the same trend, although the drop was less marked. Production of this commodity went up in North America, after a long period of decline induced by harvesting restrictions, but down by 7 percent in Europe. The steady fall in production of coniferous logs in the Russian Federation was reported to have come to a halt in 1996.

• Production of tropical logs is estimated to have remained at the previous year's level. Many tropical countries have introduced harvesting restrictions and log export bans, in view of their desire to protect the remaining natural forests. In 1996, Côte d'Ivoire, the main tropical log exporter until the mid-1980s, reinstated its log export ban on 35 wood species. Ghana introduced similar legislation in 1996. As a notable exception, in late 1996 the Malaysian state of Sabah announced the lifting of the ban on log exports, indicating that up to 2 million m^3 of logs would be available for export in 1997.

• World production of sawnwood in 1996 continued its slow downward trend. With the exception of North America and in particular the United States, where housing activity was strong, the production of coniferous sawnwood remained elsewhere at low levels. Production in the Russian Federation is estimated to have fallen by a further 10 percent, reflecting mainly a shortage of capital by the sawmill industry and higher transportation costs of wood supply from Siberia. Some signs of recovery appeared, however, in Europe and Japan in late 1996, where construction activity expanded significantly.

• Trade in coniferous sawnwood, which accounts for 85 percent of total sawnwood trade, was estimated to have declined by 2 percent as a reflection of weak demand in Europe for a good part of 1996 and owing to high stocks and competition from other products. The new trade agreement between Canada and the United States, which limits duty-free Canadian coniferous sawnwood exports to the United States (unless a specified price level is reached), caused notable uncertainty among buyers and exporters in the latter part of the year and an upward effect on prices. Total Canadian exports of coniferous sawnwood to the United States rose in 1996 by 3 percent while shipments overseas rose by 1 percent.

Exhibit 8B

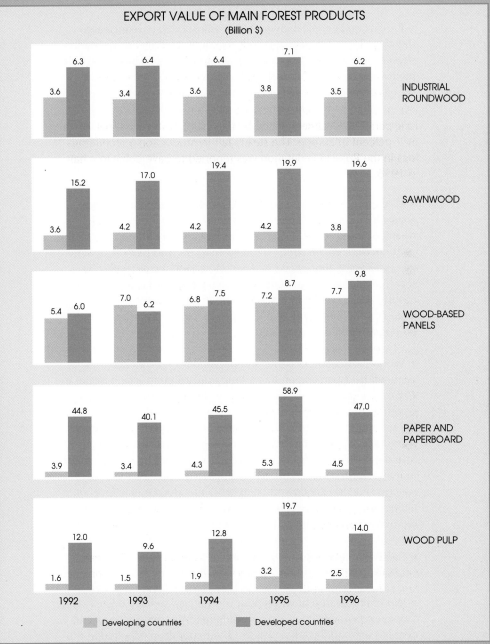

EXPORT VALUE OF MAIN FOREST PRODUCTS
(Billion $)

Source: FAO

• Production of tropical sawnwood is estimated to have increased slightly in 1996. Of the main producer countries, only Brazil reported a significant increase in tropical sawnwood production. Trade in tropical sawnwood continued to decline, as major exporters are favouring exports of more processed products such as plywood, veneer, furniture and furniture parts. For example, exports from Malaysia, the world's largest exporter, were estimated to have decreased by about 10 percent, while exports of Malaysian wooden furniture were up by 30 percent. As a notable exception, exports of tropical sawnwood from Ghana were reported to be up by 15 percent.

• World production of wood-based panels is estimated to have grown by more than 3 percent. Demand for new products, such as oriented strand board (OSB) and medium-density fibreboard (MDF), continued to remain strong in major markets, and further capacity increases were announced in developed countries as well as in some developing Asian countries. Demand for tropical plywood was robust in Asia. While Indonesian output and exports (the world's largest) were hampered by difficulties in log supply, Malaysian production and exports surged.

• World production of paper and paperboard is estimated to have declined by 1 percent, ending a long upward trend which began in 1982. The decline in production occurred only in the developed countries, where output decreased by an estimated 3 percent. With the exception of Japan and the United States, where output grew marginally, all other major producers experienced decreases. Scandinavian countries were particularly affected by weak demand in major European markets. Many mills in Scandinavia and North America had to take downtime in order to reduce a high level of paper stocks. In the last part of the year, however, some signs of recovery began to appear. Production in developing countries, on the other hand, grew by an estimated 6 percent. As in the past, countries in the Far East enjoyed the fastest growth, where large capacity expansions in the region took place.

• World production of wood pulp is estimated to have decreased by 5 percent. Markets for wood pulp suffered from oversupply, weak demand and rapidly falling prices. The major drop occurred in the developed countries, where output decreased by an estimated 8 percent. In the last part of the year, the market situation improved slightly and production started a slow recovery. Because of new capacity installed in 1996, production in the developing countries increased by 18 percent. However, trade value in wood pulp decreased with the rapidly falling prices.

WORLD REVIEW
II. Overall economic environment and agriculture

WORLD ECONOMIC ENVIRONMENT

After a pronounced slowdown in 1995, world economic growth accelerated in 1996 in both developed and developing countries. World economic activity is projected to gather strength in 1997 and remain vigorous in 1998 (Figure 1).[3] At the same time, inflation rates remained moderate throughout 1996 and early 1997, falling in many cases to their lowest levels in decades, while efforts to reduce fiscal and external imbalances were intensified, with positive results in many countries. After having risen at a dramatic pace during the previous two years, in 1996 the rate of expansion of world trade slowed markedly, reflecting mainly sluggish import demand in some industrial countries and moderate growth in a number of Asian economies. Following are some regional highlights:[4]

- In the developed countries, robust growth performances were recorded in 1996 in the United States, the United Kingdom and a number of smaller economies, along with a recovery in Japan. After disappointing growth in 1995 and much of 1996, the economic outlook improved somewhat in Europe, although high, and in several countries growing, unemployment as well as the fiscal criteria laid down as conditions to participate in monetary union within the EU remain difficult challenges for the region. For 1997 and 1998, expectations are for an acceleration in the growth rate of the United States and the EU, but a slowdown in Japan.
- Sustained growth was recorded in the developing countries overall. Growth rates remained at or exceeded 6 percent for five consecutive years (1992-1996), and similarly high rates are

---

[3] Unless otherwise indicated, economic estimates and short-term forecasts in this section are from IMF. 1997. *World Economic Outlook 1997.* Washington, DC.

[4] A more detailed account of economic developments in the developing country regions and economies in transition can be found in Part II, Regional review.

Figure 1

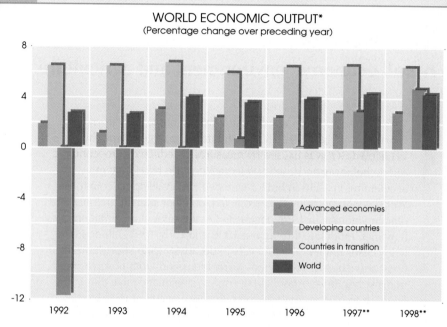

WORLD ECONOMIC OUTPUT*
(Percentage change over preceding year)

Advanced economies
Developing countries
Countries in transition
World

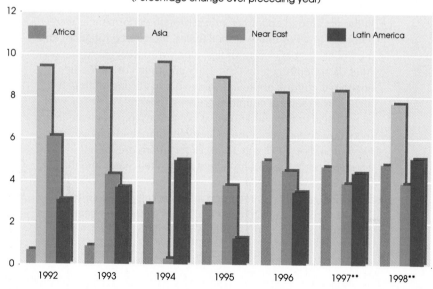

ECONOMIC GROWTH, DEVELOPING COUNTRY REGIONS
(Percentage change over preceding year)

Africa Asia Near East Latin America

Source: IMF

* Real GDP ** Projections

projected for 1997 and 1998. A remarkable broadening of the economic upturn initiated in 1994-95 was observed in Africa, where the 5 percent growth rate in 1996 was the highest in two decades, reflecting to a large extent strong performances of the agricultural sector. African growth rates are also projected to remain high by historic standards in 1997-98. The Asian economies remained dynamic, despite some slowdown since the very high 1992-95 growth rates; to a large extent, this slowdown was caused by measures to reduce macroeconomic imbalances and control overheating. The Near Eastern economies continued to recover from the slump of 1994, boosted by a significant increase in prices of crude petroleum during 1996, but growth is expected to lose momentum in 1997-98, largely in response to weakening oil prices. In Latin America and the Caribbean, a marked recovery has taken place following the gloom induced by Mexico's financial crisis, with the two countries worst hit by the crisis in 1994-95, Argentina and Mexico, recovering at a much faster pace than expected.

- In the transition economies as a whole, 1996 may have been the first year of positive, if still minor, growth since 1989, and short-term prospects are for a strengthening of economic

Figure 2

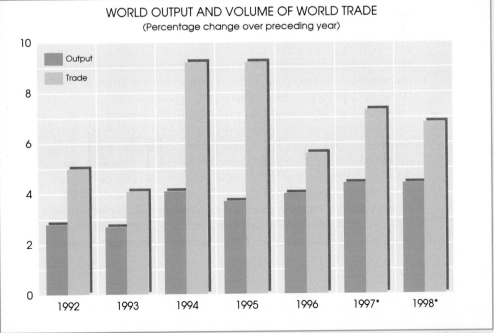

WORLD OUTPUT AND VOLUME OF WORLD TRADE
(Percentage change over preceding year)

Source: IMF

* Projections

activity. Widely differentiated performances were still observed across countries, however. Those more advanced in the reform process showed robust growth and moderate inflation. Growth rates ranged between 5 and 7 percent in Slovakia, Poland and Croatia, while the Czech Republic recorded 4.2 percent; the exception was Hungary, where GDP only rose by 1 percent following severe stabilization measures in 1995-96. On the other hand, most other economies in transition were showing continuing difficulties in emerging from the crisis. Output was estimated to have fallen again in 1996 in five countries in the CIS, including the Russian Federation and Ukraine.

Long-term interest rates continued a downward trend until early December 1996 to mid-February 1997 in most industrial countries, but increased significantly again during the first quarter of 1997, reflecting concerns about inflation risks and signs of stronger economic activity in several countries. By March 1997, nominal long-term interest rates were about 6 to 8 percent in the major industrial countries, except Japan (where they were about 2.3 percent), compared with a wider spread of 8 to 12 percent in the early 1990s. Such an overall decline in interest rates is of considerable importance, not only because of its direct effects on investment and economic activity but also, for the developing countries, because of its implications on capital flows and debt servicing.

Another factor of major importance for many developing countries is the behaviour of commodity prices. According to IMF, commodity prices in United States dollar terms rose overall by about 5 percent in 1996, with a 20 percent increase in the price of crude petroleum and a 1 percent decline in that of non-fuel primary commodities. The world index of prices for primary agricultural products[5] fell from 110 in 1995 to 100 in 1996 (1990 = 100) in nominal terms.

Reflecting different weights in total exports, the index for the developed countries fell by 5 percent and that for the developing countries by 16 percent. The bulk of the latter reduction was in coffee (-25 percent) and sugar (-8 percent). Prices of natural rubber, hides and vegetables also fell considerably. Despite such declines in prices of major commodities exported by the developing countries, the overall index for these countries in 1996 was still 20 percent higher in real terms than the depressed levels of 1990-93. Moreover, prices of several commodities, including tropical beverages, tended

---

[5] **Computed using the 1980 weights, as used by *United States Monthly Bulletin of Statistics*, and on the basis of world market prices compiled by FAO.**

BOX 1
EXTERNAL DEBT AND FINANCIAL FLOWS
TO DEVELOPING COUNTRIES

Total outstanding external debt for all developing countries, according to preliminary estimates, reached $2 177 billion at the end of 1996. This represents an increase of $111 billion, or more than 5 percent in nominal terms, over the total debt at the end of 1995 ($2 066 billion).

The ratio of debt to export earnings, however, declined to 146 percent from more than 151 percent in 1995. All regions shared in the decline, except East Asia and the Pacific, which recorded an increase in the debt to export earnings ratio because of a sharp increase in private non-guaranteed debt. In sub-Saharan Africa, this ratio declined to 237 percent from 242 percent in 1995, reflecting debt-alleviation measures in favour of this region. Debt-service ratios, which express total debt-service payments as a percentage of total export earnings, also declined in all regions except Latin America owing to the prepayment of debt from the Mexico rescue package. The aggregate debt-service ratio for all countries in 1996 was slightly more than 16 percent, almost one point below the previous year. Sub-Saharan Africa recorded an estimated 12 percent debt-service ratio, against slightly more than 14 percent in 1995. In Latin America and the Caribbean the ratio stood at 30 percent in 1996 against 26 percent the previous year. To service their total outstanding debts, the developing countries paid a total of $245 billion in 1996, of which $101 billion were interest payments.

Negotiations between debtor countries and multilateral and bilateral creditors were actively pursued in 1996, giving rise to a number of encouraging developments in debt relief and debt reduction. The heavily indebted poor countries (HIPC) initiative, established in September 1995, was endorsed in 1996 by the World Bank, IMF, the Paris Club and bilateral creditors. Under this initiative, bilateral and multilateral creditors of poor, indebted countries provide debt relief in order to reduce the debt burden to sustainable levels over the medium term. Countries qualifying must be eligible to borrow from IDA and must have a good record of economic and social policy reform, including improvements in health care and education. The World Bank has established an HIPC Trust Fund, managed by IDA, and has set aside $500 million to cover its initial contribution. IMF is participating in the initiative through its enhanced structural adjustment facility (ESAF), a concessional financing facility that supports macroeconomic and structural reform in low-income countries. The first debt relief under the HIPC initiative was approved in April 1997 for Uganda which, through the operation, will reduce its multilateral and bilateral debt by about 20 percent or $700 million. Preliminary agreements have also been made with Bolivia, Côte d'Ivoire and Burkina Faso.

The Paris Club of creditors, through which the debt-relief operations for most official bilateral debt are negotiated, has continued to play a very important role. Between mid-1995 and end-1996, five stock-of-debt operations, which reschedule concessionally all stocks of debt, and nine flow reschedulings (which reschedule debt service falling due on eligible debt) were made on the so-called Naples terms, providing for a two-thirds reduction in present value terms on certain categories of official debt for the poorest countries. Since the introduction of the Naples terms in 1994, creditors have implemented six stock-of-debt operations or exit options, covering more than $2 billion, and 19 flow reschedulings, covering about $7 billion. In addition, seven agreements were made on non-concessional terms. The Russian Federation benefited from the largest ever restructuring package by the Paris Club, covering more than $40 billion in debt.

In 1996, seven agreements between debtor countries and commercial bank creditors were concluded, restructuring $17 billion in debt and reducing outstanding debt by more than $5 billion. Other debt conversion programmes, such as debt-for-equity, debt-for-development and debt-for-nature swaps, have increased rapidly. Between 1985, when these arrangements were first institutionalized, and 1995 such debt conversion has totalled $141 billion.

FINANCIAL FLOWS

Capital flows to the developing countries, in particular private flows, reached record levels in 1996, reflecting relatively low interest rates in industrial countries, the continued development of capital markets in many emerging market economies, the investment opportunities created by privatization and, more generally, the climate of confidence created by successful stabilization and adjustment measures in many countries.

Aggregate net long-term external capital flows to developing countries reached an estimated $285 billion in 1996, an increase of 20 percent ($47 billion) over 1995. Net private capital flows, which account for 86 percent of total aggregate net long-term flows, continued to increase, reaching a record $244 billion, $60 billion above the figure for 1995. However, many of the world's developing countries still do not share, to any significant extent, in the growth of private flows. East Asia and the Pacific, together with Latin America and the Caribbean, received the largest amounts of net private flows, $109 billion and $74 billion, respectively. Net private capital flows to sub-Saharan Africa, $11 billion in 1996, while still modest, were nevertheless ten times greater than at the beginning of the 1990s. China was the largest single recipient country, followed by Mexico. Private net flows recorded increases for all instruments, such as bonds, portfolio equity investments, foreign direct investment (FDI) and commercial bank lending. The latter, which had stagnated for many years, increased by $8 billion in 1996. Almost half of new bank lending was for project financing, especially for infrastructural development.

FDI flows to developing countries reached an estimated $110 billion in 1996, $14 billion more than in 1995, representing a fourfold increase since 1990. In 1996, East Asia and the Pacific and Latin America received the largest amounts of net FDI flows, with $61 billion and $26 billion, respectively, followed by Eastern Europe with $15 billion. FDI flows to sub-Saharan Africa, generally directed to the natural resource sectors of a rather limited number of countries, remained altogether low at $2.6 billion in 1996. China continued to be the largest individual recipient of FDI flows, accounting for more than $42 billion in 1996, a dramatic increase when compared with the $3.5 billion of 1990.

Net official development finance fell by $12 billion to an estimated $41 billion in 1996, the lowest level in more than a decade. Net official concessional flows, composed of ODA and other official aid flows to low- and middle-income countries, accounted for $44 billion in 1996, $0.8 billion lower than in the previous year. The decline was mainly attributable to a $1.3 billion fall in grants. Official concessional flows in 1996 remained concentrated in sub-Saharan Africa, with 34 percent of the total. However, the share of concessional flows to Europe and Central Asia rose from zero in 1990 to an estimated 20 percent in 1996. The decrease in long-term development assistance has been accompanied by a marked shift in fund allocation. An increasing amount of funds is indeed being directed towards emergencies such as refugee relief and other emergency aid. Altogether, an estimated 12 percent of all official development assistance is now devoted to emergency aid, compared with less than 2 percent in 1990.

Figure 3

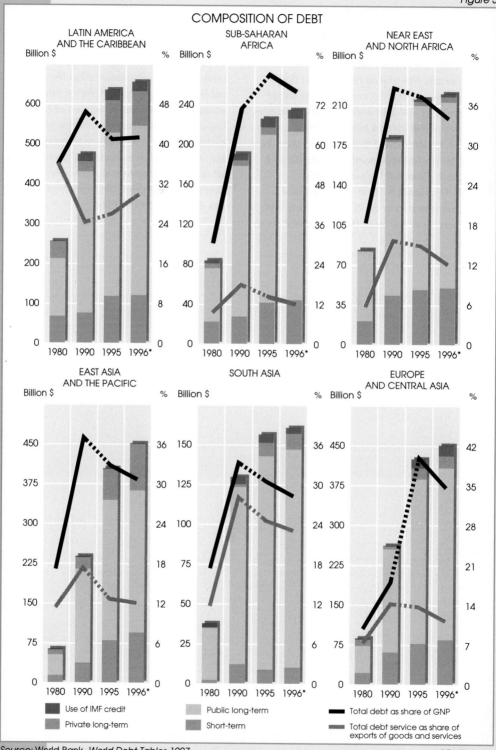

COMPOSITION OF DEBT

LATIN AMERICA AND THE CARIBBEAN

SUB-SAHARAN AFRICA

NEAR EAST AND NORTH AFRICA

EAST ASIA AND THE PACIFIC

SOUTH ASIA

EUROPE AND CENTRAL ASIA

Use of IMF credit
Private long-term
Public long-term
Short-term
Total debt as share of GNP
Total debt service as share of exports of goods and services

Source: World Bank, *World Debt Tables 1997*

* Preliminary

to strengthen during the first quarter of 1997. As regards cereals, prices rose to very high levels during 1995 and 1996 but tended to weaken in the first half of 1997 (see Exhibit 6, p. 25).

Economic outlook and the implications for agriculture

In the absence of unforeseen shocks, most analysts foresee a continuing world economic expansion into the medium term. For many developing countries, success in curbing inflation, liberalizing their economies and opening to international trade should enhance their prospects for continued or even accelerating growth. The developing countries should also benefit from the expected continued economic expansion, accompanied by moderate inflation in industrial countries, significantly lower real interest rates than during the 1980s, continued trade liberalization and a strong increase in private capital flows. However, this overall optimistic outlook masks widely diverging expectations for specific countries and regions. Much of the economic improvement in developing countries is expected in the already fast-growing East and South Asia regions, as well as in other countries in Asia and Latin America and the Caribbean that are better integrated in world financial and trade flows. For the least-developed countries in Africa, on the other hand, even an annual growth rate of about 4.5 percent[6] would be inadequate to raise their per caput incomes to any significant extent, let alone close the gap *vis-à-vis* other regions. Prospects appear particularly gloomy for many agriculture-based economies where social problems pose obstacles to the pursuance of reform policies to the extent necessary for building growth momentum and investor credibility, and these economies are therefore unable to mobilize flows of finance for economic diversification. They must also face the prospects of reduced aid and intensified competition in international markets.

For countries depending on primary product exports, a crucial determinant of their economic performance will be the evolution of commodity prices. According to World Bank forecasts, the decline in non-oil commodity prices over 1996-97 would return about two-thirds of the price gains seen in 1994-95, but a broad flattening of these prices should subsequently occur, contrasting with the major declines of the past 15 years. Moderately optimistic expectations for commodity prices overall constitute one of the basic assumptions of the agricultural projections reviewed below.

---

[6] **This rate is projected by Project LINK for the period 1998-2001 (see Agricultural outlook for the developing countries, p. 46).**

Agricultural outlook for the developing countries

Mid-term forecasts of economic and agricultural output growth in the developing countries, as elaborated by Project LINK, include the following noteworthy features:

- Prospects for the period 1998-2001 are for annual rates of GDP growth of more than 6 percent in the developing countries as a whole, somewhat above what was forecast a year earlier. The outlook for agricultural output also appears more favourable than previously forecast although, at an annual 4.5 percent, the growth rates for the sector are expected to lag well behind those of the economy as a whole. Such projected annual growth rates of 4.5 percent for the developing countries must be considered with caution, however. On the one hand, they appear optimistic in the light of long-term trends and the deceleration in agricultural production growth in some large countries such as China and India in recent years. On the other hand, they do not appear inconsistent with the projected continuation of very high GDP growth rates in the developing countries (above 6 percent yearly) over 1998-2001, and the generally strong performances of the agricultural sector in these countries in recent years. [7]
- The least dynamic performances of the agricultural sector are likely to be in sub-Saharan Africa, the region where such performances have a greater developmental and food security importance. Nevertheless, at close to 4 percent, growth in agricultural output would still exceed long-term trends by a significant margin and enable gains in per caput terms. For the other developing country regions, the projected levels of agricultural growth (about 4.5 percent annually) would also constitute a significant improvement in relation to past trends.
- The agricultural trade of the developing countries is likely to benefit from the more favourable world economic outlook and market liberalization. After a significant decline following the end of the 1994/95 commodity boom, agricultural export earnings are forecast to gather momentum in 1998-2001. In this period, agricultural exports are forecast to expand at annual

---

[7] As reviewed above, developing countries' GDP rose by more than 6 percent yearly during 1992-96. IMF projects GDP growth rates of 6.6 and 6.7 percent for these countries in 1997 and 1998, respectively, in line with Project LINK forecasts for this period. Crops and livestock production in the developing countries rose by 4 percent in 1993, 5 percent in 1994, 5.2 percent in 1995 and 2.9 percent in 1996.

BOX 2
OUTLOOK FOR THE ECONOMIES HIGHLY DEPENDENT ON AGRICULTURAL EXPORTS

Mid-term prospects for economies highly dependent on agricultural exports (EHDAEs)[1] appear generally favourable in relation to past trends. The forecast growth of their agricultural export value (5 to 6 percent yearly during 1998-2001) would more than offset the projected deterioration in agricultural terms of trade, thus enabling some improvement in the purchasing power of their agricultural exports. The outlook appears more promising for the Latin American and Caribbean countries than for the African countries of this group, reflecting in particular the commodity composition of these regions' exports. Indeed, market prospects appear to be more favourable for a number of export commodities of Latin America and the Caribbean – in particular cereals, livestock products, soybeans and fruits – than for the less diversified range of commodities that constitute the bulk of Africa's agricultural exports – chiefly coffee, cotton and cocoa.

The generally favourable prospects for the EHDAEs' agricultural exports are expected to contribute to an improvement in their overall economic outlook. IMF has prepared for FAO some short-term (1997-98)

[1] This group comprises 47 countries (24 in sub-Saharan Africa, 18 in Latin America and the Caribbean and five in the Near East and North Africa) for which agricultural, fishery and forestry exports are equivalent to at least 20 percent of their total exports, or 20 percent of their total imports.

forecasts of economic performance in these countries:

- an acceleration of GDP growth, to around 5.5 percent, up from the average 4.9 percent of the previous five years;
- a significant increase in investment rates, suggesting a consolidation of the basis for sustained growth in the years to come – gross capital formation should rise to 26 to 27 percent of GDP in 1997-98, up from less than 20 percent in the mid-1980s and 24 percent in the early 1990s;
- a dramatic decline in consumer price increases, from hyperinflationary rates in the early 1990s to single digits in 1997-98;
- a reduction in central government fiscal deficit, from 2 to 4 percent of GDP during the 1980s to less than 1 percent in 1997-98;
- an increase in the value of merchandise exports of about 8 percent in 1997 and 10 percent in 1998 (with a strong expansion in the volume of exports more than offsetting weakening export unit values) and a similarly strong expansion in the value of merchandise imports;
- widened current account imbalances, resulting from larger deficits in the trade and service balances (despite the vigorous performance of the export sector) outweighing larger positive current transfers;
- little encouragement on the external debt front: debt-service payments are forecast to climb from about $69 billion in 1996 to

about $82 billion to $85 billion in 1997-98, claiming about 40 percent of export earnings in the Latin American and Caribbean countries of this group as compared with 36 percent in 1996 (for the Latin America and Caribbean region as a whole the debt service-export ratio was 30 percent in 1996). In the case of the African countries, however, the ratio is likely to decline significantly in 1998, to 22 percent, after having climbed to 29 percent in 1997.

rates of about 4.5 percent in sub-Saharan Africa, 6 percent in the Near East and North Africa, 5.5 percent in the Far East and Oceania and more than 8 percent in Latin America and the Caribbean. In particular for Africa, which had seen its agricultural export earnings stagnate or decline over the 1980-1993 period, such growth rates would imply a marked improvement over past trends. Export earnings from agriculture should also expand somewhat faster than agricultural imports in all developing country regions except the Near East and North Africa, where the agricultural trade deficit by 2000 can be expected to rise by about 30 percent from current levels.

- Prospects for food and agricultural trade in China are of particular interest in view of the debate over possible implications for the food supply/demand balance worldwide. Project LINK forecasts accelerating growth in agricultural import demand, at an average annual rate of about 6 percent (which, again, should be viewed with caution given China's decline in cereal imports in 1997), but an even more marked expansion of agricultural exports for 1998-2001. This suggests a continuation of the trend begun in the mid-1980s, when China emerged as an agricultural net exporter. [8]

- In line with the movements in agricultural prices reviewed above, the terms of trade of agricultural exports are expected to improve in 1997 after the deterioration that took place in 1996 following the end of the price boom. Forecasts for the mid-term are for a more stable pattern of movements in agricultural terms of trade, with a slightly deteriorating trend. The cumulative deterioration during 1998-2001 is forecast to be about 3 percent for the developing countries as a whole.

[8] A large number of analyses and projections have been made of China's future food needs and the resulting trade implications. These vary widely on the sides of domestic production and demand. A recent review (by Ke Bingsheng, Vice President and Professor at China Agricultural University) reveals that the gap between the most pessimistic and optimistic estimates of China's future cereal import needs in the various studies are almost 80 million tonnes for the year 2000, 111 million tonnes for 2010 and more than 300 million tonnes for 2030.

WORLD REVIEW
III. Selected issues

FORESTS IN A GLOBAL CONTEXT[9]

Globally, forestry faces difficult challenges as we enter the next millennium. Population growth, changes in population distribution, economic pressures and efforts to alleviate poverty and ensure food security are leading to the intense scrutiny of forests' actual and potential contribution to development and of the relative benefits of retaining land under forest as opposed to converting it to other land uses. The most obvious challenge within the sector is how to meet the growing demand for forest products while safeguarding the ability of forests to provide a range of environmental services, including the maintenance of soil and water resources, protection against desertification, the conservation of biological diversity and mitigation of global climate change. Conflicting demands and differences in opinion about the relative importance of the goods and various services provided by forests must be addressed. Easily quantified economic benefits from forests, including the production of wood and non-food forest products and the generation of employment, must be weighted against environmental and social benefits, all of which have a value but only some of which are easily expressed in monetary terms. Demands for a more equitable distribution of the benefits from forests, for safeguarding the rights of forest dwellers and indigenous peoples and for widespread participation in decision-making related to forests will add to the complexity and challenge of forest management and policy-making in the coming years.

Major current trends that are having an effect on forests include continued population growth and urbanization, higher rates of global economic growth after the sluggish first three years of this decade, the continued progress of many former centrally planned economies towards a market economy and trade liberalization.

---

[9] The material in this section is taken from FAO. 1997. *State of the World's Forests 1997*. Rome. This biennial report provides a comprehensive view of global forestry, with policy-relevant information on the state of the world's forests today and on recent developments in the sector.

Over the past few years, the structure and functions of public institutions, including forestry and related departments, have continued to undergo significant changes. Trends in decentralization, the privatization of functions previously assigned to the public sector and a movement towards a more pluralistic, or multipartner, institutional environment have become more apparent. Budget reductions have affected forestry departments in developed and developing countries alike. Environmental concerns increasingly are influencing natural resource policies and practices and even, to some extent, international trade. Finally, the "internationalization" of issues continues; attention at the highest policy-making levels has been drawn to the interactions between development and environmental and social issues through four international summits held within the last two years: the World Summit for Social Development (Copenhagen, March 1995); the Fourth World Conference on Women (Beijing, September 1995); Habitat II – the Second United Nations Conference on Human Settlements (Istanbul, June 1996) and the World Food Summit (Rome, November 1996). The importance accorded internationally to forestry is reflected in the establishment of the Intergovernmental Panel on Forests in April 1995 by the UN Commission on Sustainable Development (CSD) to encourage international consensus on key issues related to forests. Set up to monitor the implementation of the agreements made at the United Nations Conference on Environment and Development (UNCED – Rio de Janeiro, June 1992), the CSD reported to a special session of the UN General Assembly in June 1997 on progress made over the last five years. This meeting was attended by many heads of state and has kept the discussion of sustainable development prominent on the agenda of policy-makers.

The effect of population and economic growth on demand for food and forest products is clearly illustrated by past consumption trends. Between 1960 and 1995, world population almost doubled in size and the world economy (as measured by GDP in real terms) tripled. Over the same period, world production of grains more than doubled while that of fuelwood doubled and that of paper more than tripled. Looking ahead, today's population of 5.7 billion is expected to grow to seven billion by the year 2010. Nearly all of this increase will occur in the developing world, where constraints to agricultural and forestry production are particularly challenging and national economic imperatives and disparities in income distribution are already putting intense pressure on natural resources. These factors will certainly affect the ability of countries to attain long-term food security and to maintain the productivity of their natural resource base, including forest resources.

Figure 4

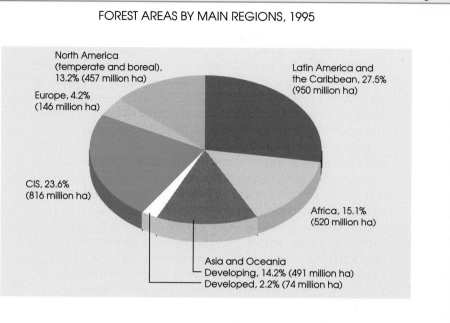

FOREST AREAS BY MAIN REGIONS, 1995

North America
(temperate and boreal),
13.2% (457 million ha)

Latin America and
the Caribbean, 27.5%
(950 million ha)

Europe, 4.2%
(146 million ha)

CIS, 23.6%
(816 million ha)

Africa, 15.1%
(520 million ha)

Asia and Oceania
Developing, 14.2% (491 million ha)
Developed, 2.2% (74 million ha)

Source: FAO

Figure 5

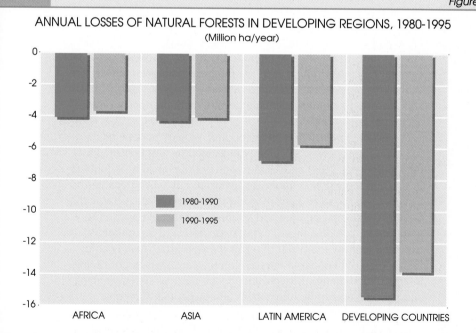

ANNUAL LOSSES OF NATURAL FORESTS IN DEVELOPING REGIONS, 1980-1995
(Million ha/year)

1980-1990

1990-1995

AFRICA   ASIA   LATIN AMERICA   DEVELOPING COUNTRIES

Source: FAO

New information on global forest cover was released in 1997 by FAO's Forest Resources Assessment Programme, including: the area of forests in 1995; changes in forest area between 1990 and 1995; and revised estimates for changes in forest area between 1980 and 1990.[10] Forests (natural and plantation) are estimated to have covered 3 454 million ha (26 percent of the world's total land area) in 1995, 57 percent of which were in developing countries. The distribution of forest area by main regions is shown in Figure 4.

Worldwide, there was a net loss of 56 million ha between 1990 and 1995. This was due to a decrease of 65 million ha in developing countries and an increase of 9 million ha in developed countries over the five-year period. Considering only natural forests in developing countries, which is where most deforestation is occurring, the new estimates indicate that:

- the annual loss of natural forests between 1980 and 1990 was lower than the estimate made earlier in the Forest Resources Assessment 1990 (15.5 million versus 16.3 million ha); and
- the annual loss of natural forests was lower during the 1990-1995 period than the 1980-1990 period (13.7 million versus 15.5 million ha) as indicated in Figure 5.

In short, although deforestation continues to be significant in developing countries, it appears that the rate of loss of natural forests may be slowing. While this is a positive sign, it will be difficult to know whether it is the beginning of a trend until more data are available from FAO's Forest Resources Assessment 2000, now in progress.

Recently released information[11] on the causes of deforestation between 1980 and 1990 shows that key factors in forest cover change are rural population growth, coupled with agricultural expansion (especially in Africa and Asia), and large economic development programmes involving the resettlement of people, agricultural expansion and infrastructure development (in Latin America and Asia). Although timber harvesting is generally not a direct cause of deforestation, it is known to be a facilitating factor in some areas, particularly through the construction of roads which make previously remote areas accessible to agricultural colonizers.

Demand for food to feed the world's increasing population will continue to put pressure on forest lands. FAO estimates that the

---

[10] These data are published in FAO, op. cit., footnote 9, p. 50. This work also analyses of these figures and provides data on forest cover by country.
[11] FAO. 1996. *Forest resources assessment 1990: Survey of tropical forest cover and study of change processes.* FAO Forestry Paper No. 130. Rome.

increase in world food production to meet rising demand, mainly in developing countries, is likely to be in the order of 1.8 percent per year from now until 2010. In some countries, supplies will be increased by importing food or by intensifying production on existing agricultural land. For countries where neither option is feasible and where opportunities for land expansion exist (mainly sub-Saharan Africa and Latin America), food supplies will also be increased by putting more land into agriculture. The need for increased production and improved access to food in developing countries is also drawing greater attention to the ways in which forests and trees can contribute to household and national food security, in particular their role in protecting the natural resource base on which agriculture depends.

On the other hand, in some developed countries the levelling off of demand for agricultural products, coupled with continued intensification of production, is resulting in the release of marginal agricultural lands from production and therefore new opportunities for afforestation.

Despite overall positive economic performances in much of the developing world in recent years (see World economic environment, p. 37), poverty, hunger and malnutrition persist in parts of the world and among various sectors of the population because of an uneven distribution of wealth and access to resources. Many of the world's poor live near forests and are dependent on forest lands and resources for their livelihoods. Forests do and will continue to play a particularly important role in providing products and income for these people. Competing demands for forests to continue to provide for local needs while meeting increasing national demands for industrial forest products, which will be stimulated by rising overall income levels, may well intensify.

The combined impact of economic growth and increasing population size on demand for forest products is likely to be significant, particularly so since per caput consumption of industrial forest products is especially responsive to changes in low-level incomes. There was a 36 percent increase in consumption of wood products between 1970 and 1994. Slightly more than half the wood harvested each year is consumed as fuelwood, while the rest is used for industrial wood products. Today, demand for fuelwood continues to increase at a rate of about 1.2 percent per year (the average annual rate of increase for 1992-94). Demand for industrial wood products seems to be levelling off in developed countries but it continues to rise steadily in developing countries. Preliminary figures from the forthcoming issue of FAO's *Global Outlook Studies* indicate that the increase in demand for wood products (fuelwood and industrial wood) between 1990 and 2010 will be in the order of

20 percent, driven primarily by expanding populations and economic growth in developing countries.

One of the most pressing questions regarding the future outlook for the forest sector is whether there will be sufficient wood to meet expanded demand in the future and whether it can be supplied without unacceptable social and environmental costs. Various factors are having an impact on forest product supply, including increased plantation establishment and improvements in processing (both of which help ease the situation), and an apparent, sharp decrease in timber removals in the Russian Federation this decade (which has had a significant impact on world wood production). In addition, restrictions placed on timber harvesting in natural forests in response to environmental concerns are reducing industrial roundwood supplies in some countries.

The area under plantations in developing regions has doubled between 1980 and 1995 (from 40 million ha to 81 million ha), and industrial wood production from farm forestry and agroforestry systems is becoming increasingly important in several countries. Increased demand for forest products is likely to reinforce these trends.

Improvements in forest industries have resulted in significant increases in output of finished products per unit of raw material. These improvements include the diversification of raw materials (e.g. an increasing use of coconut wood and rubber wood in forest industries), greater use of wood residues, the increased recycling of paper and paperboard and the development of more efficient processing technologies. International trade, which has increased steadily in volume (see Figure 6) and value over the past few decades, is expected to become even more important as a way to compensate for shortages in many countries' wood supply. Although developed countries still dominate world trade in forest products on both the export and import sides, developing countries, particularly in Asia and Latin America, are becoming increasingly important. Asian countries are expected to become even more important importers of wood products to offset predicted major wood deficits.

The dissolution of the USSR and subsequent efforts by newly independent countries to move from a centrally planned to a market economy are having major impacts on forestry. First, there have been serious disruptions in forest management and production systems as well as forest product processing and trade in some of these countries. Particularly significant are the changes in the Russian Federation, which accounts for more than one-fifth of the world's forests and is a major producer of industrial roundwood. The sharp decrease (recorded removals in 1994 were only about half of those in 1990) in industrial roundwood removals in the CIS and the

Baltic states contributed to the decline of about 15 percent in world industrial roundwood production over the same period. Second, major reorganizations are taking place in the forestry sectors of the countries in transition in Central and Eastern Europe and the CIS, including the reorientation of forestry policies and institutions, the privatization of forest operations and state-owned forest enterprises and the restitution of nationalized forest land to former owners or to their heirs.

The impact of rapid infrastructure development and of urbanization on land use, land cover and environmental conditions in urban and peri-urban areas is evident in many areas of the world, but especially in Africa and Asia where the rates of urbanization are highest. The effect of urbanization on overall demand for forest products and on rural land use, however, has been studied less and is less well understood than the relationships between forest resources and population or economic growth; it is unclear whether the patterns evident in developed countries as they became urbanized will hold true for developing countries, which are urbanizing at a much faster rate and have populations at much lower income levels. What is apparent, however, is that there is considerable scope for forestry to improve the environmental

Figure 6

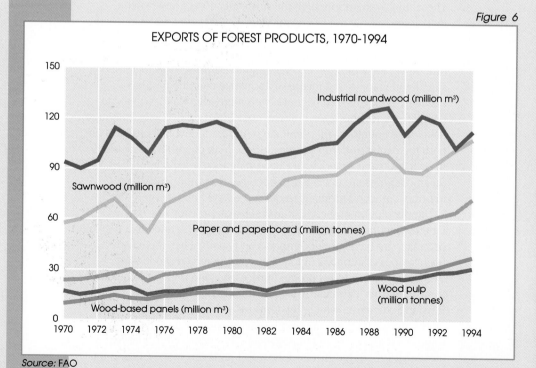

EXPORTS OF FOREST PRODUCTS, 1970-1994

Source: FAO

conditions and livelihoods of urban dwellers and, in some places, there is a potential productive role that peri-urban plantations can play in providing urban populations with wood products. While rapid urbanization is no longer an issue in most developed countries, in recent years an increased awareness of the potential environmental and social benefits of forests and trees in urban areas has led to the development of strong urban forestry programmes in many countries such as the United States and in Europe.

Environmental awareness and public pressure have continued to have an impact on all aspects of the forestry sector: on forest management, harvesting and post-harvest activities, markets and trade in forest products. Concern that forests should be managed in such a way as to ensure that their productive functions, environmental services and social benefits are sustained over the long term has led to efforts to develop criteria and indicators for sustainable forest management.[12]

There is a trend towards the management of forests as ecological systems that have multiple economic benefits and environmental values, and management objectives put more weight on environmental protection and the conservation of biological diversity. More attention has been drawn to the potential environmental and social benefits which might result from the development of non-wood forest products. Restrictions have been placed on harvesting in national forests in North America and some tropical Asian and South Pacific countries. Reduced-impact logging systems are being advocated to minimize harmful effects of timber harvesting. Some initiatives, such as certification schemes and the listing of timber species in appendixes of the Convention on International Trade in Endangered Species of Wild Fauna and Flora, are being implemented in an attempt to link trade to forestry-related environmental concerns.

The increased importance ascribed to the environmental functions of forests and their integral role in sustainable forest management was highlighted by Chapter 11 of Agenda 21 (Combating deforestation) and the "Forest Principles" adopted at UNCED. It is also reflected in recently enacted international conventions, including: the International Convention to Combat Desertification; the Convention on Biological Diversity; and the UN Framework Convention on Global Climate Change. These conventions are

---

[12] A special section in *State of the World's Forests 1997* provides a comprehensive discussion of recent global, regional and national efforts to develop criteria and indicators of sustainable forest management.

expected to reinforce ongoing national, regional and international activities related to forests.

Both the socio-cultural benefits of forests and the social implications of the distribution of forest benefits continue to be issues of international attention and national action. The questions range from how to meet the needs and respect the rights of indigenous groups, forest-dwelling and forest-dependent people to the more universal question of how to take into consideration the range of demands for forest goods and services by a variety of interest groups. These concerns have resulted in the further development and institutionalization of various participatory forest management systems, in the devolution of ownership of forest resources and in the recognition of access rights of local communities and user groups. In many developing countries in particular, local communities are playing an increasingly important role in the day-to-day management and protection of forest resources and, in the case of indigenous peoples, efforts are being made to minimize outside interference with traditional resource management practices. Increasingly, in developed and developing countries alike, action is being taken to develop means by which the opinions of a wide range of interest groups can be considered in forestry policy and management decision-making.

The forestry sector is undergoing a dynamic evolution in a rapidly changing world. The world's forests and forestry sector are shaped as much by external economic, political, demographic and social trends as by forces working within the sector itself. Both the present and the future of forests must be considered within the wider context of development, which has as its ultimate goal the improved well-being of present and future generations of human beings.

RAISING WOMEN'S PRODUCTIVITY IN AGRICULTURE
Introduction
Women play an extremely important role in agricultural development, accounting for an estimated 40 percent of the agricultural labour force in Latin America and the Caribbean and between 60 and 80 percent in both Asia and the Pacific and Africa.[13] A lack of adequate research casts serious doubts on estimates of women's full contributions to farm activities. Additionally, women's low participation in national and regional policy-making, their invisibility in national statistics and their lack of participation in extension services (with the exception of home economics programmes) has meant that issues of most concern to women are often neglected in the planning, appraisal, implementation, management and evaluation of many rural development policies and programmes. Other reasons why

agricultural development efforts have failed to be reoriented towards women include limited female leadership and resources in recipient governments as well as gender biases within donor agencies.[14] This neglect of women results in losses in potential productivity gains and economic growth.

The challenge to include women in development efforts was first taken up at the 1975 World Conference on Women in Mexico and again in Copenhagen in 1980. In the wake of the UN Decade for Women (1975-1985), many international initiatives have since contributed to a greater recognition of women's key participation in rural and other domains of development. The Fourth World Conference on Women, held in Beijing in 1995, reconfirmed a global commitment towards the advancement of women.

In response, most governments have signed various international agreements, treaties and conventions, pledging to pay greater attention to the needs of women, particularly rural women, and to focus more efforts and resources on raising their productivity. A wider understanding of gender issues, and of the role of women in agriculture and food security, has become part of mainstream development thinking. For example, many governments and agencies now have women-in-development units and gender policies and specialists. There have also been improvements in the collection of gender-disaggregated data, research on female-headed households and the role of women in agriculture, and methods for including the activities of women in national accounts. Additionally, effective women's organizations are helping female farmers gain better access to credit and resources.

Despite these public displays of commitment, change has been slow and many development efforts are still not reaching a significant number of women. When women have been targeted as beneficiaries, it has generally been in their reproductive capacity or as targets of welfare interventions. Until recently, small, dispersed

---

[13] Based on estimates from the UN regional economic commissions: the Economic Commission for Africa (ECA); the Economic and Social Commission for Asia and the Pacific (ESCAP); and the Economic Commission for Latin America and the Caribbean (ECLAC). The estimates are aggregates from micro level studies that examined the full farming system, not just the measured agricultural labour force. Cited in R.L. Blumberg. 1989. *Making the case for the gender variable: women and the wealth and well-being of nations.* Washington, DC, USAID.

[14] M. Snyder, F. Berry and P. Mavima. 1996. Gender policy in development assistance: improving implementation results. *World Development,* 24(9).

"women-specific" projects, or project components, focusing on their productive role in agriculture have remained isolated from national agricultural planning and policies. Given the crucial role they play in food production and provisioning, efforts to increase women's productivity are vital to global food security. Key among these efforts is increasing women's access to agricultural education, extension and training, as human capital development has been shown to be a prerequisite for increasing agricultural productivity. Ensuring full participation of women in the Special Programme for Food Security pilot demonstration projects and in constraints analyses is essential for short-term benefits.

The role of women in agricultural development

Although there is diversity in household production patterns, women in all regions of the world play a predominant role in household food security through agricultural and food production. It is estimated that women in developing countries spend up to two-thirds of their time in traditional agriculture and marketing, with their work hours tending to exceed those of men. In these countries, women in rural areas grow at least 50 percent of the world's food. They work in all aspects of cultivation, including planting, thinning, weeding, applying fertilizer and harvesting as well as post-harvest activities such as storage, handling, stocking, marketing and processing. They are also involved in poultry and livestock production. In Southeast Asia and the Pacific, as well as in Latin America, women's home gardens represent some of the most complex agricultural systems known. While nearly all tasks associated with subsistence food production are performed by women, their share in cash crop farming is also significant.

The findings of a UNDP/World Bank project in Burkina Faso, Kenya, Nigeria and Zambia on raising productivity of women farmers in sub-Saharan Africa concluded that women are so important to African agriculture that initiatives to raise the sector's productivity cannot afford to ignore them. Women farmers in this region produce more than three-quarters of its basic food supply. In addition, they are now cultivating crops (e.g. coffee and other cash crops), taking on tasks (such as land clearing) traditionally undertaken by men and, increasingly, making decisions on the daily management of farms and households.[15] This is partly due to males

---

[15] K. Saito. 1994. *Raising the productivity of women farmers in sub-Saharan Africa.* World Bank Discussion Paper No. 230, Africa Technical Department Series. Washington, DC, World Bank.

migrating away from farms in search of more remunerative activities. While women produce much of the developing world's food supply and are the backbone of food production and provisioning for family consumption, their productivity is generally low and based on long work hours on small landholdings. They also have restricted access to training, technology, credit and inputs and, for the most part, use traditional and unimproved agricultural methods. Closing the gap between current and potential productivity levels may be the most effective means of promoting agricultural development. The opportunity to do so in the low-income food-deficit countries is presented by the Special Programme for Food Security pilot phase.

Investing in education: effects on productivity

Investing in human capital is one of the most effective means to reduce poverty and bring about sustainable economic growth. Research suggests that increasing the average amount of education of the labour force by one year raises GDP by 9 percent. This is true for the first three additional years of education, in which case a 27 percent increase in GDP can be expected.[16]

Virtually all studies on agricultural productivity show that more educated farmers earn a higher return on their land. According to one study,[17] four years of primary education increased the productivity of farmers by 8.7 percent overall, and by 10 percent in cases where a modernizing environment was prevalent, largely in Asia. (A modern environment was characterized by the availability of new crop varieties, innovative planting methods, erosion control and the availability of capital inputs such as insecticide, fertilizer and tractors or machines. Market-oriented production and exposure to extension services were also indicators.) In analysing Malaysia, Thailand and the Republic of Korea, Jamison and Lau[18] estimated that one year of schooling is on average associated with a net increment to farm product of 5.1, 2.8 and 2.3 percent, respectively.

---

[16] The return thereafter of an additional year of education diminishes to a GDP increase of approximately 4 percent, or a total of 12 percent for three years (World Bank. 1991. *World Development Report 1991.* New York, Oxford University Press).

[17] Lockheed, D. Jamison and L. Lau. 1980. Farmer education and farm efficiency: a survey. *Economic Development and Cultural Change,* 29(1): 37-76.

[18] D. Jamison and L. Lau. 1982. *Farmer education and farm efficiency.* Baltimore, USA, The Johns Hopkins University Press for the World Bank.

A World Bank study estimates that the rate of return on investments in women's education is in the order of 12 percent in terms of increased productivity, the highest rate of return of possible investments in developing nations. The researchers estimated that if women and men received the same education, farm-specific yields would increase from 7 to 22 percent. Increasing women's primary schooling alone would increase agricultural output by 24 percent.[19]

Education also plays a major role in improving the status of women, the nutrition of their families and national food production. Female education brings significant social returns, with associated improvements to household health and nutrition, lower infant and child morbidity and mortality and slower population growth.[20] Women's education also typically pays off in wage increases, with a consequential rise in household incomes. A recent ILO report indicates that each additional year of schooling raises a woman's earnings by about 15 percent compared with 11 percent for a man.[21]

For agriculture, female education is crucial to higher productivity and increased implementation of environmental protection measures. Education is most effective in increasing productivity and aggregate output when technological inputs, training and access to information are readily available. Increasing agricultural production is therefore contingent not only on education but also on ensuring women equal access to extension, agricultural credit and other inputs and support services.

Agricultural extension: the current situation

Agricultural extension programmes bridge the gap between technical knowledge and farmers' practices. Generally, they are free public services, but user fees and private extension services do exist. Numerous studies show that extension is generally cost effective and has significant and positive impacts on farmers' knowledge and adoption of new technology, and hence on farm productivity and rural incomes. Without technical assistance, information and training, farmers are limited in their ability to adopt new technologies and plant varieties. They may be forced to use low-input/low-output cultivation techniques, thereby reducing the

---

[19] K. Saito, op. cit., footnote 15, p. 60.
[20] K. Subbarao and L. Raney. 1995. Social gains from female education: a cross-national study. *Economic Development and Cultural Change*, 44(1).
[21] L. Lim. 1996. Women swell ranks of working poor. *World of Work*, Vol. 17. Geneva, ILO.

intensity of cultivation. This results in lower crop yields and may be linked to environmental degradation.

Given women's role in agriculture, including female farmers in extension makes sense for a variety of reasons. First, agricultural extension programmes that ignore women's farming roles risk low returns, inefficiency and, in the long term, failure to achieve development objectives. Second, extension activities that are carried out without the participation of female farmers risk having negative impacts on women and their families. Accordingly, the productivity and welfare of rural households can be maximized when both female and male farmers participate in extension activities that are relevant to their roles as agricultural producers.

The present situation, however, is that agricultural information is not reaching or benefiting women effectively. FAO estimates that rural women's access to agricultural extension worldwide is currently only about one-twentieth of that of men.[22] The belief that information will trickle down to them through households and communities is still widely held. Studies in Asia and the Pacific, Africa and Latin America and the Caribbean, however, show that such transmission is often poor.[23] FAO survey data (1989) show that about 5 percent of all agricultural extension resources worldwide are directed to female farmers and 15 percent of the world's extension agents are women, which is a sharp contrast with the proportion of agricultural work carried out by women (Table 2). Whether by design or default, the result is a male-to-male system for transferring agricultural training, technologies and information.

The lack of female extension agents is one of the biggest constraints to African women in gaining information and training. FAO found that women accounted for less than 11 percent of extension staff in Africa. Very few of the female agents surveyed had agricultural training; most specialized in home economics. Only 7 percent of all agricultural extension services were allocated to women farmers, and extension services traditionally available to women – home economics – received only 1 percent of total extension resources.[24]

According to a recent FAO report on the Near East region, where

[22] FAO. 1996. *Farmers' rights in the conservation and use of plant genetic resources: who are the farmers?* By S. Bunning and C. Hill. Rome.

[23] B. Hertz. 1989. Bringing women into the mainstream. *Finance and Development,* (December): 22-25.

[24] FAO. 1995. *Women, agriculture and rural development – a synthesis report of the Africa region.* Rome.

TABLE 2

Percentage of agricultural work carried out by women versus percentage of women extension staff

Country	Female agricultural work	Female extension staff
	(percentage)	
Benin	60-80	8
Congo	60	10
Morocco	50	9
Namibia	59	9
Philippines	26	44
Sudan	49-57	22
Tanzania, United Rep.	54	16
Tunisia	24	4
Zimbabwe	70	8

Source: FAO. Women, agriculture and rural development fact sheets (for the respective countries).

women represent an important source of agricultural labour, the majority of extension officers in the region are male and most of their target farmers are males.[25] In Egypt, women perform 53 percent of the agricultural labour, but women extension officers constitute less than 1 percent of the total. Extension to female farmers is often limited to traditional home-based activities, such as health, hygiene and home management. In India, agricultural extension services largely bypass the 40 percent of the country's farm workers who are female. Studies of extension services in Latin America and the Caribbean find similar biases.

Gender barriers in extension and training

Extension messages that ignore the unique role, responsibilities and workloads of women farmers are inappropriate for them. According to an FAO report on women, agriculture and development in Africa, the primary focus of extension is oriented towards commercial crops, which are traditionally grown by men, rather than on food and subsistence crops, which are the primary concern of women farmers and the key to food security. Women working in agriculture generally undertake extremely diverse activities and so require a wider range of information and training than men. Most extension

---

[25] FAO. 1995. *Women, agriculture and rural development – a synthesis report of the Near East region.* Rome.

programmes lack the breadth of content needed to interest or benefit large numbers of women.

Another result of male-dominated extension services is the oversight of the practical constraints facing women. Male extension agents in many countries do not consider the dual roles of women in farming and the family, and they consequently schedule meetings and demonstrations at times and places that are inconvenient for women farmers. A lack of child care services and the need to perform household chores mean women often cannot attend. Extension meetings may also interfere with income-generating activities. In eastern Nigeria, for example, local markets operate on a five-day cycle, and few women can afford to forgo the income of a market day in order to meet an extension agent.

Distance from extension sites can pose a serious problem for women because of transportation costs and cultural restrictions on their mobility. For instance, in eastern Nepal, few females attended training courses because they lacked experience in social interaction; in their communities, it is the men who primarily deal with the outside world.[26] In other cases, women may not be able to change their work schedules without permission from village elders.

Underlying these problems is a lack of recognition that men and women are often responsible for different crops, livestock, tasks and income-generating activities, and therefore have different extension needs. As an example of flawed assumptions about gender roles, in Zambia, extension agents provided special beakers for measuring fertilizer to male farmers, although it was the women who actually applied the fertilizer. Consequently, the women continued to apply the fertilizer without the beakers and the problem of inaccurate measurements persisted.[27]

The lack of women extension agents severely curtails the spreading of vital information to women farmers since, in many societies, they are discouraged from speaking individually with male extension agents. Even where extension contact between the sexes is relatively unrestricted, male agents may encounter difficulties in dealing with women, resulting in services being skewed away from female clients, as occurred in a forestry project in Honduras.[28]

---

[26] P.P. Bhattarai. 1989. *Women's roles – a case study of Tankhuwa Panchayat.* PAC Occasional Paper No. 1. Kathmandu, Pakhnibas Agricultural Centre.
[27] V. Nayak-Mukeherjee. 1991. *Women in the economy – a select annotated bibliography of Asia and the Pacific.* Kuala Lumpur, Asian and Pacific Development Centre.
[28] Ibid.

Where women are hired, however, they often face lower pay and other inequities. Socio-cultural restrictions may also pose difficulties for women agents by, for example, preventing them from travelling by motorbike or applying for posts away from families and communities.

The lack of female staff can be attributed in part to male-dominated extension and research organizations that fail to understand the need to target services directly to women farmers. The "glass ceiling" limiting promotions for women in these agencies may exacerbate the situation. One study points to examples in the Department of Agricultural Extension in Bangladesh, where women made up only 5 percent of staff with college degrees, and in the Caribbean Agricultural Research and Development Institute, where 22 percent of the staff were women. Furthermore, opportunities to hire women are declining as these agencies face reduced budgets and staff cutbacks.[29]

Perhaps the greatest problem is in recruiting qualified women from agricultural educational institutions to fill positions in extension services. Although the enrolment of women in agricultural programmes is generally lower than that of men, their proportions are substantially higher than the proportions employed in extension would indicate. For example, in Lebanon 47 percent of bachelor's degree recipients in agriculture and veterinary science and 59 percent of master's degree graduates in these fields are women. In Peru nearly 30 percent of the university-level agriculture graduates are female. In Zimbabwe, 22 percent of those enrolled in agriculture and 18 percent of those in veterinary science at the college or university level are women. In Tunisia 12 percent of those receiving agricultural training are women. In Honduras, at the university level women make up 12 to 42 percent of students in various agricultural majors. In the Sudan, while few students are enrolled in graduate-level agricultural or veterinary studies, one-third are women.

Existing women-oriented extension services tend to concentrate almost exclusively on women's reproductive role. As such, they provide women with training in traditional home-based activities such as child care and home management, but little or no training in income-generating activities, such as crop and livestock production, agro-industries or sustainable agriculture. In settlement schemes in Sri Lanka and Malaysia, for example, rural women were trained in cake-making and embroidery, despite their high degree of participation in agricultural activities.

---

[29] V. Nayak-Mukeherjee, op. cit., footnote 27, p. 65.

However, the need for agricultural extension services directed at women is only increasing. A World Bank study of Burkina Faso, the Gambia, Mali, Mauritania and Senegal reveals that women in the Sahel are increasing their labour input in agricultural production as a result of male migration, changes in gender responsibilities, intensification of farming and environmental degradation. Despite this increase in responsibility, these women have not received a commensurate increase in access to resources and services.[30] One of the major reasons for this is that rural surveys are designed or administered to identify men as heads of households. Thus, female-headed households are ignored and excluded from projects and funds. This is particularly striking given that, in some regions of Africa, 60 percent of households are headed by women.

In Asia and the Pacific, while many extension efforts have successfully reached women over the past 20 years, serious constraints still limit women's access to information and technical assistance. For example, women involved in small-scale livestock rearing – a major activity in almost all Asian countries – cite a lack of both livestock-related extension services and access to veterinarians.[31]

Even when contacted, many women are unable to utilize extension recommendations fully because of limited access to land, credit, inputs, technologies and markets. Very few credit-lending arrangements in the Near East, for example, have been set up especially for women farmers, and only a small number apply for credit. This is mainly attributable to weak institutional structures, traditional beliefs and cultural practices, a high degree of illiteracy and poor education as well as women's lack of collateral. In many developing countries, rural women often do not have the necessary education or skills, such as functional literacy and management experience, to understand extension literature or to participate fully in activities.

The failure of governments and donors to provide these women with agricultural inputs and support services results in considerable in agricultural productivity and output losses. Although some changes have been made over the past few years in terms of women's access to extension services, women's contact with extension has not had as positive an impact on output as has that of men. These disappointing results point to the need for strategies to

---

[30] **World Bank. 1995. *Rural women in the Sahel and their access to agricultural extension – sector study*. Report No. 13532. Washington, DC.**
[31] **V. Nayak-Mukeherjee, op. cit., footnote 27, p. 65.**

improve not only the quantity but also the quality of extension packages for female farmers.

Improving extension services for women

Several strategies or combinations of strategies can dramatically improve the quality of extension services for women and increase the number of female participants. In many cases, relatively simple and cost-effective adjustments to extension services and delivery mechanisms can yield enormous improvements. Some of these are outlined in Box 3.

A number of encouraging initiatives have been taken by some countries. In Egypt, for example, the recent establishment of a strong Policy and Coordination Unit for Women in Agriculture in the Ministry of Agriculture has begun to address some of the above-mentioned constraints. Efforts to increase the number and technical competence of women extension agents have achieved some success in Burkina Faso, Kenya and Morocco. In the Gambia, after concerted efforts to target women, the proportion of female extension participants rose from 5 percent in 1989 to 60 to 70 percent by 1994. In Zimbabwe, the development of a more appropriate extension package for female farmers and the inclusion of women as candidates for master farmer certificates boosted their participation from 44 percent in 1990 to more than 60 percent in 1993.

In Asia and the Pacific, the explicit targeting of women for agricultural extension services has coincided with a growing number of female farmers. During the late 1980s, almost all Asian and Pacific countries produced extension publications directed at women; of note was an extensive series for women produced by the International Rice Research Institute (IRRI) in the Philippines.

Conclusion

Women farmers are by no means a homogeneous group. They represent different socio-economic situations with different extension needs. The nature and extent of their involvement in agriculture certainly varies greatly from region to region. However, regardless of these variations, there is hardly an activity in agricultural production in which women are not actively involved.

Within the agriculture sector, there is no doubt that the returns from investing in women are very high. Since education, extension and training are all mutually supportive and reinforcing contributing factors to agricultural productivity, efforts to assist rural women and improve their opportunities should concurrently focus on all of these areas. Educated women have a foundation for further technical training and are better equipped to seek out and obtain credit and

BOX 3
RECOMMENDATIONS TO IMPROVE EXTENSION
FOR WOMEN

- *Increase the number of female agents* by recruiting more and providing them with access to training, resources and logistical support equal to that of male agents.

- *Increase the pool of women qualified to provide extension* by promoting the teaching of science and technical subjects to females, targeting females for intakes to agricultural colleges and providing more facilities for them at such colleges.

- *Retrain and redeploy female agents,* for example home economists or rural development staff, to provide agricultural extension. In Nigeria, home economists (who had detailed knowledge of rural women and were farmers in their spare time) were successfully transferred to an extension service. This involved little additional cost, since they were already on the government payroll.

- *Increase the number of women contacted* by specifying targets. In Burkina Faso, measures to target women farmers resulted in an increase in the number of women directly contacted by extension agents from 15 000 to 299 000.

- *Adjust the selection procedures or criteria* for "contact farmers" so more women qualify for extension services. In Kenya, for example, agents were encouraged to accept contacts with the wives of men who were identified as contacts but worked off the farm or farmed only part-time.

- *Provide extension services to women's groups* where it is more efficient than individual contact or where women indicate a preference for group extension. In Kenya, studies estimate that group extension can reach twice as many as farmers at the same cost as individual extension.

- *Make more efficient use of scarce female agents* by having them introduce womens' groups to the extension system and services as well as the male extension agent assigned to the area.

- *Improve the content of extension services to women farmers* by ensuring that they receive agricultural information and that messages and recommendations are relevant to women's production activities. Improve farm technology to make it more appropriate for women.

- *Adjust the timing and location of extension meetings and training sessions* so that they are convenient and accessible for women (e.g. held in the evenings and sited at markets or grain mills). Shorter modules and mobile training units brought to the villages can also help.

- *Train and sensitize male extension agents to work with women farmers.* Male agents should have technical training in women's activities and crops and training to help them work with women. As an example, male agents in Nigeria met regularly with female Subject Matter Specialists to discuss extension messages from the perspective of women farmers.

• *Offer incentives to encourage extension agents to meet with female farmers.* In Nigeria, donor support for women and positive feedback made extension agents feel that, by extending their services to female farmers, they were part of an effective, ground-breaking strategy.

• *Diagnose and identify women's extension needs* by collecting and analysing gender-disaggregated data and use this information to plan and implement policies and interventions.

• *Monitor and evaluate extension programmes* with feedback from the participants and gender-sensitive extension agents to ensure that the programmes are helping women farmers as intended.

Source: K. Saito, op. cit., footnote 15, p. 60.

other resources. Women who have access to extension services are more receptive to new technologies and are more likely to adopt environmentally sustainable farming techniques. Trained women are in a better position to pass on useful information to other women, thereby diffusing relevant technical information. The link between education and training and extension for female farmers and higher economic productivity and output underscores the value of investing in women. During the past decade, structural reform programmes have justifiably called for the elimination of government subsidies, taxes, regulations and inefficient state enterprises that distort the functioning of markets. However, intervention is called for to improve market performance and social welfare where underinvestment occurs owing to market failures or distortions.

If subsidized extension services are to continue, these services must be directed at the farmers who have the greatest impact on global and household food security, i.e. women farmers. To do this, more contact is needed with women farmers and the quality of this contact must be improved. Both of these can be accomplished by increasing the proportion of women agents, sensitizing and training male agents and having both male and female agents provide information relevant to women farmers. In addition, access to complementary inputs, credit and technology is vital for realizing production gains.

GLOBAL CLIMATE CHANGE ABATEMENT POLICIES: IMPLICATIONS FOR DEVELOPING COUNTRIES
Introduction
In recent years a consensus has developed that the increasing accumulation of greenhouse gases in the environment is likely to lead to undesirable changes in the global climate. Signatories to the UN Framework Convention on Climate Change[32] recognize the need to reduce greenhouse gas emissions and have agreed that developed countries, in the first instance, should aim at reducing emissions to 1990 levels by 2000 and beyond, although caveats provide exemptions to this for some countries. It is becoming clear that the developing countries will need, at some point, to take an active role in abating global greenhouse gas emissions. Because of the prominence of agriculture in these countries, its dependence on climate and its role as an emitter of greenhouse gases, the sector deserves special attention.

---

[32] **UN. 1992.** *United Nations Framework Convention on Climate Change.* **New York.**

The UN Framework Convention on Climate Change distinguishes between developed and developing countries. It commits members of the Annex 1 group (comprising 37 developed countries and European economies in transition) to develop policies "with the aim of returning individually or jointly to the 1990 levels of ... anthropogenic [human-induced] emissions of carbon dioxide and other greenhouse gases ...". Furthermore, developed country parties are obliged to "... provide new and additional financial resources to meet the agreed full costs incurred by developing country Parties in complying with their obligations ...". In addition, recognition is given to the priorities of "economic and social development and poverty eradication" in developing countries.

The role of the agricultural sector is given particular attention in the framework convention, which states in its preamble that "arid and semi-arid areas or areas liable to floods, drought and desertification ... [are] ... particularly vulnerable to the adverse effects of climate change" and requires that developed countries assist in the "protection and rehabilitation" (Article 4) of such areas, many of which are in developing countries, particularly in Africa.[33]

Nonetheless, in spite of the emphasis on developed countries reducing their emissions and assisting developing countries, the latter group will have to address the problem within the next few years. Most of the growth in carbon emissions will come from developing countries.[34] Indeed, if OECD countries were to reduce their emissions to zero, in the absence of any policy changes global carbon dioxide emissions would still be above 1990 levels (22 billion tonnes) by 2010 because of the rapid growth in emissions from some developing countries. Thus, developing countries must certainly have a role in emission abatement if global warming is to be adequately addressed. Because of the pervasiveness of energy use, all sectors of an economy will be affected, positively or negatively. As an emitter of carbon, methane and nitrous oxide and provider of carbon sinks that absorb or sequester carbon, but also as a beneficiary of an additional CO_2 fertilization effect, the agricultural and forestry sectors will be affected in complex ways.

A further role for developing countries relates to so-called joint implementation. The framework convention allows countries to fulfil their obligations jointly. Thus, two or more countries may cooperate

---

[33] UN, op. cit., footnote 32, p. 71.
[34] World Bank. 1995. *World Development Report 1995.* New York, Oxford University Press; AsDB. 1993. *Electricity Utilities Databook.* Manila.

to reduce their aggregate emissions or enhance sinks, through afforestation for example, to absorb greenhouse gases by the required amount. Empirical estimates suggest that the costs of abatement tend to be lowest in developing countries, for example China and India. Such countries could therefore be potential partners in jointly implemented emission abatement projects.

In addition to undertaking emission abatement and joint implementation, a third issue for developing countries concerns the impact that policy changes in other countries have on them. Opinions vary as to the costs of reducing emissions to 1990 levels by 2000 and beyond in Annex 1 countries (the so-called stabilization approach and a common interpretation of the framework convention's requirements), but some observers suggest that reductions in growth and in demand for developing country exports may make developing countries worse off. This is in spite of the absence of abatement policies in developing countries and the relocation of industries that may occur as a result of changes in international competitiveness. For these various reasons, policies to abate global climate change are an important issue for developed and developing countries alike.

Climate change and agriculture
Various degrees of uncertainty exist about several technical aspects of climate change (see Box 4). While most agree that anthropogenic emissions of carbon dioxide (CO_2), methane (NH_4), nitrous oxide (N_2O), chlorofluorocarbons and other substances are warming the globe, there is still much uncertainty about the likely magnitude or impact of the global warming on climate. Changes in precipitation and sea level are uncertain, as are the regional and temporal distribution of changes and their impacts. Some regions of the world may benefit from a warmer climate and the beneficial fertilization effect of higher carbon dioxide levels on plant growth and yields. Some regions may also suffer damages from inundation as a result of rising sea levels; an increased frequency and magnitude of natural hazards such as storms, floods and droughts; an increase in human and animal diseases such as malaria; and decreases in biodiversity. As a result of these uncertainties, the magnitude and distribution of the benefits of abating emissions are unclear. Despite the uncertainties, policy-makers have been sufficiently convinced of the consequences to agree to make considerable efforts to reduce the growth of emissions.

The potential impact of climate change on agriculture and forestry is noteworthy because changes in climate affect production directly. Furthermore, the production phase of crops and forests acts as a carbon sink, taking up carbon that would otherwise contribute to

BOX 4
GLOBAL WARMING: SOME CAUSES, MODULATING FACTORS AND PHYSICAL RESPONSES

CAUSAL MECHANISMS
Fossil fuel use
Production of CFCs
Changes in land use
Population growth

MODULATING FACTORS
Concentration and persistence of gases
Role of clouds
Role of oceans
Role of ice
Role of land cover

PHYSICAL RESPONSES
Changes in temperature
Changes in precipitation
Changes in sea level
Regional and temporal distribution
of vegetation changes

increased atmospheric CO_2 concentrations and an enhanced greenhouse effect.[35]

General circulation models (GCMs) of global climate suggest that projected increases in global average surface temperatures of 1° to 3.5°C are likely to occur over the next 100 years, shifting the climate zones away from the equator, raising sea levels (probably less than 1 m by 2100) and increasing the likelihood of storms, floods and droughts.

While changes in temperature and precipitation are important from an agricultural perspective, other factors influencing yields include a reduction in soil moisture and increases in plant transpiration. In addition, higher levels of atmospheric CO_2 should increase photosynthesis rates, thereby increasing yields in favourable conditions.

Average temperatures are expected to increase by a greater amount nearer the poles than the equator. In the temperate zones,

[35] An earlier perspective on the possible effects of climate change on agriculture, forestry and fisheries is provided in FAO. 1994. *The State of Food and Agriculture 1994*, p. 55-62. Rome.

each degree of warming is expected to shift the climatic zone by 200 to 300 km. Regional climatic changes imply that the production of crops for which temperature is a limiting factor could increase in the higher latitudes. Wheat production could therefore possibly extend into Canada, Scandinavia, the Russian Federation and Argentina, reflecting the longer growing season.

For many crops, particularly in tropical agriculture, the limiting factor is precipitation. While the area affected by monsoonal rains is likely to extend, climate models are unable to predict with any certainty the regional distribution of rainfall. If rainfall increases in marginal areas that have fragile soils or mountains or over the sea, increases in production may not offset decreases resulting elsewhere from reduced rainfall or soil moisture.

A warmer climate might reduce soil moisture. Evaporation rates in mid-latitudes increase about 5 percent for each 1°C increase in temperature. Crops in arid zones are likely to be sensitive to this factor. Some estimates indicate that yields may fall considerably in some instances. However, these often neglect adaptation towards more suitable varieties or crops as well as the fact that the per unit productivity of water of C4-type crops such as maize or sugar cane, especially, increases with increased CO_2 through reduced evapotranspiration.

Increased concentrations of CO_2 also have a fertilization effect on productivity. A doubling of CO_2 may increase photosynthesis by 100 percent in some instances, allowing plants to grow faster and to a greater size.[36] This applies particularly to wheat, rice and soybeans and, to a lesser extent, to low-latitude crops such as maize, sorghum, millet, sugar cane and pasture grasses.

A further issue relating specifically to agriculture concerns methane. Little attention has been given to this issue to date because of data limitations, the overriding importance of carbon for (energy-dependent) economic growth and the relatively slow growth in methane emissions. However, the framework convention specifies that there should be reductions in methane emissions. Policies relating to methane emissions may be particularly important for many developing countries that are dependent on rice and livestock production.

Methane is the second most important greenhouse gas, accounting for more than 15 percent of the enhanced greenhouse effect. Recent estimates suggest that annual emissions are around 380 million tonnes per year, compared with 80 million tonnes in

---

[36] UNEP. 1996. http:/www.unep.ch/ipcc/fs101.html.

pre-industrial times.[37] However, methane remains in the atmosphere for a considerably shorter time than carbon. The major anthropogenic sources of methane emissions are livestock farming, natural gas and oil production, coal mining, rice cultivation, the burning of biomass, landfills and sewage. Hoofed animals, mainly cows, contribute perhaps 100 million tonnes or 25 percent of human-induced emissions.[38] Per animal emissions vary tremendously depending on diet, species, age, weight and health. Typically, cows in developing countries that are fed on a sparse diet produce perhaps more methane and nitrous oxide per unit of meat or milk than animals in intensive production.

Wetland rice production accounts for an estimated 60 million tonnes of methane per year, although estimates are regarded with considerable uncertainty. Most rice is produced in developing countries, with China and India making a substantial contribution.

Policies to reduce methane emissions are likely to impact more significantly on developing countries, which tend to have large agricultural sectors, often with substantial amounts of rice and livestock production. Increasing meat consumption in developing countries may lead to increased livestock production and hence increased methane emissions in these economies, unless the additional consumption is partly based on increased imports from developed countries.

There are also limited means with which to reduce methane emissions. There is some scope for dietary supplements for livestock, and in time this may be significant, particularly for intensive producers. There seems to be less scope in rice cultivation, although the development of cultivars that require less time under water, or a switch in favour of wheat consumption, may have some impact.

Nitrous oxide is another greenhouse gas emitted mainly from agriculture. It is released naturally from forests, wetlands and termite mounds as well as from human sources such as biomass burning, land clearing, nitrogen-fertilized pasture and crops, leguminous crops, cattle in intensive production systems, animal waste and fossil fuels. Although nitrous oxides have a long atmospheric lifetime, similar to carbon and in contrast to methane, present-day levels are little higher than pre-industrial levels and annual growth is

[37] **D. Stern and R. Kaufman. 1995. *Estimates of global anthropogenic methane emissions, 1860-1993*. Working Paper No. 4. Boston, USA, Center for Energy and Environmental Studies.**
[38] **UNEP. 1996. http://www.unep.ch/ipcc/fs032.html.**

relatively low. About 90 percent of global emissions are attributable to agriculture.

Emission abatement polices: carbon leakage, terms of trade and welfare effects

Current efforts towards abating emissions are primarily concentrated in the developed countries. This reflects the historical contribution of these countries to the stock of atmospheric greenhouse gases. Of interest are the likely effects that such policies may have on developing countries and their agricultural sectors. For developing countries not implementing abatement measures, two effects of developed country abatement policies are noteworthy: carbon leakage and changes in terms of trade.

First, "carbon leakage" refers to the fact that emission reductions in one country may be partially or completely offset by an increase in emissions from another non-abating country, whose continuous recourse to fossil fuel-intensive techniques would enhance its relative competitiveness. Clearly, a high rate of carbon leakage undermines the effectiveness of an emission abatement policy overall, but non-abating developing countries may benefit from this effect. Empirical estimates of the magnitude of carbon leakage if emission abatement policies were widely implemented in developed countries range from next to nothing to 100 percent or more, although estimates at the lower end of this range, from about 10 percent to 35 percent, seem more plausible.[39]

A second effect of abatement policies concerns changes in terms of trade, the ratio of export to import prices. A deterioration in terms of trade implies that a greater quantity of exports are needed to purchase a given quantity of imports. Abatement policies can be expected to affect import and export prices in all countries, even in those not implementing abatement policies. Prices of fossil fuel-intensive products (such as chemicals, rubber and plastics, iron and steel, non-ferrous metals and manufactured goods) could be expected to rise as the implicit or explicit tax on fuel combustion is passed on. However, the tax-induced fall in demand for fossil fuels would lower their prices. Finally, lower economic growth in emission-abating countries would lower their import demand,

[39] ABARE/Government of Australia. 1995. *Global climate change: economic dimensions of a cooperative international policy response beyond 2000.* Canberra; A. Manne and J. Oliveira-Martins. *OECD Model Comparison Project (II) on the Costs of Cutting Carbon Emissions.* Economics Department Working Paper No. 146. Paris, OECD.

negatively affecting exports from all countries, including agricultural exports from developing countries. The overall impact depends on the composition of imports and exports. Countries that export large quantities of fossil fuel (such as OPEC members), or products requiring intensive use of fossil fuel, are likely to experience worsening terms of trade, while countries that import these products (e.g. Japan) are likely to gain.

Changes in terms of trade can offset changes in output induced by carbon leakage. In other words, the decline in developed countries' demand for developing country exports may more than offset gains to developing countries that are attributable to carbon leakage.

The substitutability of agricultural inputs versus use of these inputs in other industries, both domestically and in other countries, is another important factor. In developing countries, capital and labour resources may be drawn away from the agricultural sector towards the more internationally competitive and profitable fossil fuel-intensive industries, such as iron and steel. The composition of industry across the economy will determine the extent to which the agricultural sector is affected.

Efficient outcomes reduce welfare losses to abaters and non-abaters alike

Whether developing countries gain or lose from climate change abatement policies, a more relevant question is whether there are alternative policies that could benefit all countries. Recent international negotiations between parties to the UN Framework Convention on Climate Change have focused on countries making cuts in their greenhouse gas emissions in proportion to their emission growth since the base year 1990. Addressing the enhanced greenhouse effect through the so-called stabilization of emissions to 1990 levels by 2000 ignores a fundamental feature of the problem, namely that climate change is truly global in scope. Analysts are largely in agreement that the enhanced greenhouse effect is a global problem in the sense that the environmental impact of greenhouse gas emissions is independent of location. Greenhouse gases are a stock pollutant – it is the atmospheric concentration of gases that determines the enhanced greenhouse effect, not the flow of emissions. Therefore emissions released in the tropics are assumed to have the same impact as those released in temperate climates.

The location of the reductions in emissions does not influence their environmental impact. However, the cost of abating greenhouse gas emissions does vary considerably from country to country owing to differences in technologies in use, the availability of alternative methods of energy generation, the composition of industry, the distribution of energy resources and markets, dependence on exports and other factors. Even at the margin, costs may differ significantly.

Perhaps of greater importance from a global perspective is the fact that the costs of abatement tend to be lower in developing than in developed countries, reflecting the considerable scope for improvements in energy efficiency through the application of more modern technologies.[40] For example, China has many small-scale coal-burning power plants, and its iron and steel sector is relatively inefficient and out of date. Some empirical estimates suggest that marginal costs of abatement in China could be less than 20 percent of total OECD marginal costs.[41]

A similar argument applies to sinks. The costs of providing sinks, such as forests, will vary with the availability and potential alternative uses of land. Land values and the costs of establishing sinks vary tremendously, but are likely to be greatest where the land is used most intensively. Countries such as Australia, New Zealand, Brazil and Argentina would appear to provide the greatest scope for sink enhancement.

Given the global nature of the enhanced greenhouse effect, the substantial differences in costs in different countries and the different rates of economic and emissions growth in different countries, it makes economic sense for countries with the largest potential contribution to the global problem to attempt to reduce or contain emissions. From a global perspective, any given target can be achieved at minimum cost only if the least-cost opportunities for reducing emissions are utilized first. An efficient outcome would require much of the abatement in emissions to be located in developing countries.

According to some estimates, welfare losses under an efficient outcome in 2020 are $47 billion (constant 1988 United States dollars), just 40 percent of the losses that would be sustained if developed countries were required to locate their emission-reduction activities within their own country.[42] An earlier OECD study puts this figure at 20 percent.[43]

---

[40] IEA. 1994. *World Energy Outlook.* Paris, OECD.

[41] Z.X. Zhang. 1996. *Macroeconomic effects of CO_2 emissions limits: a computable general equilibrium analysis for China.* Wageningen Economic Papers 1996-1. The Netherlands, Wageningen Agricultural University.

[42] ABARE/Government of Australia, p. 112 in op. cit., footnote 39, p. 77.

[43] J.-M. Berniaux, J. Martin, G. Nicoletti and J. Martins. 1991. *The cost of policies to reduce CO_2 emissions: initial simulation results with GREEN.* Working Paper No. 103. Paris, OECD.

This does not imply, however, that the costs of emission abatement should necessarily accrue wholly or mainly to developing countries. That costs of abatement are relatively lower in the developing countries does not detract from the fact that these countries also have relatively less margin for bearing abatement costs in terms of competitiveness and income losses. It remains true, however, that the problem is global in scope, and all countries have their share of responsibility in controlling it.

Implications and conclusions

The enhanced greenhouse effect is an environmental challenge that is perhaps unique in scale. It features global causes and effects and will require widespread cooperation if atmospheric concentrations are to be reduced. However, the problem of abating global greenhouse gas emissions seems intractable. Most developed countries see the need to reduce global emissions, and political and economic realities dictate that these countries set an example in the abatement effort. However, many have yet to demonstrate the political will to accomplish reductions. Many developing countries see the problem as a legacy of industrial development, whereby developed countries took the opportunity to develop in a period when greenhouse gas emissions were not seen as a constraint, and they regard other priorities as more pressing. This is in spite of the observation that most of the increase in emissions in future will come from countries currently regarded as developing countries. Nonetheless, to increase the international abatement effort, it will be necessary at some stage to broaden participation to include countries not currently committed to emission abatement.

Although uncertainties remain as to the nature and importance of the problem, there is no doubt that abatement policies will have an impact on developing countries. While in some cases such an impact will be positive, resulting from the relocation of carbon- and methane-intensive industries, in others it may be negative if the demand for developing country exports falls. Negative impacts are most likely to be minimized by encouraging efficient and equitable outcomes. A willingness to participate actively in the negotiation process and in jointly implemented projects is likely to be in the best interests of developing countries individually and collectively. Throughout the prolonged negotiation process, improvements in energy efficiency and better use of energy-saving technologies would appear prudent. The removal of subsidies on energy consumption would also be desirable.

Agriculture and forestry will remain an important area in the climate change debate because the physical effects are most apparent in these sectors. Evidence to date suggests that the impact of climate change on net global agricultural productivity is difficult to assess, with higher yields owing to adaptation and the CO_2 fertilization effect, in some cases, and lower yields attributable to lower rainfall and soil moisture in other cases. The impacts of global abatement policies on the agricultural sector are also likely to vary between regions and countries, although constraints on methane and nitrous oxide emissions could impact negatively on agricultural growth.

Meanwhile, in the agricultural sector consideration should be given to the impact on carbon, methane and nitrous oxide emissions when assessing prospects for forestry, livestock and crop development. In addition to their effect on emissions, improved land management practices through better use of water, fertilizer and fuel and through the conservation of organic matter are likely to prove beneficial to developing countries.

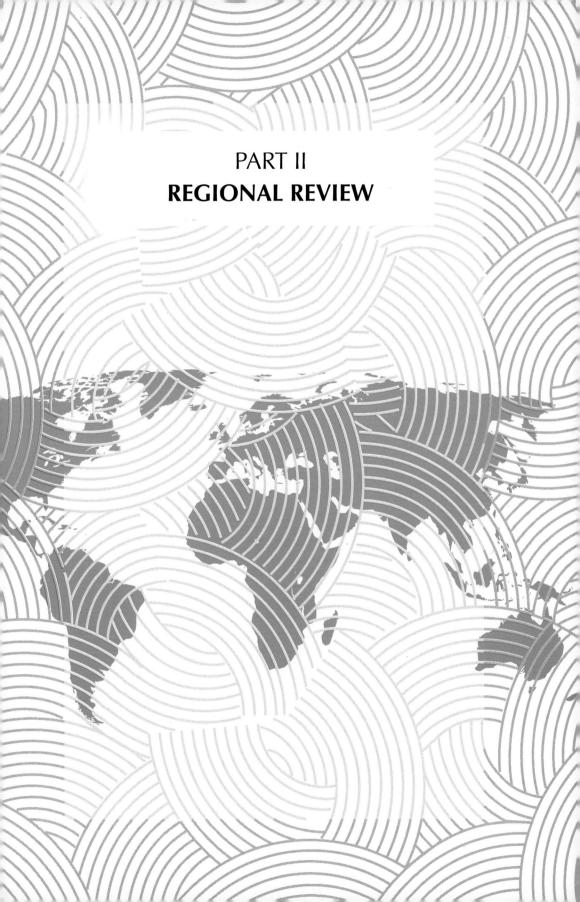

PART II
REGIONAL REVIEW

REGIONAL REVIEW

AFRICA

REGIONAL OVERVIEW

The global community has recognized the development of Africa, especially sub-Saharan Africa, as the world's foremost development challenge. This recognition manifested itself most forcefully at the 1996 World Food Summit, which stressed the need to address the multifaceted factors underlying food insecurity and placed a special emphasis on sub-Saharan Africa. The approval of the World Food Summit Plan of Action, along with a number of recent favourable economic and agricultural developments in many countries in the region, has raised hopeful expectations for the emergence of a more positive trend in economic development and food security in the years to come.

General economic performance

Economic performance in Africa improved significantly in 1996, with GDP estimated to have increased by 5 percent compared with 2.9 percent in 1995 and an average of only 1.7 percent over the period 1990-94. In sub-Saharan Africa, in particular, against the background of more than a decade of deep recession, the growth performance over the past two years is encouraging.[1] The change in GDP in 1996 was estimated to have increased by about 4.4 percent[2] (5.6 percent excluding Nigeria and South Africa), up from 4 percent the previous year and the strongest growth rate in 20 years. GDP growth rates of 5 percent or more were recorded in about 20 of the countries in sub-Saharan Africa, exceeding by a significant margin the yearly population growth rate of 3 percent. Negative growth rates were only experienced in Burundi, the Central African Republic and Djibouti. While still remaining very high, consumer price inflation for the region as a whole dropped from 39.6 percent in 1995 to 31.5 percent in 1996.

[1] The remaining part of the section focuses on sub-Saharan countries, as the North African countries are discussed in the context of the regional review for the Near East and North Africa.
[2] IMF. 1997. *World Economic Outlook*. Washington, DC.

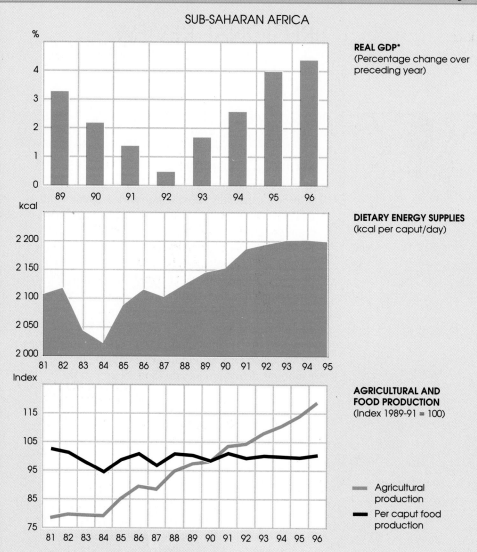

SUB-SAHARAN AFRICA

REAL GDP*
(Percentage change over
preceding year)

DIETARY ENERGY SUPPLIES
(kcal per caput/day)

**AGRICULTURAL AND
FOOD PRODUCTION**
(Index 1989-91 = 100)

Agricultural
production

Per caput food
production

Source: FAO and IMF

*Including South Africa

Figure 7B

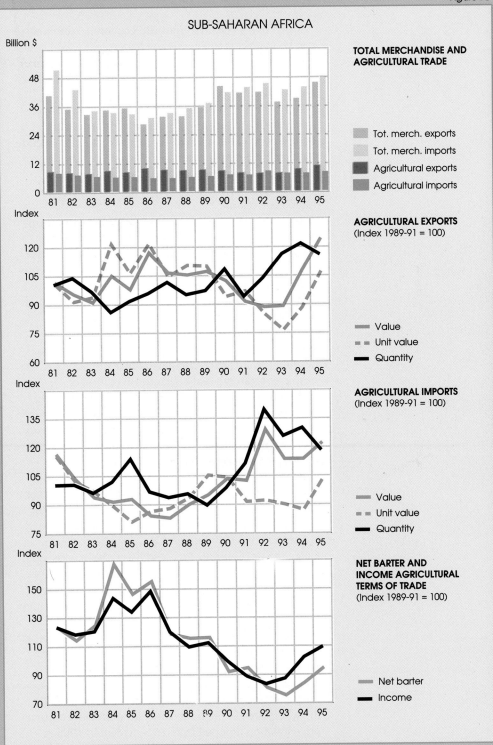

SUB-SAHARAN AFRICA

Billion $

**TOTAL MERCHANDISE AND
AGRICULTURAL TRADE**

- Tot. merch. exports
- Tot. merch. imports
- Agricultural exports
- Agricultural imports

Index

AGRICULTURAL EXPORTS
(Index 1989-91 = 100)

- Value
- Unit value
- Quantity

Index

AGRICULTURAL IMPORTS
(Index 1989-91 = 100)

- Value
- Unit value
- Quantity

Index

**NET BARTER AND
INCOME AGRICULTURAL
TERMS OF TRADE**
(Index 1989-91 = 100)

- Net barter
- Income

Source: FAO

AFRICA

Much of the region's improved economic performance can be attributed to the primary export sector, which was particularly strong in 1996 owing to favourable weather and a productive agricultural season. Such a strong link between overall economic and agricultural performances underlines the relevance of emphasizing agricultural production in the region. Other factors contributing to the improved economic situation include the notable progress made towards macroeconomic stability in a number of countries and the success of the CFA franc devaluation in several countries in the franc zone region.

The year witnessed stronger stabilization and reform efforts in an increasing number of countries. Ghana, Uganda, Malawi, Senegal, Benin and Côte d'Ivoire, for example, strengthened policies favouring private sector involvement in the economy as well as trade liberalization. Several of these countries have achieved unexpectedly strong and sustained economic performances accompanied by lower inflation, suggesting, in the view of some analysts, that the long-awaited rewards of reform may now be forthcoming. For example, Uganda's real GDP growth of 7 percent in 1996, one of the highest in the region, followed two years of even more striking growth (11.5 and 9.8 percent in 1994 and 1995, respectively), thus further enhancing the credibility of the country's macroeconomic policies. Moreover, inflation was held at 5 percent, the freely convertible currency remained steady, foreign reserves rose to nearly five months import cover and investment was buoyant, boosted by donor support amounting to more than $500 million a year.

Most countries of the CFA franc zone, in particular Côte d'Ivoire, Senegal, Togo and Benin, have witnessed a remarkable turn around in their economies since the January 1994 devaluation. The real GDP rate of growth of the CFA franc zone in 1996 was about 5.2 percent, up from 2.6 percent in 1994 and 4.6 percent in 1995. Inflation at first erupted in the zone with the devaluation, hitting the urban areas the hardest, but was contained relatively quickly through tight fiscal and monetary policies, price controls, the limiting of wage increases in the public sector and a reduction of some tax rates. For the whole area of the franc zone, for example, consumer price inflation dropped from 15.3 percent in 1995 to 6 percent in 1996; however, inflation still remained in

AFRICA

the double digits in a few countries such as Chad and the Congo.

Several factors explain the economic turnaround in countries of the CFA zone. In addition to increases in exports, contributing factors included debt forgiveness and increased official and private inflows of financial resources. Other coinciding events that were not related to the devaluation also contributed to the improved economic situation: for example, new oilfields started production in Côte d'Ivoire and Equatorial Guinea while the socio-political situation improved in both Chad and Togo.

Of all the countries in the zone, the Niger benefited least from the devaluation partially because of adverse climatic conditions and low export earnings from uranium, which continues to command a low market price. Cameroon likewise has not enjoyed the post-devaluation takeoffs that other countries have.

Varied performances are found elsewhere in the region. South Africa's economy continued to grow steadily as it reintegrated into the world market. However, the growth rate of 3 percent in 1996 was somewhat weaker than had been expected, considering the vigorous expansion in private investment, exports (owing in particular to a successful agricultural season) and manufacturing output. However, a high unemployment rate of about 40 percent constitutes a serious economic challenge as well as a factor of socio-political instability.

The Nigerian economy, still rather unstable, grew by 2.1 percent in 1996, down from 2.5 percent the previous year. After a sharp rise to 70 percent in 1995, inflation fell to 29.3 percent in 1996, its lowest rate of increase since 1991. An appreciable rise in oil production and exports, coinciding with higher than expected world oil prices, improved the short-term outlook.

Economic conditions remained difficult in the Sudan, the Democratic Republic of the Congo and Zambia. The Democratic Republic of the Congo experienced triple-digit inflation, with the total rise in consumer prices amounting to well over 600 percent in 1996. Zambia had to deal with a sharp drop in copper prices and the need, in the first half of the year, to import substantial quantities of maize following the 1995 drought. It also had to contend with the depreciation of the kwacha, persistently high inflation, high interest rates and,

consequently, little interest on the part of international investors.

African countries still continue to suffer from high external indebtedness. Despite some countries' buoyant commodity exports and improved current account balances in 1996, export growth still did not keep pace with the growth of external debt in many countries. The total debt-service ratio for the region, however, declined from 14.9 percent in 1995 to 12.1 percent in 1996. The debt burden in sub-Saharan Africa continues to exert significant pressure on public finances; according to the International Monetary Fund (IMF) 33 out of the 41 heavily indebted countries are in sub-Saharan Africa. A large debt breakthrough, however, came in September 1996 when bilateral creditors (the Group of Seven industrial nations) and IMF officials agreed to a minimum $5 billion plan to offer more generous relief to as many as 20 of the world's poorest debtor countries.

Agricultural performance
Agriculture has continued to dominate the livelihood and economic performance of African countries, and weather conditions continue to be the major determinant of agricultural performance. After droughts in 1995, good rainfall generally returned to southern Africa and a favourable agricultural season was experienced by the majority of sub-Saharan African countries, with the notable exception of those affected by civil strife. Improved weather and other factors, such as farmers' response to favourable market conditions for export crops in 1994/95, enabled agricultural production in the region to increase by 4.2 percent in 1996, up from 3 percent in 1995 and 2.3 percent in 1994. While the overall production increase accrued mainly to non-food crops in 1995, the increase in 1996 stemmed from a more balanced growth of both food and non-food crops.

After many years of unfavourable production conditions, all members of the Southern African Development Community (SADC) enjoyed exceptional rainfall levels in 1996, with the exception of Namibia which was still suffering from a persistent drought. As a result, coarse grain production in the subregion was 88 percent above the 1995 drought-reduced level and 39 percent above the average. Wheat production was 32 percent higher than the previous year.

Maize production rose considerably throughout

AFRICA

southern Africa. South Africa, for example, produced a record maize crop, estimated to be 112 percent larger than in 1995, and a wheat crop that was 32 percent larger. Lesotho's maize production doubled while grain production in Zimbabwe also rose significantly, thereby contributing to the country's return to self-sufficiency. Similarly, Malawi's 1996 maize crop harvest of 2 million tonnes (up from 1.5 million tonnes in 1995) more than met the domestic requirements of the country and therefore enabled stockpiling.

In West Africa in 1996, record cereal crops were reported in Benin, Côte d'Ivoire, Ghana, Cameroon and Nigeria. The subregion (in particular Côte d'Ivoire, Senegal and Liberia) reached a record rice production of 7.1 million tonnes, 27 percent higher than the previous year. Nigeria's agricultural output, however, is estimated to have grown by only 1.7 percent compared with 3.3 percent in 1995. Although Nigeria maintained its lead in world cassava production, its production of maize and rice was affected by an endemic shortage of fertilizers.

With a record wheat crop, the total grain harvest in Ethiopia almost covered domestic needs and some reports claim that food imports may soon be unnecessary. Kenya also achieved record levels of wheat production.

Despite the fact that 1996 food production levels reached an all-time high in a number of sub-Saharan African countries, several of which significantly reduced their food import needs, food supply problems remained acute or worsened in parts of the region.

Burkina Faso and the Niger registered major cereal deficits. For the second year running, inadequate rainfall and locust invasions left more than 2 700 villages with cereal shortages in the Niger. Namibia experienced one of its worst rainy seasons ever: very few parts of the country receiving even half of the normal rainfall, which left approximately 180 000 people in need of drought relief food aid. While the 1995/96 maize crop in the United Republic of Tanzania increased from the previous year, the rice and wheat harvests declined, and 280 000 people were left in need of food assistance. A poor year of rainfall in Mauritania left the country with an estimated food deficit of 115 000 tonnes of cereals in 1997.[3] Although the agricultural sector in Kenya has grown by a modest amount this past year, the overall food security situation is said to be weakening.

[3] **Economist Intelligence Unit.** *Country Report – Mauritania* **(1st quarter 1997).**

AFRICA

Production of the country's most important food items (maize, wheat and sugar) has failed to keep pace with the growing demand of its soaring population.

Some sub-Saharan African countries enjoyed a particularly successful production year for cash crops, in particular cocoa, coffee and cotton. In addition to higher than average production levels in Cameroon and Nigeria, Côte d'Ivoire, the world's top cocoa producer, produced an all-time record cocoa crop while Ghana produced its largest cocoa crop in 30 years. Cotton also had a record year in Cameroon as well as South Africa, Zimbabwe and Mali, which enjoyed increased net exports of cotton stemming from a substantial increase in area under cotton. In Ethiopia, despite a record volume of exports, total earnings from coffee in 1995/96 were slightly down from the previous year because of lower world coffee prices. Production surpluses were in fact experienced in all the largest coffee-producing countries such as Côte d'Ivoire, Uganda and Kenya. Production and exports of groundnuts, sunflower seeds, soybeans, sugar and dried beans also expanded in South Africa, aided by the devaluation of the rand.

While currency devaluation has stimulated exports and economic growth in a number of countries, it has also negatively affected food consumers in the short term. Such situations have been observed after the devaluation of the CFA franc[4] and, more recently, in countries such as Nigeria and South Africa. In the case of Nigeria, the food index (which accounted for nearly 70 percent of total household expenditure) rose by 71.8 percent in 1996 compared with 46.8 percent in the preceding year, without a corresponding increase in income levels. The strong depreciation of the South African rand also resulted in pronounced consumer food price increases, inevitably accentuating food insecurity, particularly among the 20 percent of urban and 60 percent of rural populations still living at minimum subsistence levels.

Policy developments
The overall trend of strengthening macroeconomic reform also extended to the agricultural sector. Privatization continued to be a major policy objective as a means to improve productivity and reduce government subsidies on public enterprises that run at a loss. However, the overall degree of government intervention

---

[4] See FAO. 1995. *The State of Food and Agriculture 1995.* Rome.

BOX 5
POLITICAL STABILITY, DEMOCRACY AND FOOD SECURITY

Despite the democratization process in many countries in Africa (1996 was a pivotal year, with a record 18 multiparty elections held), the region continued to experience political instability and protracted civil wars in many areas. This past year saw political instability resurface in some countries such as Sierra Leone, while in other countries, for example Liberia, civil war was intensified and had devastating effects with respect to cereal production and food supply. Food aid operations were in fact cut back owing to repeated looting and intimidation by the militias, and rice and other basic foods were well beyond the reach of most Liberians as shortages sent prices rocketing in the capital city. Conflict and resulting population displacements continue to disrupt food production and supplies in Burundi, the Democratic Republic of the Congo (former Zaire), Somalia, Uganda and the Sudan, where ongoing insurgency persisted. Overall cereal production in Somalia, for example, was 37 percent lower than the pre-war average. In the Central African Republic, a 7 percent GDP

growth estimate for 1996 was forced down to 2 percent, with a fall in fiscal revenue of well over 50 percent owing to a military rebellion in April.

Compounding the obvious effects of war on production, an embargo imposed on Burundi by neighbouring countries not only stifled agricultural production by rendering agricultural inputs inaccessible, but the country's inability to export tea and coffee (which provides 90 percent of its hard currency) resulted in a devastating revenue collapse. In July 1996, at a summit in the Tanzanian city of Arusha, Kenya, Rwanda, the United Republic of Tanzania, Uganda, (former) Zaire, Ethiopia and Cameroon agreed to impose sanctions on landlocked Burundi until civilian rule returned. On a more positive note, with the resolution of longstanding conflicts in Angola, Ethiopia and Mozambique, countries that had been plagued by civil wars for almost two decades, dramatic recoveries were made this past year in grain production as farmers returned to their homes and land. In Angola, however, despite the large increases in production, the overall economic environment remains fragile and the food supply situation problematic, with several hundred thousand people still relying on external assistance. This is also true for Rwanda, where the influx of hundreds of thousands of refugees returning from neighbouring countries strained the already delicate and unstable food situation, and where more than half a million people were still in need of food aid. Although the agricultural sector is recovering, and agricultural production increased by 15 percent from the previous year, harvests were still 23 percent down on their pre-war levels.

Despite good harvests in Eritrea, 750 000 people were in need of food assistance.

Progress towards democratization and the resolution of civil wars and ethnic tensions will no doubt have a favourable impact on economic performance and development in the region. The emergence of a new regime in the Democratic Republic of the Congo has raised new uncertainties but also new hopes in this context. Among other things, continued peace should bring benefits through increased flows of investment and trade, as recently seen in the growth path of the Horn of Africa and southern Africa.

AFRICA

in the economy and in agricultural markets remained significant within the region.

A case in point is Kenya where, despite a strong push for full liberalization in the agricultural sector since late 1992, the government continued to control the trade of vital commodities such as maize, wheat and dairy products. Domestic prices remained low, resulting in a lack of incentives for farmers to expand production. The milling of coffee was opened up to competition, but marketing and grading remained effectively in the hands of the Coffee Board of Kenya. A March 1996 agreement between the donor community and the Kenyan Government included the privatization of agricultural parastatals and the reduction of government intervention in agricultural markets.

Numerous examples may be cited of recent privatization moves in the region. Uganda's Coffee Marketing Board, formerly a state monopoly, was privatized in 1996. In addition, as part of the process of revitalizing its cotton industry, the Ugandan Government sold a further 11 parastatal ginneries to the private sector; nine plants had already been privatized prior to 1996.

After much controversy, South Africa's Marketing of Agricultural Products Act was finally implemented in November 1996. It set a 13-month timetable for the dismantling of all state-controlled marketing boards for a wide range of agricultural products, including fruit, cotton, maize, meat, lucerne, wheat, oilseeds and wool.[5]

South Africa intends to bring about a free market for agricultural produce with as little government intervention as possible. As part of this initiative, the government moved towards liberalization by allowing the private sector to export maize. Domestic maize market prices were deregulated and imports freed in May 1995, while in 1996 export permits were issued by the South African Maize Board, which only two years ago was responsible for the buying and selling of maize on both the domestic and international markets as well as for setting producer and consumer prices.

In Zambia the National Milling Company was fully privatized in December 1996. In Zimbabwe, now that all government marketing parastatals have been converted into wholly owned government companies (with the exception of the Grain Marketing Board), discussions are focusing on how best to change these

[5] **Economist Intelligence Unit.** *Country Report – South Africa* (1st quarter 1997).

BOX 6
DEVELOPMENTS IN REGIONAL COOPERATION

Positive developments were recorded in 1996 with respect to the establishment of intraregional trade alliances. At their annual summit, held in Lesotho in August, all the 12 member countries of SADC adopted a free trade protocol which provides for the phased reduction and eventual elimination of trade barriers over the next eight to ten years with a view to building a common market similar to the European Union (EU). The pledge is an essential part of SADC's strategy to reduce its dependence on aid and to encourage regional and foreign private sector investment. To focus their energies more on SADC, Lesotho, Mozambique and Namibia have decided to withdraw from the Common Market for East and Southern Africa (COMESA).[1]

---

[1] COMESA now groups Angola, Burundi, Comoros, the Democratic Republic of the Congo, Eritrea, Ethiopia, Kenya, Madagascar, Malawi, Mauritius, Rwanda, the Sudan, Swaziland, the United Republic of Tanzania, Uganda, Zambia and Zimbabwe.

The SADC agreement comes at a time when Zimbabwe and South Africa have also agreed in principle to renew a bilateral trade agreement that provides preferential treatment to Zimbabwean exports but which expired in 1992. South Africa is Zimbabwe's single largest foreign trading partner. The South African/EU deliberations for a preferential trade agreement continue in parallel, with the EU reluctant to allow many agricultural products into the agreement.

March 1996 marked the inauguration of the Commission for East African Co-operation, established by and for the East African subregion and made up of Kenya, Uganda and the United Republic of Tanzania. The commission seeks to establish closer economic ties, coordinate efforts to develop the region, increase agricultural trade within the subregion and lead to the eventual creation of a single common market. It aims to strengthen business ties and create a favourable environment for activities led by the private sector. To initiate the drive to revive the East African Community (which had collapsed in 1977 as a result of political and economic divergences) as well as reducing business costs, the currencies of countries in the subregion were declared convertible in June. It may be several years, however, before the three countries begin lowering tariffs, reducing non-tariff barriers and establishing a common external tariff.

The West African Economic and Monetary Union (WAEMU) ratified a plan for a preferential customs area, aimed at encouraging trade between its member countries, Benin, Burkina Faso, Côte d'Ivoire, Mali, the Niger, Senegal and Togo.

The Government of Ghana signed the Free Zone Act of 1995 into law. This promotes Ghana as a gateway to Europe and West Africa. Through this export processing zone, similar to those of both Togo and Côte d'Ivoire, it is hoped that Ghana will eventually reach a positive trade balance as exports by Ghana and through Ghana increase.

Six coastal states, Cape Verde, the Gambia, Guinea, Guinea-Bissau, Mauritania and Senegal, all members of the Subregional Commission on Fisheries, pledged in April to harmonize their fisheries policies. In particular, they agreed to improve protection and conservation of common fishing grounds by sharing their air surveillance information and equipment.

companies to privately owned concerns. The privatization programme in Côte d'Ivoire has been completed for rubber production and palm oil production and is in the initial stages for cotton, sugar and livestock. The government has now announced a privatization plan for the parastatal cotton company Compagnie Ivorienne pour le Développement des Textiles (CIDT). This plan may set the tone for other franc zone cotton companies. The cotton industry in Senegal is still dominated by the ginning parastatal Société de Développement des Fibres Textiles (SODE-FITEX), the privatization of which is one of the objectives outlined in Senegal's new Agricultural Sectoral Adjustment Programme (PASA). Another objective is the privatization of the oilseed processing firm Société Nationale de Commercialisation des Oléagineux du Sénégal (SONACOS), and this programme is already under way.

In Ethiopia the parastatal Fertilizer Industry Agency, responsible for the marketing and distribution of agricultural fertilizers, has announced that the controversial fertilizer subsidy scheme would be modified so that only wholesale prices would be regulated. It is hoped that this measure will introduce competition between private fertilizer merchants and allow price reductions for farmers.[6]

Another important area of policy liberalization has been external trade. Here again, many recent examples illustrate the efforts made by countries in the region towards reforming the trade regime for agricultural products and inputs.

The Government of Zimbabwe further liberalized the trading of agricultural products by allowing producers both to export and import wheat and soybean directly without going through the government marketing board. Now that most of the restrictions on access to foreign currency have been removed, the number of farmers with access to "off-shore" financing for covering production costs and the availability of input items, such as crop chemicals and tractors, have significantly increased. Prior to this last policy development, the government had only permitted those farmers who produced export products to have access to this source of funding. The Government of Zimbabwe, however, retained exclusive rights to export maize even though the domestic marketing of maize has been liberalized.

[6] Economist Intelligence Unit. *Country Report – Ethiopia* (1st quarter 1997).

AFRICA

On the whole, unless agricultural produce is imported by a government parastatal (or former parastatal), it is still subject to import duties.

In Côte d'Ivoire, although flour imports were liberalized in January 1996, the 30 percent protection tariff (which is only 5 percent for wheat) acts as a disincentive to imports. By January 1997, rice imports were also freed. The government will remove its annual rice import quota but taxes will be levied on imports at variable rates based on world prices to protect local growers and encourage self-sufficiency. In April 1997 an electronic auction system was implemented for export permits for cocoa and coffee, the intention being to make the awarding of export permits more transparent.

In Senegal, the Caisse de Péréquation et Stabilisation de Prix (CPSP), which acted as the state rice-importing agency, was closed in 1996. In addition to rice, export subsidies were eliminated and imports liberalized for sugar, wheat and flour. The wheat market remains highly protected, however, with a 45 percent import tariff on wheat flour.

In Zambia, the ban on maize exports was lifted in May 1996, but farmers were reported to have been refused export licences during July and August, when the price of maize was at its lowest. In Lesotho, price controls on cereals were lifted in June, along with the ban on maize meal imports.

As mentioned previously, Nigeria experienced an endemic shortage of fertilizers owing to the government's decision to extend a ban on fertilizer imports in 1996. Although the government has been subsidizing fertilizers, various entrepreneurial practices have prevented the fertilizers from reaching farmers at low costs.

AFRICA

MOZAMBIQUE AND ANGOLA

Mozambique and Angola are often paired together by the development and donor communities because of their similar and concurrent colonial heritage, socialist experimentation, prolonged and exceptionally destructive civil wars and recent transition to liberalized market economies. For more than 25 years, they have endured almost continuous instability as a result of these events. Both countries have evoked images of extreme hardship in the form of widespread war and drought-induced poverty and hunger, vast numbers of displaced and conflict-affected people and numerous war amputees. At last there is some promise for peace and stability. Only by maintaining the current peace and carefully reconstructing their economic base will Mozambique and Angola be able to move forwards and emerge as self-determined nations with distinct and viable economies.

Colonial heritage

Angola's experience. Angola was the Portuguese colonial seat in Africa. During much of the colonial era Angola's agricultural sector was dependent on slavery and forced labour until the Portuguese abolished slavery in the late nineteenth century and forced labour in 1961. Up until independence (1975), the economy was strong and diverse, with a solid export base. Angola was the third largest exporter of coffee and sisal, while vegetable oil, tea, tobacco and meat were also exported. Trade extended beyond the limits of Portuguese markets to Europe and elsewhere. In addition, Angola was self-sufficient in all food crops except wheat, and it even produced maize surpluses for export. Livestock played a critical role in the country's agriculture long before the arrival of the Portuguese. Cattle were used for animal traction and also represented an important store of wealth.

Supporting Angola's agricultural success was an excellent integrated transport system including port, rail and primary and secondary road linkages. There was a substantial network of Portuguese bush traders who bought produce and extended credit to semi-subsistent peasants as well as to Portuguese medium-sized commercial farmers. There were numerous agricultural input suppliers as well as agro-industries such as breweries, oil processing plants and mills, which

AFRICA

provided local outlets for agricultural surpluses. The colonial government had also established a number of agricultural research stations. Oil reserves, and to a lesser extent timber resources, of Cabinda district, provided substantial export revenue; however, the district of Cabinda was only integrated into the colony in 1946. Although representing a much smaller percentage of GDP than oil or agriculture, diamond mining also contributed to the generation of foreign exchange.

Mozambique's experience. As a Portuguese colony, Mozambique's economy functioned predominantly as a supplier of raw material for Portuguese-based agro-industries (e.g. cotton, copra, tea, sisal and cashew) with a few notable exceptions, such as sugar which was processed locally. The agricultural sector comprised a few plantations, several thousand commercial concessions (settler farms with long-term, liberal usufruct rights) and approximately 1.5 million African smallholder farms. The colonialist economy operated on a system of forced labour. Mozambican peasants were obligated to provide free labour to cotton and rice production or, alternatively, to public works projects located in various, and often distant, regions of the country. The institution of rural taxes induced Mozambicans to seek employment on plantations and at the mines in neighbouring South Africa. In addition to the exploitation of agriculture, the colonial authorities extracted significant revenue from transport services provided to British landlocked colonies as well as from the export of prawns.

Independence and agriculture under socialist systems
The socialist system. After more than a decade of multiple independence struggles, Portugal granted all of it's African colonies independence in 1975. A high percentage of Portuguese settlers fled the newly liberated colonies and deliberately destroyed the property and animals they were forced to abandon. As a result, this mass exodus of Portuguese left an enormous economic and managerial vacuum. Mozambique and Angola initially established similar soviet-style, one-party, Marxist-Leninist regimes: FRELIMO (*Frente para a Libertação de Moçambique*) and the MPLA (*Movimento Popular de Libertação de Angola*). Factories and processing facilities were nationalized, plantations were

AFRICA

converted into state farms, prices and marketing margins were administered at nearly every stage of the production and distribution chain and all marketing of produce and agricultural inputs was centralized and controlled by government-owned marketing boards or parastatals. Both countries established *lojas do povo* which were stores that sold goods at government-fixed prices through a rationing system. In Mozambique, FRELIMO attempted to collectivize widely dispersed rural communities into communal villages and production cooperatives.

Agricultural performance under socialism. Both the Angolan and Mozambican Governments favoured state farms, ignoring peasant farmers while spending scarce foreign currency on imported agricultural equipment and inputs for highly mechanized state farms. Neither government had the managerial capability to run the state farms effectively and, as a consequence, both productivity and production rapidly declined. Angolan coffee production suffered a great infestation one year after independence because beans were not picked on time but left to rot and attract pests. Coffee prices were set so low that farmers dug up coffee trees and replaced them with cassava; coffee exports fell from 218 700 tonnes in 1973 to just 47 200 tonnes in 1980, a mere 21 percent of the 1973 level. In the case of maize, Angola went from being a net exporter (112 000 tonnes) in 1973 to being a net importer (142 700 tonnes) in 1980.[7] Similarly, Mozambique's cashew, rice and maize production dropped more than 50 percent between 1975 and 1980. Sisal and copra production dropped by 15 and 25 percent, respectively, over the same period.[8] It has often been noted that, given their extremely limited human resource capacity, one mistake of both FRELIMO and the MPLA was to overcentralize and overadministrate.

Civil war. Another important factor contributing to the poor economic performance of these newly formed socialist countries was civil unrest. The degree of insecurity caused vast numbers of rural households to abandon their farms and relocate to urban centres. In Angola, UNITA (*União Nacional para a Independência Total de Angola*) was one of several factions which fought against Portuguese colonialism and was later the

[7] World Bank. 1994. *Angola strategic orientation for agricultural development: an agenda for discussion.* Washington, DC.
[8] World Bank. 1996. *Mozambique agricultural sector memorandum. Volume II. Main report.* Washington, DC.

AFRICA

sole form of opposition to the MPLA government. It was well organized, highly disciplined and adequately supplied by many loyal farmers. UNITA exploited coffee-, oil- and timber-producing areas that were under MPLA control. Angola soon became geographically, as well as politically, divided with MPLA controlling urban centres and UNITA controlling rural areas. In contrast, RENAMO (*Resistência Nacional Moçambicana*), the opposition to FRELIMO in Mozambique, was formed after independence and sometimes looted rural communities and sabotaged economic activity by repeatedly blowing up transport and hydroelectric power infrastructure. RENAMO was not well organized and did not forge strong links with agricultural producers. These prolonged civil wars demolished the physical and economic infrastructure of both countries, particularly in Angola when the war resumed and intensified after the 1992 presidential election results were released.

Economic liberalization in Mozambique
Mozambique began a process of market liberalization in the early 1980s. A landmark conclusion of the Third Party Congress in 1983 was that the current agricultural development strategy emphasizing state farm production was not working and that more support should be granted to the private and family farm sector. In order to provide greater production and marketing incentives to this sector, price controls on fruits and vegetables were removed and fixed prices on other agricultural commodities were increased. The following year, Mozambique joined IMF and the World Bank and, within three years, had launched a structural adjustment package of broad market reforms known as the Economic Rehabilitation Programme (PRE).[9] The programme addressed macroeconomic distortions and imbalances, market liberalization and privatization.

Market liberalization. Beginning in 1988, producer and consumer prices were gradually liberalized. Many fixed prices were replaced by mandatory minimum prices and later by recommended minimum prices. The latter were to serve merely as a reference to traders and to provide some leverage for farmers. Prices of 22 agricultural products were freed in 1993, and consumer price controls were retained only on bread and wheat flour.

[9] Tinker, V. 1992. Structural adjustment and agricultural pricing in Mozambique. *Review of African Political Economy*, 53: 25-42.

There were, and still are, a number of non-agricultural consumer goods, such as cooking fuel, which remain under price controls.

During the same period, international trade was progressively liberalized. Cotton and cashew prices have always been controlled, even during the colonial era. However, the method of calculating boarder prices of cashew and cotton was adjusted to reflect the international market more closely in 1994. In accordance with the 1991 tariff code, import tariffs were to be simplified into five rates ranging from 5 to 35 percent. The definition of product groups was to be clarified and exemption criteria minimized in order to reduce the need for discretion to be used in applying tariffs. The code also stipulated that all export taxes, with the exception of those levied on raw cashews, would be limited to 0.5 percent in 1991 and, at a later stage, completely eliminated. The government also instituted a significant reduction in the export tax on raw cashews, which was expected to result in improved farmgate prices and increased production. Under PRE provisions, there should be no export tax on any commodity beyond the year 2000. Currently, the raw cashew tax is the only one remaining. Although export licence restrictions have been substantially reduced, the application process for import licences continues to be complex and cumbersome.

Privatization. The 1989 privatization programme began the process of selling off state farms and enterprises. To date, nearly all state farms and more than 500 small-, medium- and large-scale enterprises have been privatized, including all cashew processing plants and the customs offices. *Lojas do povo* have also been abolished, and the government has become progressively more tolerant of private traders. The state still has interests in sugar production, cotton ginning and fishing. Ginneries historically had contracting relationships with small-scale cotton producers. Currently, these ginneries are operating under joint venture concessions with the government. While traditionally supplied by large estates, joint venture sugar mills are considering contracting arrangements with small farmers as well. It is important to note that while farming operations have been privatized, all land is still owned by the state.

AFRICA

The 1991 law providing for the restructuring all state enterprises changed those firms that had not yet been privatized into "public" enterprises that are required to operate along commercial lines with improved record-keeping and greater financial accountability. The Foreign Investment Law, enacted in June 1993, cleared the way for greater foreign investment in Mozambique. The largest investors to date are Portugal and South Africa, and the most favoured sectors have been agriculture and tourism.[10] This law also allowed for the opening of two foreign banks and an insurance company in Maputo.

Correcting macroeconomic distortions and imbalances. In an effort to address macroeconomic distortions and imbalances, the Mozambican Government has enacted a series of standard structural adjustment measures. Devaluation of the national currency has reduced the difference between the parallel and official exchange rates from 2 100 percent in 1989 to 3.6 percent in 1995. While devaluation makes Mozambican export crops more attractive to foreign buyers, there is a cost in terms of the increased burden of importing equipment and other material required for reconstruction and rehabilitation. Such is the case for revitalizing sugar mill operations. Credit extended to parastatals had previously been essentially unlimited and unmonitored, but limits have now been imposed and more standard international banking and reporting procedures have been adopted. The government has also raised interest rates and set controls on growth in the money supply. Largely as a result of these measures, inflation dropped from 163 percent in 1987 to less than 50 percent in 1996.

The Mozambican Government has instituted a hiring freeze, expanded and improved tax collection and reduced the level of spending on certain programmes in order to close the gap between government revenue and spending and to decrease the deficit. External debt was 400 percent of GDP in 1994, while the debt service ratio has been almost continually declining since 1990: from 162 percent in 1990, it had reached 77 percent in 1996.[11]

A strategy for agriculture. Mozambique has good agricultural potential for basic grains as well as a number of cash crops such as cashew, cotton, sisal, tea,

[10] *South African Economist.* July 1993. Drumming up investment.
[11] World Bank. 1993. *Mozambique policy framework paper for 1994-96.* Washington, DC.

AFRICA

tobacco, groundnuts, sunflower oil, citrus and vegetables. The northern portion of the country has more reliable rains and better soils, while livestock is limited to tsetse fly-free areas of the south. Communications and transport links between the north and the south are weak: at present each region is better connected to international markets. Although transport, energy, fisheries and tourism hold excellent economic promise, agriculture represents approximately 30 percent of GDP and employs 80 percent of the active population. The vast majority of Mozambican farmers have approximately 1 ha of land; yet, together, these plots comprise 95 percent of all cultivated land area. Most farmers are very poor and seasonally food-insecure. Fewer than 30 percent have off-farm income opportunities.

Given the importance of agriculture, the development strategy for Mozambique logically centres on the agricultural sector. In cooperation with donors, the government has designed a five-year sector-wide programme, PROAGRI, which lays out priorities and strategies in dealing with the expansion of agricultural production, poverty alleviation and natural resource conservation. The emphasis of the programme is on planning, coordination and capacity building within the Ministry of Agriculture and Fisheries.[12] There has been some concern expressed that the programme is too narrowly focused on production at the expense of off-farm opportunities and post-production aspects of agriculture such as marketing and processing.

Issues in Mozambican agriculture today
Revitalization of agricultural production. The peace accord to end the protracted civil war was finally signed in 1992. Vestiges of the war, however, haunt rural areas in the form of hidden landmines,[13] banditry, demolished infrastructure, poverty and virtually non-existent markets for producer and basic consumer goods. Exacerbating the problem was a severe drought in 1992. As a result, approximately 80 percent of total cereals available in 1992 was derived from food aid (72 percent) and commercial imports (8 percent).[14] Since then, food aid has been slowly tapering off with lingering programmes for the extremely vulnerable, such as food-for-work arrangements on specific rehabilitation projects and the provision of seeds and agricultural tools for resettlement.

[12] *Programa Nacional de Desenvolvimento Agrário (PROAGRI): Draft III.* 1996. Maputo, Ministry of Agriculture and Fisheries.
[13] Some 10 000 Mozambicans have been landmine victims, with 8 000 of them amputees. It is estimated that hundreds of thousands of landmines are yet to be found.
[14] *Boletim de Segurança Alimentar.* 1991/92. Maputo, Department of Food Security, Ministry of Commerce.

Preliminary estimates for 1996/97 suggest that food aid and commercial imports have dropped to just 10 percent of cereal supplies. Local cereal production has displayed repeated increases, rising from a 3.4 percent increase in 1994 to a 30 percent increase in 1995 and a further 34 percent increase in 1996. Continued growth in agricultural output will depend increasingly on the availability of productivity-enhancing inputs such as fertilizer or improved seeds and less on area expansion. Cashew, copra, cottonseed and sugar-cane production have been expanding at a more gradual rate than grains. The future performance of the agricultural sector will depend largely on input and credit availability, the rehabilitation of processing facilities and rural infrastructure and market outlet development.

Marketing. Less than 30 percent of Mozambican farmers market surplus production. Groundnuts and then maize are the most commonly traded commodities. A number of significant constraints impede the diversification and expansion of agricultural marketing. The rural trade network is composed of an estimated 9 564 commercial establishments, of which only 61 percent were in operation in 1995. Transport costs are very high, while movement throughout the country is still restricted by instances of banditry. Owing to war-related sabotage and neglect of maintenance, only 30 percent of the road network is suitable for travel, and storage facilities are severely limited. Warehouses of the Instituto Moçambicano de Cereais (IMC), the Mozambican grain marketing board, are seriously underutilized. Irregularly enforced pan-territoral minimum reference prices prejudice the marketability of produce. The lack of liquidity and absence of rural credit limit the volume and geographic spread of trade, and transaction costs are soaring as traders resort to the use of barter. Circulation taxes and outdated and burdensome licensing requirements discourage new entrants to rural markets.

Land tenure. Mozambique's current land law dates back to the colonial period. A new law has been drafted but is still to be reviewed by Parliament. All land is currently owned by the state, which issues 50-year renewable leases granting liberal usufruct rights whereby the holder may sell and bequeath improvements and access rights.

RECENT DEVELOPMENTS IN MOZAMBIQUE'S CROP AND FOOD SUPPLY

An FAO/World Food Programme Crop and Food Supply Assessment mission visited Mozambique in April 1997 to estimate the country's 1996/97 production of food crops, forecast cereal import requirements for 1997/98 and determine the likely food aid needs. The mission found encouraging developments in the crop and food supply situation, but nevertheless estimated that considerable amounts of food aid would still be needed.

Reflecting the natural increase in population and the timely reintegration of returnees and demobilized soldiers, the total area planted to cereals and other food crops in 1996/97 is 6 percent higher than last year. The total 1996/97 production of cereals is estimated to be 11 percent higher than the previous year. Production of cassava, the other major staple, has also increased, while the production of beans and groundnuts is estimated to have increased by 8.5 percent over the previous year.

Owing to these increases in both cereal and other food production, the overall food supply situation in Mozambique in the 1997/98 marketing year (April/March) is expected to be better than last year, with a coarse grain surplus of an estimated 63 000 tonnes. However, in 1997/98 the country will have an estimated import requirement for rice and wheat of 205 000 tonnes.

The mission estimated that approximately 172 000 people will require food assistance for four months and that a further 77 000 people might require assistance for an additional three months, contingent on the evaluation of the second-season crop performance since the crop fields of the first harvest were inundated by floods. Heavy rains in several areas in the central region caused floods that brought considerable damage to crops, notably on farms along the Zambezi, Pungue and Buzi Rivers.

Even with a promising second harvest, however, there would still be a significant number of people who would have difficulty coping with shortages without receiving assistance. There are families in some areas in the normally food-deficit south as well as in parts of other provinces who are not likely to be able to meet their consumption needs from their own production or afford to purchase food on the market. The population in the south has never been self-sufficient and, therefore, has usually depended on the market to secure its requirements. For many food-deficit rural areas, lack of infrastructure remains a serious bottle-neck. As a result, prices tend to be high for those who rely on the market. While families that grow cash crops such as cotton and cashew nuts and those who find employment in non-farm sectors can afford to buy the food they need, many low-wage earners and the unemployed are unable to have access to adequate food.

The mission estimates that, out of the total cereal import requirement, 102 000 tonnes will be covered by commercial imports, leaving a deficit of 103 000 tonnes to be covered by food aid. Emergency food aid is estimated at 10 000 tonnes, including 1 000 tonnes of pulses, which can be secured through local purchases. Overall, the 1997/98 food assistance requirement represents 46 percent of that provided in the previous marketing year.

Authority to assign access rights and the issuance of a title depends on the size of the landholding. Although the actual limits vary according to land use, smallholdings are under the jurisdiction of provincial authorities and do not require titles, while larger holdings are titled and administered by the Ministry of Agriculture and Fisheries and holdings exceeding 10 000 ha are in the domain of the Land Commission. Although Mozambique is generally considered a land-abundant country, only 3 to 4 million of an estimated 36 million cultivable hectares are classified as good-quality and easily accessible to markets. The more densely populated Maputo, Gaza and Inhambane provinces all have imminent land constraints, especially when fuelwood collection, hunting and grazing needs are factored in.

Economic liberalization in Angola

In 1984 the Government of Angola acknowledged the failure of state farms and began to allocate land and other resources such as inputs and technical assistance to farmers' associations. Discussions arose concerning liberalizing prices, increasing the role of the private sector, decentralizing management and allowing more financial autonomy for public enterprises. The drop in international petroleum prices in 1985 and 1986 had disastrous effects on the already troubled balance of payments. This prompted the government to initiate an economic and financial "cleansing programme" (*Programa de Saneamento Económico e Financeiro*), and later that year the government applied for membership in IMF and the World Bank. Similar to Mozambique, Angola adopted PRE, a reform programme which addressed market liberalization, macroeconomic distortions and imbalances and privatization.

However, Angola's route to market liberalization has been more circuitous, utilizing a longer succession of occasionally awkward policy instruments to reach a similar end. Planning in Angola was further hampered by a resurgence of the civil war in 1992. Although the government and UNITA signed a new accord in 1994, not all negotiated terms have been fulfilled. The deadline for the complete demobilization of soldiers and withdrawal of the UN peace-keeping forces (UNAVEM III) was extended, and the country remains physically and politically divided. The fact that long-lasting peace

AFRICA

is not yet assured impedes the implementation of market liberalization measures and compromises economic performance.

Market liberalization. Market liberalization began gradually in 1988 with the removal of price controls on fruits and vegetables. In 1991, the government disbanded all price controls with the exception of seven basic products (flour, bread, rice, sugar, cooking oil, condensed milk and soap), which were assigned margin restrictions a short time later. The government also maintained fixed prices for another group of basic consumer items, including rent, public transport fares, electricity and water. There are currently three sets of price systems: fixed, free and fixed margins. Adding a further complication, parallel market prices diverge widely from administered prices. The international donor community continues to apply pressure to eliminate all price controls. In 1991, the government created the Caixa de Crédito Agropecuario e Pescas, an agricultural and fisheries credit programme for small and medium-sized farms and enterprises. Unfortunately, the war undermined the successful implementation of the programme, and rural credit remains virtually non-existent today.

The Foreign Investment Law restructured taxes so that they are more favourable to foreign investors. Import quotas and authorization from the Ministry of Commerce have been abolished. Nevertheless, serious impediments to trade persist. There are taxes, fees, licensing requirements and a heavily bureaucratic process of documenting all transactions. The complexity of the system lends itself to instances of abuse.

Privatization. Two laws enacted in 1988 and 1991 governed the process of privatization. The laws granted preferential treatment to Angolan nationals, imposed a ceiling of 49 percent on private ownership and created a system of allocating shares of the enterprises being privatized to managers and workers. By 1992, hundreds of state-owned companies and farms had been divided into smaller private units through a less than completely transparent bidding process. Private investment is expected to increase with a greater assurance of long-lasting peace.

AFRICA

Correcting macroeconomic distortions and imbalances.
Correcting macroeconomic distortions in Angola has not
been as straightforward or successful as it has with
Mozambique. In battling hyperinflation, the government
issued a new currency in 1990 which was devalued by
95 percent the following year. The government then
established a complex system of multiple exchange rates
which functioned through taxes levied on imports and
exports at different rates depending on the type, use and
destination of the commodity. In order to curb spending,
the government instituted a hiring freeze and tightened
access to credit by state enterprises. Over the past six
years, approximately two-thirds of the budget has been
spent on defence and administration. In contrast,
agriculture has received on average just 1.5 percent. The
share of the budget allocated to defence recently fell by
50 percent while the share allocated to administration
increased. Although accounting and auditing standards
were introduced in 1989, IMF and the World Bank
continue to exert pressure for de facto improved banking
practices and reporting procedures.

Despite the war, Angola has managed to demonstrate
some limited improvement in a number of standard
macroeconomic measures. The differential between the
parallel and official exchange rates has diminished
substantially. Inflation dropped from 4 000 percent in
1995 to approximately 2 000 percent this past year.[15]

Issues in Angolan agriculture today
Revitalization of agricultural production. Angola has
excellent agricultural potential. The diversity in agro-
ecological regions allows for the production of both
temperate and tropical crops, and livestock is expected
once again to play an important role within the sector.
Although mining, including oil and diamonds,
constitutes the largest share of GDP, agriculture is still a
significant sector of the Angolan economy, representing
approximately 20 percent of GDP. Despite war-related
disruptions, more than 80 percent of the population is
still dependent on agriculture.

With the resurgence of the war in 1992, violence,
banditry and crop vandalism rose sharply; rural
infrastructure was completely demolished; and the
country was littered with landmines. As a result, farmers
and even whole villages chose to flee to the relative
safety of urban centres, and agricultural production

[15] FAO. 1996. *Agriculture and
macroeconomy: linkages and
sector policy.* Angola
agricultural recovery and
development options review.
Working Paper No. 14. By
S. Kyle. Rome.

AFRICA

plummeted, particularly in MPLA areas. Because UNITA was dependent on local sources for its food supply, UNITA disturbed producers as little as possible and even provided some extension services. Until now, the country remains divided, despite the removal of most check points. The worst year in terms of production of cereals and cassava was 1993/94. Since then, output has been expanding, yet nearly half of 1996/97 cereal needs will nonetheless be met by aid and commercial imports, even though cereal production increased by 100 percent between 1995/96 and 1996/97.

Angola is in an early phase of resettlement. Many rural families have settled in temporary locations and plan to continue their migration in stages. WFP and non-governmental organizations (NGOs) continue to distribute food and agricultural seeds and tools. WFP expects 1998 to be its final year of involvement in food aid. There is some concern that the youth who are currently concentrated in urban centres may not return to the rural lifestyles they left behind. Nevertheless, rural areas are beginning to normalize and, as a result, marketing activities have gradually picked up. This is expected to continue as greater freedom of movement is gained.

The government's current programme for agriculture logically focuses on rehabilitation and capacity building; however, the funds for such activities are derived mostly from donors and not from the national budget. The donor community, in collaboration with the Angolan Government, has developed the Community Rehabilitation Programme. Like Mozambique's PROAGRI, but not limited to the agricultural sector, it is an integrated programme that coordinates donor efforts.

Given the current attention on markets, the scarcity of agricultural labour and historic patterns, the Ministry of Agriculture and Rural Development has proposed a programme which emphasizes animal traction, fertilizer use and private commercial farm enterprises. Currently, donors, NGOs and international research institutes are working to rebuild and improve local seed stocks.

Confidence building. One major impediment to progress in Angola is the lack of confidence in nearly all aspects of Angolan life: political, economic and social. The reigniting of the war in 1992 and the continued postponements in the reconciliation process cast doubt

AFRICA

on future prospects for consolidating peace. Many Angolans fear for their physical safety. In 1990, the government dealt a devastating blow to the public's already shaky confidence in the currency. In issuing new kwanza notes, old notes were exchanged at par with the new ones but only 5 percent of the value was distributed in cash: the rest was to be converted to government securities. Rural people who were unable to make the exchange ended up with worthless old notes, while, for those who were able to secure new notes, the maximum 5 percent provided insufficient cash to cover immediate expenses, including food.

Oil and diamond wealth. Angola is blessed with oil and diamonds. Oil alone accounts for as much as 90 percent of exports and half of GDP.[16] Ironically, it is the extreme lucrativeness of this sector that acts as a curse as well. The huge concentrated export earnings tend to cause chronic overvaluation of the local currency and inflationary pressure, especially when the government spends rather than invests these earnings. Some argue that the government is preoccupied with this sector at the expense of socially more important sectors such as agriculture, education and health.

Land tenure. Angola recently enacted a new land law. Like the case of Mozambique, the state owns all of the land and grants liberal access rights in the form of long-term release leases. Unfortunately, the law is not without fault. It allows multiple ministries to grant access rights independently, and there are several different cadastres mapping and recording land information. Under this form of administration, multiple users are likely to be assigned rights to the same parcel of land and conflicts are bound to arise.

CONCLUDING REMARKS

Macroeconomic reform and market liberalization have undoubtedly contributed to economic stabilization in both Mozambique and Angola. However, after more than three decades of civil unrest, the most significant factor is clearly the establishment of peace. The emphasis is now on rehabilitation and the creation of conditions that will induce development, including fine-tuning recent macroeconomic reforms. Currently, rehabilitation programmes are being sponsored by the

---

[16] **World Bank. 1994.** *Angola: strategic orientation for agricultural development.* Washington, DC.

AFRICA

donor community. The future of both countries depends heavily on the form of this reconstruction. With respect to the agricultural sector, the most important issues are the guarantee of personal safety, recapitalization, production increases and productivity improvements, marketable output diversification, creation of market opportunities and agro-industrial linkages, and human and institutional capacity development. Underlying these issues is the need for rural finance and clearer, less-conflicting land rights.

ASIA AND THE PACIFIC

REGIONAL OVERVIEW
Economic developments

Developing Asia and the Pacific continued to outperform other regions in economic growth in 1996, although growth in some of the region's economies moderated. Average real GDP growth in Asia and the Pacific was 8.2 percent in 1996, slightly lower than the 8.9 percent recorded in 1995 but still strong enough for substantial per caput income growth. The region's cumulative growth between 1991 and 1996 added up to more than 50 percent. Growth in China continued to decline marginally in 1996, including in Taiwan Province of China, but at 9.7 percent, it still increased the size of the Chinese economy relative to the rest of the world. India, Asia's other giant, grew at 6.8 percent. The newly industrializing economies (NIEs) of Hong Kong, the Republic of Korea and Singapore suffered a slowdown in their important export sectors, and their overall growth rate declined from 7.5 percent in 1995 to 6.3 percent in 1996. Southeast Asian economic growth declined from 8.1 to 7.1 percent, affected by the export slowdown as well as tighter monetary and fiscal policies. In South Asia, structural reforms continued, and the economies posted an aggregate 6.5 percent growth in 1996. Real economic growth in Asia and the Pacific is expected to be roughly stable at slightly more than 7 percent per year in 1997 and 1998.[17]

Trade and investment continued to play a key role in the region's development. In 1996 it again reinforced its position as the leading destination among all developing regions for foreign direct investment (FDI), accounting for more than half of all inflows to developing countries. Where current account deficits in the region have widened, they have generally reflected increasing imports of capital goods to support the region's high level of investment, rather than reflecting increased consumption. For developing Asia and the Pacific as a whole, export growth fell from 21.8 percent in 1995 to just 4.6 percent in 1996. This decline from unsustainably high export growth rates in 1995 was largely due to a slump in demand for some of the region's major export items, notably electronics, in the

[17] The country data and projections in this section are based on AsDB. 1997. *Asian Development Outlook 1997 and 1998.* Manila.

ASIA AND THE PACIFIC

more industrialized countries. Other factors included slower economic growth and import demand within the region (caused, in the notable case of China, by measures to prevent overheating, with knock-on effects for Hong Kong's exports) and import restrictions to maintain the trade balance within prescribed limits.

A major issue for developing Asian economies is the extent to which the export slowdown also reflects a loss of competitiveness or, in other words, the extent to which it reflects structural rather than cyclical factors. High investment, education and economic growth rates in the region have made it natural for the comparative advantage of countries to shift. Over time, domestic supply bottlenecks, fiscal policy changes, a continued appreciation in the real effective exchange rate, relative factor price changes or changes in the composition of export demand can affect export performance negatively if structural adjustments do not occur. For some countries, such as Thailand, there is increasing competition from lower-cost producers within Asia (such as China and Viet Nam), and the maintenance of strong economic growth in these countries will depend on their continually adjusting their mix of products and production technologies – the same challenge faced by other industrializing or industrialized countries.

For almost two decades, China, with the world's largest population, has pursued reforms and experienced extraordinary economic growth and improved living conditions. At 9.7 percent, the country's real GDP growth in 1996 remains the envy of most other countries but has been gradually brought down from its 1992 peak of more than 14 percent in an effort to keep inflation under control. This has been accomplished through tight fiscal and monetary policies as well as new standards for bankruptcy of state-owned enterprises. China continues to be the most popular destination for FDI in the developing world, and continues to increase its export share of world markets in garments, textiles and light machinery.

India has continued to show enormous improvements resulting from the liberalization programme begun in 1991. Real GDP growth in 1996 remained strong at 6.8 percent, led by a 9 percent growth in the industrial sector and helped by the ninth favourable monsoon in a row. If the monsoons remain favourable, continued annual growth of about 7 percent is expected over the

Figure 8A

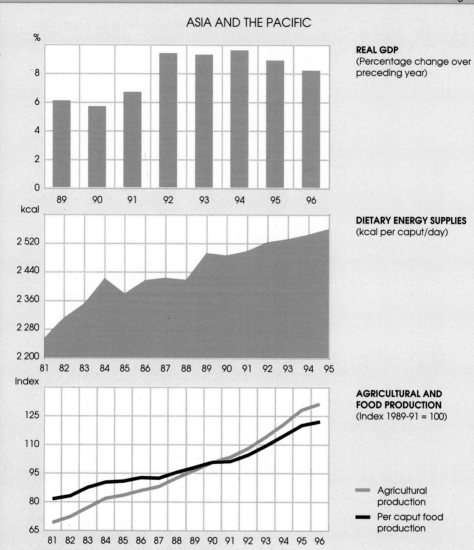

ASIA AND THE PACIFIC

REAL GDP
(Percentage change over preceding year)

DIETARY ENERGY SUPPLIES
(kcal per caput/day)

AGRICULTURAL AND FOOD PRODUCTION
(Index 1989-91 = 100)

Agricultural production

Per caput food production

Source: FAO and IMF

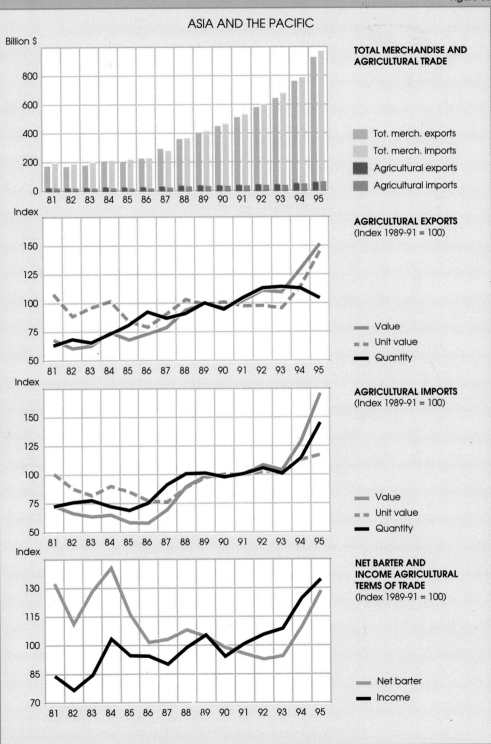

Figure 8B

ASIA AND THE PACIFIC

TOTAL MERCHANDISE AND AGRICULTURAL TRADE

- Tot. merch. exports
- Tot. merch. imports
- Agricultural exports
- Agricultural imports

AGRICULTURAL EXPORTS
(Index 1989-91 = 100)

- Value
- Unit value
- Quantity

AGRICULTURAL IMPORTS
(Index 1989-91 = 100)

- Value
- Unit value
- Quantity

NET BARTER AND INCOME AGRICULTURAL TERMS OF TRADE
(Index 1989-91 = 100)

- Net barter
- Income

Source: FAO

ASIA AND THE PACIFIC

next two years. Mobilizing sufficient investment resources to finance the country's massive infrastructure investment needs will remain a major challenge in the medium term.

Growth in the NIEs slowed slightly in 1996, mainly as a result of weak demand for electronics in the United States and Europe, which negatively affected exports from the Republic of Korea, Singapore and Taiwan Province of China. An appreciating US dollar, to which Hong Kong pegs its own currency, and a fall in China's exports (and Hong Kong's re-exports) reduced exports and overall growth in the territory. However, domestic demand picked up in the second half of 1996, and consumer and business confidence appeared to be high as Hong Kong entered its transition to the status of a Special Administrative Region of China. Growth in the Republic of Korea's economy slowed, affected by a slowdown in investment and export growth, as well as by a more than doubling of the current account deficit. Economic liberalization related to the 1996 Korean accession to the Organisation for Economic Co-operation and Development (OECD) will promote further structural changes in the coming years. Growth in Singapore also slowed in 1996 as demand for electronics exports weakened and the financial and business services sector slumped.

Southeast Asia has generally been following the manufactured export-led growth path of the NIEs, but in most cases with substantially larger domestic markets and more robust agricultural sectors. Economic growth in Cambodia remained at a healthy 6 percent in 1996, led by power generation and construction and supported by a substantial increase in investment, particularly foreign investment. Real GDP growth in Indonesia declined slightly to 7.8 percent in 1996, as tighter monetary and fiscal measures were implemented to constrain inflation and reduce the current account deficit. However, prospects for the near future remain bright in view of strong domestic demand, increasing foreign investment flows and progress in deregulation. In Laos, real GDP growth rebounded to 7.2 percent as investment remained strong, trade and revenue collection increased and inflation remained moderate. Agriculture, particularly rainfed agriculture, remains the dominant economic sector, keeping overall economic performance subject to the vagaries of weather.

ASIA AND THE PACIFIC

Malaysia experienced a slowdown in GDP growth to a still high 8.2 percent, as monetary policy was tightened to limit the current account deficit, but plans for massive infrastructure projects should sustain growth. Myanmar achieved 6 percent growth in 1996, reflecting good weather and a resulting large harvest which yielded substantial rice exports. Reform measures introduced after 1990 have made this the fifth good year of economic growth. Under the influence of ongoing reforms in the Philippines, GDP growth has been improving, reaching 5.5 percent in 1996, and high rates of investment are being fed by both foreign and domestic capital flows. Viet Nam maintained economic growth at 9.5 percent in 1996, led by the industrial sector. Agricultural output met its target, despite bad weather in parts of the country, and inflation moderated to 6 percent.

In South Asia, the economic reform process began later than in most other parts of Asia, and the reforms, while positive, remained unfinished. Even so, real GDP continued to grow at 6.5 percent in 1996, up slightly from 6.4 percent in 1995. At 4.7 percent, growth was modest in Bangladesh, as reforms were delayed in implementation, investment and aid disbursements were below target and exports slowed. Recovery in the agricultural sector following improved weather spurred overall economic growth in Nepal in 1996, supported by growth in industry and tourism. Real GDP growth increased to 5.9 percent in Pakistan in 1996, but inflation remained in double digits as a persistent budget deficit again resulted from difficulties in revenue mobilization. Domestic savings declined, as did export growth, culminating in the introduction of a new stabilization effort. Sri Lanka continued to suffer from the strains of high defence expenditures, compounded by drought, while a declining agricultural output and weak performance in the industrial sector constrained export growth.

Reform measures undertaken throughout South Asia, together with the possible expansion of intraregional trade being advocated in the South Asian Association for Regional Cooperation (SAARC), have put the subcontinent on a sound footing for further growth. Expansion and further implementation of reforms will determine the sustainability of improved growth rates.

Agricultural performance

At 436 million tonnes, in 1996 China's cereal harvest reached a record for the second year in a row, helping to hold down grain imports and increase stocks as well as narrowing the gap between state procurement and market prices. Cereal imports are estimated to decline sharply to about 12.9 million tonnes in 1996/97, down from 26.9 million tonnes in 1995/96. Agricultural production grew by 3.4 percent, significantly below the 1993-95 average of 8.9 percent, reflecting in particular poor performances of non-food crops. Food production rose by 4.2 percent, helped by good weather and higher procurement prices. The record cereal harvest and high government agricultural expenditures boosted rural incomes substantially, thereby helping to slow the widening rural-urban income disparity. A poor cotton harvest and rising cotton prices contributed to weaker textile exports in 1996.

Agricultural output in India increased by a marginal 0.5 percent in 1996, with cereal production remaining virtually unchanged from the previous year at 214 million tonnes. From 1990/91 to 1996/97 growth in annual cereal production only averaged 1.7 percent, less than the country's 1.9 percent annual population growth. Record rice exports in 1995/96, together with the country's first net wheat exports since 1947, pushed total agricultural exports up to $5.7 billion while agricultural imports, which are limited by tariffs, licensing, state trading arrangements and an array of other non-tariff barriers, fell to $1.9 billion, although vegetable oil imports more than tripled. Estimates for 1996/97 point to India's return to being a net wheat importer and to a decline in the overall cereal surplus. The first budget under the United Front coalition government contained higher subsidies for irrigation, fertilizer and agricultural equipment, as well as provisions for supplying families classed below the poverty line with grain at 50 percent below the prevailing issue price. It also enhanced credit supplies for rural infrastructure and investment in horticulture, floriculture and food processing. Agriculture continues to employ nearly 70 percent of the economically active population and accounts for roughly 30 percent of GDP.

Despite wide variations in recent years, agricultural production in the Republic of Korea has generally exceeded population growth and it enabled an average

ASIA AND THE PACIFIC

1.6 percent yearly increase in per caput food output during the period from 1991 to 1996. The country is a large and growing market for consumer foods. Consumer-oriented food imports exceeded $2 billion in 1995 before declining substantially but still exceeding $700 million in 1996. High tariffs and non-tariff barriers protect domestic producers, who are generally high-cost, small-scale family farmers, with a policy emphasis on rice production. However, under its Uruguay Round Minimum Market Access (MMA) commitments, the Republic of Korea will be required to import rice at least in accordance with its MMA schedule. To help the country's rural sector adjust to the impacts of its Uruguay Round commitments, the government has passed a ten-year special tax, the proceeds of which will be targeted at hard-hit rural villages, and a Five-Year Agricultural Development Plan emphasizing improved international competitiveness, the promotion of rural industry and improved welfare for rural people.

In the Democratic People's Republic of Korea the domestic food supply situation was extremely precarious after several years of poor agricultural performances (per caput food production fell by 3 percent yearly between 1991 and 1996). The outlook for 1997 also appeared grim in the wake of severe floods over two consecutive years. Although grain production in 1996 was estimated to be slightly greater than in 1995, a large part of the harvest was consumed prematurely owing to the severity of food shortages.

In accordance with the benefits perceived in Southeast Asia from unilateral liberalization measures and to control inflation, the Government of Indonesia has been deregulating and lowering the tariffs on many bulk-product agricultural imports as a step towards meeting its commitments to the World Trade Organization (WTO), the Asia-Pacific Economic Cooperation Council (APEC) and the Common Effective Preferential Tariff, set by the Association of Southeast Asian Nations (ASEAN). The government has also set standards for maximum allowable pesticide residues as well as for the handling, labelling and sale of all foodstuffs. Wheat milling, animal feed, food processing and textile industries are all continuing to expand at a rapid pace. Although agriculture has increased at significantly faster rates than population over much of the past decade, the sector's contribution to GDP has

ASIA AND THE PACIFIC

declined to about 17 percent, down from 24 percent in the early 1980s. Agriculture still accounts for almost 45 percent of employment, however.

Also following ASEAN's direction towards a more liberalized economic environment, Malaysia's Seventh Plan strives for greater private sector investment to expand capacity and increase mechanization. Under this plan, agricultural production programmes aim to increase export competitiveness by reducing costs, and to increase production of high-value commodities. Agricultural production has expanded at annual growth rates of about 2.8 percent in recent years, with the much faster growth of the industrial and services sectors. However, agriculture now only accounts for 14 percent of GDP, down from 22 percent in the early 1980s.

The Philippines' agricultural sector recovered in 1996, with both higher output and higher prices on average. Rising incomes are reflected in increasing demand for meat and other imported foods and inputs (including feedgrains). The effects of the long shortage of public investment in rural infrastructure, human resources and research and development are becoming obvious as domestic production is increasingly unable to meet the food needs of the rapidly growing population. In 1996, the government replaced quantitative restrictions on imported agricultural goods with tariffs, taking a significant step towards eventually complying with WTO agreements and integrating its agricultural sector into the global economy.

Lower prices limited growth in the value of Thailand's agricultural exports in 1996, thus adding to the country's trade difficulties. Agricultural imports increased, notably livestock feedstuffs, despite the fact that the maize import window was shortened to April-June and the tariff-quota regime on maize and soybean products was maintained.

Pakistan's agricultural sector grew by 6.7 percent in 1995/96, up from a relatively strong 5.9 percent growth in 1994/95 and spurred by growth in crop production and fisheries. The growth occurred despite a price rise and a shortage of fertilizer following a subsidy withdrawal as the sector benefited from better weather, fewer pests and an expansion of improved production technologies. Cotton area increased as sugar cane area declined and increased raw cotton exports boosted the share of primary commodities in total exports.

ASIA AND THE PACIFIC

Issues and prospects for regional agriculture

For a vast majority of people in Asia and the Pacific, food security is largely linked to the performance of the cereals sector. Rice and wheat account for, respectively, about 37 and 19 percent of the region's calorie consumption. As a result of relatively good performance in the region's cereal production, its self-sufficiency ratio has remained high, decreasing slightly in East Asia (including China) between 1969-71 and 1988-90 from 97.9 to 96.2 percent, and increasing slightly in South Asia over the same period from 98 to 102 percent. As cereal self-sufficiency has remained high and total exports have grown, the share of the region's export earnings spent on food imports declined from 16.1 percent in 1970-72 to just 5.1 percent in 1990-92.

Improvements in the region's food availability helped reduce the share of the population suffering from nutritional deficiencies, yet about half a billion people in Asia and the Pacific are still chronically undernourished while many more suffer from other dietary deficiencies. For the food security of these people in particular, and the region's population in general, supply disruptions arising from natural or market forces can be catastrophic.

An increasing population density, environmental degradation, migration to vulnerable areas and climatic variations have made Asia and the Pacific the most disaster-prone region in the world. An average of 35 natural disasters occur in the region each year, representing roughly 60 percent of the world's total. A flood in Bangladesh in 1987 reduced rice production by 35 million tonnes to 82 percent of normal national output. In 1991, 5 percent of China's annual harvest was destroyed by floods as 4 000 state grain warehouses were washed away and another 3 400 were swamped by water. In China it has been common to experience droughts in the north and floods in the south. Cyclones, earthquakes, volcanic eruptions, fire, pest infestations and other natural hazards have also taken their toll in the region. Physical losses from natural disasters in Asia and the Pacific were estimated by the Asian Development Bank (AsDB) to have reached about $10 billion in 1990-91.

These damaging natural phenomena disrupt production, storage and marketing or distribution systems and have both immediate and longer-term

ASIA AND THE PACIFIC

consequences. Their effects can be particularly devastating for poorer families, whose household strategies play an important role in coping with them. To mitigate the effects of drought, for example, households attempt to diversify income, borrow, share, sell assets and reduce or diversify consumption.

National flood and storm prevention and management strategies require both structural and non-structural measures, many of which need to be integrated into rural development plans. Structural measures may involve the construction of reservoirs, dykes, submersible embankments and river channel improvements. Non-structural preparedness measures involve maintaining a minimum adequate reserve stock, effective national food information and early warning systems, emergency relief capability and a food relief contingency plan. These elements are frequently poorly developed and are lacking, or not well integrated, in poorer countries. Longer-term efforts can include minimizing deforestation, undertaking reforestation and other conservation measures, restricting or reducing settlements in disaster-prone areas and investing in appropriate physical infrastructure, education, employment and income-generation activities in those areas.

Public distribution systems have played an important role in protecting vulnerable groups in Asia and the Pacific, accounting at times for 25 percent of consumption in China, 12 percent in India, 8 percent in Indonesia, 9 percent in the Philippines and up to 35 percent in Malaysia. As these systems are cut back to increase efficiency, the importance of better targeting is becoming more apparent.

Imports play an important role in supply stabilization for many cereal-deficit countries, including non-wheat producers and traditionally large cereal importers such as Bangladesh, China, Pakistan and the Republic of Korea. Projections from the study *World agriculture: towards 2010*[18] suggest that, by the year 2010, Asia will need to rely on substantial imports of wheat in its tropical countries, of rice where production costs are high and multilateral trade commitments limit or prohibit protectionism, and of maize where livestock production is growing rapidly.

Relying on imported supplies may be a cost-effective way of meeting demand but may involve the risk of

---

[18] FAO. 1995. *World agriculture: towards 2010.* Edited by N. Alexandratos. Rome, FAO and Chichester, UK, Wiley.

ASIA AND THE PACIFIC

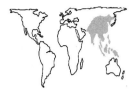

price hikes or production shortfalls in supplying nations, war or other shipping hazards and politically motivated trade sanctions or diversions. There are also more normal trade difficulties relating to exchange rate fluctuations, foreign reserve shortages, port capacity and storage and handling constraints. Some of these risks may be mitigated by increasing incentives for privately held stocks, prepositioning government stocks in deficit areas, forming regional food security plans, improving early warning systems and negotiating long-term food import agreements. Steps in these directions have already been taken by ASEAN and SAARC, which have established food information exchanges, food loans and subregional emergency food reserves.

Reduced losses and improved inventory control measures may reduce what are considered necessary emergency stock levels. In addition, many developing countries in Asia and the Pacific could improve the efficiency of their food marketing systems. In part, this will occur with improvements in transport, marketing and energy infrastructure. The region's trend towards reduced state intervention is also yielding clearer incentive structures and greater allocative efficiency.

To reduce the threats of supply shocks to regional food security the main steps that should be taken are to increase food production, generate employment and incomes, improve water control and mitigate the short- and medium-term negative effects that natural disasters have on the nutrition situation by implementing the measures mentioned above. The rapidly spreading regional cooperation efforts throughout Asia and the Pacific, together with the Asian Disaster Preparedness Centre, provide important venues for reducing trade barriers and sharing information, technology and emergency food resources as a means to achieve these goals.

ASIA AND THE PACIFIC

[19] World Bank. 1996. *World Development Report, 1996.* New York, Oxford University Press.

[20] Government of Bangladesh. *Bangladesh Food and Agriculture.* Document prepared for the World Food Summit, November 1996, FAO, Rome.

[21] The poverty line in Bangladesh is defined by the 1991-1992 Household Expenditure Survey and is calculated on the basis of a per caput minimum daily intake of 2 122 kcal (as recommended by WHO), with a 30 percent allowance for non-food basic needs. Those defined as the "hard-core" poor have a daily intake of <1 805 kcal (M.O. Hossain, 1991. Poverty alleviation. *In* R. Sobhan, ed. *Report of the task forces on Bangladesh development strategies for the 1990s, Volume 1.* Dhaka).

[22] Economist Intelligence Unit. 1996. *Bangladesh country profile, 1996-97.* London.

[23] UNDP. 1996. *Report on Human Development in Bangladesh: A Pro-Poor Agenda.* Dhaka.

BANGLADESH
Socio-economic characteristics

Despite significant economic and social progress over the past 20 years, Bangladesh remains among the poorest countries in the world. With a per caput gross national product (GNP) of $220, less than that of both Pakistan ($430) and India ($320), Bangladesh ranked as the 13th poorest among 133 countries covered by World Bank[19] rankings in 1996. With a population of 120 million living within a limited land area of 147 570 km^2, Bangladesh is one of the most densely populated countries in the world, supporting 800 people per km^2. At current rates of population growth (2.17 percent), it is estimated that the total population could reach 175 million within 25 years from now.[20] The urban population has been growing rapidly, by 5.3 percent per year from 1980 to 1993, but 83 percent of the people still live in rural areas.

Fifty percent of the Bangladeshi population lives below the absolute poverty line[21] and approximately 40 percent of the effective labour force is underemployed. Poverty in Bangladesh is closely associated with landownership. Functionally landless (less than 0.2 ha) households comprise 65 percent of the poor, while the marginal landowners (with between 0.2 and 0.6 ha) account for another 21 percent. The number of absolute and hard-core poor increased between 1985 and 1992, especially in the rural areas, but later studies suggest a slight improvement in the levels of poverty in recent years. The proportion of the population living below the poverty line is reported to have fallen from 57.5 percent in 1987 to 51.7 percent in 1994.[22] The prevalence of extreme poverty is far higher among female-headed households, whose total population may exceed four million. More than 95 percent of these female-headed households fall below the poverty line, of which one-third are among the hard-core poor.[23] Their incomes, on average, are 40 percent less than those of male-headed households.

More than 62 percent of the population in Bangladesh is illiterate, and the country suffers from some of the highest undernutrition and malnutrition levels in the world. Although infant and child mortality rates have improved since the mid-1980s, 84 percent of children under the age of five are still considered malnourished. For centuries, predominant cultural perceptions in this

ASIA AND THE PACIFIC

region have disadvantaged women. Eating last and least is an all-too-common occurrence, with the result that, contrary to the global norm, life expectancy for women in Bangladesh is less than that for the men. Bangladeshi women are the most vulnerable to dietary deficiencies and, as a result, have one of the highest maternal mortality rates in the world – 490 per 100 000 live births in rural areas – largely as a result of the poor nutrition of expectant mothers. The nutritional status of the population points to significant gaps in food consumption.

Notwithstanding these stubbornly difficult socio-economic indicators, there have been some positive developments in recent years. The economy has grown by more than 4 percent annually since 1992, compared with an average annual growth rate of 2.1 percent over the previous 12 years. Although still relatively low, the percentage of literacy increased from 32 percent in 1991 to 38 percent in 1995; primary school enrolment has increased by more than 50 percent since 1990, of which almost half is accounted for by girls; the infant mortality rate (per 1 000 live births) has come down from 94 in 1990 to 77 in 1994; the fertility rate has declined considerably from 4.3 children per woman in 1990 to 3.4 in 1995; and family planning coverage has been quite phenomenal: 45 percent of currently married women under 50 years of age are now using contraceptives versus 25.3 percent in 1985.[24]

Macroeconomic policy and performance
Economic policy in the 1970s and 1980s was contained in a series of five-year plans. Economic policy aims of the various governments in those years were rarely achieved, partly because of unrealistic objectives and partly owing to a combination of problems arising from the rise in world oil prices, natural catastrophes and political disorder.

Since the late 1980s, Bangladesh has been undergoing structural adjustment reforms. Policies have been aimed at liberalizing the economy and making it market-based in order to raise growth, mainly by reducing the role of the government and giving encouragement to the private sector.

Bangladesh has initiated a number of structural reforms which encompass fiscal, financial, trade, institutional and industrial policy reforms, public

[24] **Government of Bangladesh, op. cit., footnote 20, p. 128.**

ASIA AND THE PACIFIC

resource management and privatization. Efforts are being made to restructure and/or privatize state-owned enterprises, most of which are incurring operating losses. Fiscal policy seeks to raise additional revenue (through the improvement of tax laws, structures and management), contain and switch public expenditure and enhance incentives for private investment. The external trade sector has been liberalized through steady reductions in import tariffs, and the government has been pursuing a flexible exchange rate policy in an effort to improve international competitiveness. Its monetary policy also aims at flexible and indirect management of money and credit growths. With the exception of three lending categories (agriculture, small industry and exports), interest rates have been decontrolled.

The reforms have contributed to significant economic progress over the past decade. Up until 1993/94, the economy was responding favourably. The inflation rate fell from 9.8 percent in 1985/86 to 5.3 percent in 1990/91 and down to 1.8 percent[25] in 1993/94. There was a sharp decline in the current account deficit as a result of a rapid rise in exports of non-traditional items, such as garments and fisheries, combined with a slow growth rate in imports. Thus, the current account deficit dropped from 6.7 percent of GDP in 1984/85 to 4.5 percent in 1989/90 and again to 1.6 percent of GDP, an all-time low, in 1993/94. The country's foreign exchange reserves stood at $3.2 billion, enough for covering more than seven months of imports, in 1993/94. Government revenues increased to about 12.2 percent of GDP (1993/94) as opposed to 9 percent during the 1980s, and the budget deficit, as a percentage of GDP, declined from 8.4 percent in 1986/87 to 6 percent in 1993/94.[26]

A sudden turnaround in these positive performances, however, took place in 1994/95 and 1995/96, the years in which Bangladesh experienced devastating foodgrain shortfalls. The rate of inflation climbed back to 5.2 percent, export growth slowed, the current account deficit increased considerably (owing to increased foodgrain purchases from abroad) and the foreign exchange reserve declined to $2.03 billion by the end of 1995/96.

Since 1989, annual GDP growth has consistently remained between 4 and 4.5 percent, but below the target rate of 6 percent considered essential for any

[25] Inflation mainly reflected the price of rice which accounts for 62 percent of the consumption basket for CPI measurement. (Cited in Government of Bangladesh/ FAO. 1996. *Strategies and programme framework for agricultural development in Bangladesh – Draft.*)
[26] Government of Bangladesh/ FAO, op. cit., footnote 25.

ASIA AND THE PACIFIC

significant impact on poverty alleviation. The main sources of this modest growth have been in large-scale industry, construction, transport and allied services and trade services. Despite impressive industrial growth in the 1990s (led by the export-oriented garments industry), the industrial sector still accounted for only 11.5 percent of GDP in 1995/96, with 34 percent of the sector's contribution coming from small-scale, usually traditional, industry.

For the short to medium term, the primary objective of the new government's economic policy is to increase the growth rate to 6 or 7 percent, while keeping inflation down, through manufacturing, services and agro-based industries. The government has identified three broad areas covered by the reform programme to attain these goals: i) private sector development; ii) improvement of public sector management; and iii) poverty alleviation, human resource development and enhancement of environmental resources.

Agriculture in the Bangladeshi economy

Agriculture is the single most important sector of Bangladesh's economy. It is the principal source of income and livelihood of the vast majority (80 percent) of the population, employing approximately 66 percent of the labour force. Fifty-seven percent of the labour force is engaged in the crop sector which represents about 78 percent of the value added in the agricultural sector. The share of agriculture in GDP has fallen from around 57 percent in the 1970s to 35 percent in recent years but is still the largest economic sector.[27] It is also the source of many of the small industrial sector's raw materials, such as jute, and accounts for 32 percent of the value of exports. In short, agriculture is the driving force behind economic growth in Bangladesh and, as a result, increasing food and agricultural production have always been major concerns of Bangladeshi policy-makers.

Within the crop sector (rice, wheat, pulses and jute), rice dominates, with an average 71 percent share of the gross output value of all crops. As a result, growth in the agricultural sector essentially mirrors the performance of rice production, although the share of livestock and fisheries has increased steadily in recent years to 22 percent of the value added in agriculture.

The possibility of natural disasters is a constant threat

[27] **Government of Bangladesh,** op. cit., footnote 20, p. 128.

ASIA AND THE PACIFIC

for Bangladesh. The country has been, and will continue to be, particularly vulnerable to sudden floods, cyclones and even droughts. Vulnerability to natural disasters and a heavy reliance on annual rains for the main crop performance are the cause of severe fluctuations in foodgrain production and prices and also very erratic GDP growth. Losses of both food and cash crops are a common occurrence, seriously disrupting the entire economy by precipitating unanticipated food import requirements. This in turn reduces the foreign exchange availability necessary for imports of essential inputs for manufacturing and industry and, as a result, causes shortfalls in exports.

Bangladesh is the world's leading exporter of raw jute and jute products, including carpet backing, twine and sacking. It accounts for as much as 25 percent of world jute production, 85 percent of world jute fibre exports and 44 to 55 percent of exports of jute manufactures. The fibre's prominence in agriculture, as well as in the economy of Bangladesh, slipped during the 1970s and 1980s as world demand fell as a result of competition from synthetic substitutes. Consequently, the jute industry, which contributed 54 percent of total export earnings in 1984/85, accounted for only 11 percent a decade later. Overtaking jute in 1987/88 as an export earner, the garments industry has emerged as the country's most important export sector. Garment exports comprised 57 percent of export earnings in 1994/95, up from 11 percent a decade earlier. Since garments exports require corresponding imports of other items, such as fabrics, yarn and buttons, the net benefit of the garments industry to export earnings in 1994/95 was, however, only 29 percent of the sector's gross export earnings.[28] There are clear indications that the industry is beginning to lose momentum and speculations that pressures on the industry are likely to intensify as countries such as China and Viet Nam develop their garments industries.

Export earnings from fish and fish products, in particular shrimp, are also sizeable (See Box 8, The fisheries sector in Bangladesh, p. 148), followed by export earnings from the leather industry. Natural gas production is of increasing importance. Its major product, urea fertilizer, has more than doubled in output in the last decade and the country now exports fertilizer, mainly to neighbouring Asian countries. Within the agricultural sector, tea follows jute as an important cash

[28] **Economist Intelligence Unit, op. cit., footnote 22, p. 128.**

crop and export product; however, it represented only 1 percent of the country's total export earnings in 1994/95.[29]

Bangladesh has a narrow resource base, except of course its human resource potential. Industry in the country is at present not large enough to support the country through export earnings, or by employment generation. The opportunities for diversifying the economic base in Bangladesh are limited and the country continues to run up a heavy trade deficit, reflecting its dependence on imports for most essential goods, such as machinery, equipment and petroleum products, and the decline in the real prices of its traditional staple exports of jute, jute manufactures and tea. Although levels of domestic saving and investment have been growing in the 1990s, they are still low and act as a constraint to the country's economic growth and development.

Towards self-sufficiency

Bangladesh became a perennially food-deficit country in the late 1950s. Until then, farmers were able to produce enough grain to meet the food needs of the population, with the help of imports in times of natural disasters, crop failures, war, etc. Afterwards, however, population pressures began to take their toll. Threats of mass starvation have been felt several times since independence owing to droughts and severe floods, but a famine of significant proportion only struck the country in 1974 when world food production fell to an all-time low and world food prices rose sharply. At that time, there was insufficient food aid and the country did not have enough foreign exchange resources to buy all the grain it needed in the world market. Because of the subsequent combination of increased food aid allotments from donors and the government's import programme and increased capacity to finance food imports, the days of severe famine were put to an end. However, persisting, widespread and endemic malnutrition as well as semi-starvation among the majority of the rural population are still far from over. In fact, a downward trend in the daily per caput intake of cereals, pulses, vegetables, fruits and meat can be seen over the last few decades in rural areas as well as at a national level. For example, rice intake in rural Bangladesh in 1995/96 was 427 g per caput. In

[29] Ibid.

ASIA AND THE PACIFIC

1981/82, 1975/76 and 1962-64, the levels of intake were 451, 493 and 505 g, respectively. There was only a slight increase in cereal intake in urban locations in 1995-96 compared with 1962-64.[30]

Bangladesh's dependence on food imports and, in particular, food aid throughout the years has been cause for concern. Food imports in Bangladesh currently represent approximately 18 percent of total imports (down from 26 to 30 percent during the 1980s) and absorb 34 percent of total export earnings (down from 50 to 70 percent during the 1980s). In 1990/91, food aid represented 98 percent of total food imports but this has been reduced considerably to representing 30 percent of total food imports in 1995/96.[31] The significant difference has essentially been made up by private sector imports which began in 1992/93.

The overriding objective of all agricultural policy and development since independence in Bangladesh has been to achieve self-sufficiency in foodgrains and, in particular, rice production. In reality, what has actually been sought is a substantial acceleration in the growth rate of domestic food production and a decreased dependence on or elimination of food aid in the long term. The emphasis on accelerating food production in Bangladesh stems from the country's excessive dependence on food imports, its precarious external account situation and its perceived comparative advantage in food production. Bangladesh has excellent soils, rechargeable aquifers that are easily tapped for irrigation, an abundance of low-cost labour in its rural areas and a climate that allows crops to be grown the year round.

With the availability of high-yielding varieties (HYVs), rice has contributed significantly to the progress towards self-sufficiency. Despite the significant inroads wheat has made in the Bangladeshi diet, rice has been and continues to be the favoured foodgrain in the country. A large percentage of the wheat consumed in the country has been distributed in kind through welfare programmes, and this practice has restricted market demand. Moreover, wheat yields, which are very sensitive to the weather, require long and cool winters which are not found in Bangladesh.

Rice is the principal staple food of the Bangladeshi people and constitutes 95 percent of the cereals consumed. Rice cultivation is the major source of

[30] K. Jahan. 1996. *Nutrition survey of Bangladesh, 1995-96 – a preliminary report.* Institute of Nutrition and Food Science, Dhaka University, Dhaka.

[31] WFP. 1997. *Bangladesh Foodgrain Digest – February 1997.* Dhaka.

ASIA AND THE PACIFIC

[32] **M.M. Rashid.**
Achievements, constraints
and future activities in rice
research and production in
Bangladesh. Bangladesh Rice
Research Institute. Paper
presented at the 18th Session
of the International Rice
Commission, September 1994,
FAO, Rome.
[33] **Z. Karim. Accelerating**
agricultural growth in
Bangladesh. Paper presented
at the Seminar on Agricultural
Research and Development in
Bangladesh, February 1997,
Bangladesh Agricultural
Research Council, Dhaka.
[34] **Government of Bangladesh/**
FAO, op. cit., footnote 25,
p. 130.
[35] **WFP. 1995.** *Bangladesh*
country strategy outline. **CFA**
40/SCP, 15/8/OMA/Add.1.
Rome.
[36] **Government of Bangladesh/**
FAO, op. cit., footnote 25,
p. 130.

livelihood for the large majority of farmers of Bangladesh and it accounts for more than 74 percent of cultivated area, 83 percent of all irrigated area and 88 percent of the total fertilizer consumption in the country.[32] In the Bangladeshi diet, rice accounts for approximately 68 percent of caloric intake and 54 percent of protein intake. The weight of rice in the consumer price index (CPI) is about 62 percent. In a social, political and economic context, rice is a significant crop in Bangladesh; it dominates all other economic activities and consumes a considerable amount of foreign exchange.

Although Bangladesh continues to be a net importer of food, importing on average 1.5 million tonnes of rice annually,[33] it has achieved substantial gains in foodgrain production during the last two decades. From 1969/70 to 1992/93, the cropping intensity increased significantly, with foodgrain production almost doubling.[34] Rice, the dominant crop, increased from 11.2 million tonnes in 1970 to an average of 18.2 million tonnes in the early 1990s.[35] In the crop years from 1989/90 to 1992/93, Bangladesh produced bumper harvests of foodgrains, averaging 19.1 million tonnes per year, with a record production in 1992/93 of 19.5 million tonnes (much higher than the average of 16.4 million tonnes during 1985-89). For the first time in history it appeared that Bangladesh was close to attaining self-sufficiency in foodgrains.

In 1993/94 and 1994/95, foodgrain production declined as a result of droughts and floods as well as the farmers' response to the fall in the price of rice from the bumper harvest of the preceding year. This was evidenced by more than a 2 percent reduction in the area sown, a decline in irrigation demand and more than a 4 percent decline in fertilizer consumption.[36]

The country faced one of its largest foodgrain shortfalls ever in 1994/95, owing in part to a severe fertilizer crisis and leading to a resurgence of large food imports and high cereal prices. In both 1994/95 and 1995/96 crop years, Bangladesh imported (through food aid, private sector imports and commercial imports by the government) approximately 2.5 million tonnes of foodgrains. The shortfalls sent foodgrain prices soaring, a situation which continued until April 1996 when good boro (dry season) harvest prospects started to dampen the market.

The recent trend in foodgrain production has not been positive. The agricultural sector is now confronted with low and stagnating yields of most crops, including rice, and the food gap between domestic production and demand has actually widened (Figure 9). In spite of the fact that rice production has increased at a higher rate than the rate of population growth during the last decade, and despite the fact that there are both public and private imports each year, the daily per caput food availability of foodgrains in Bangladesh has not reached the standard foodgrain requirement or target consumption level of 454 g since 1991/92 (Figure 10). Given that food availability is not equitably distributed, it is clear that the situation is worse for the poor than these figures would lead one to believe.

The pattern of agricultural growth over the past two decades suggests that virtually the entire growth achieved in crop agriculture has been due to the increase in foodgrains. The principal sources of growth came predominantly from boro rice, followed by aman (wet season) rice and, to a small extent, wheat (output of wheat grew from about 100 000 to 1.3 million tonnes between 1971/72 and 1995/96). The success in accelerating rice production in the 1980s can be attributed almost entirely to the conversion of local varieties to modern HYVs and, as a result of changes in the policy environment, the adoption of irrigation and fertilizer technologies, which has enabled intensive use of the boro months.

As a result of the heavy emphasis on rice production, yields of other non-cereal crops such as pulses, potatoes, oilseeds and vegetables have stagnated. Land used previously for pulses has been converted for rice production. There have been modest increases in the yields of local rice but the average local yields have been 50 percent of those of the HYV rice. However, of late, it is the yield of modern varieties that is showing signs of stagnation.

Agricultural policy reforms
The focus of government agricultural policy has so far been on foodgrain production. In the early 1960s, the government launched a "grow more food" campaign, with a package of policies that included direct state involvement in the procurement and distribution of modern agricultural inputs at highly subsidized prices,

Figure 9

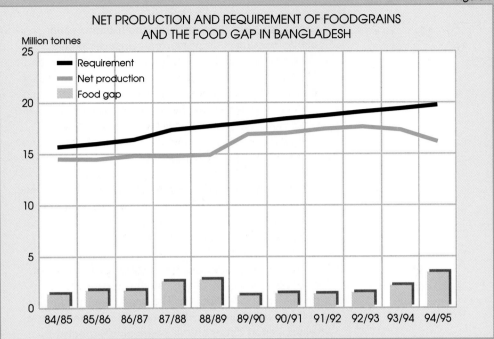

Source: Bangladesh Bureau of Statistics

Figure 10

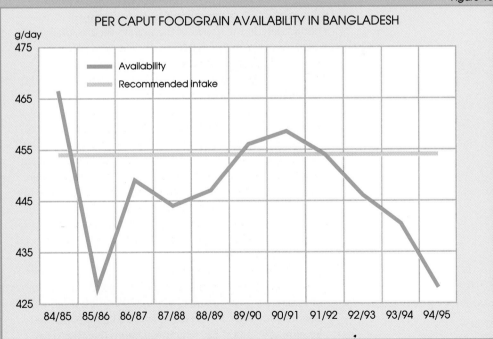

Source: Bangladesh Bureau of Statistics

ASIA AND THE PACIFIC

support to agricultural research and extension and public investment on water resource development. Recent reforms in the agricultural sector have been an essential and integral component of the ongoing market liberalization policy reforms.

These current reform measures support the main objectives of the government's food policy, which includes:

- attaining food self-sufficiency;
- ensuring food price stability with less subsidization;
- improving food availability to vulnerable groups;
- promoting greater private sector participation in foodgrain trade.

During the last two decades, government control of fertilizers, pesticides and irrigation equipment has gradually been withdrawn. The import and distribution of these inputs are now the responsibility of the private sector. Import duties on other agricultural inputs, machinery and parts have also been gradually reduced. With the exception of certain nationalized tea estates, the production of agricultural produce is now completely in the hands of the private sector. A fair amount of agricultural processing, for example rice processing, is also carried out by the private sector. However, some facilities, such as jute mills and sugar factories, are still state-controlled.

The overriding impact of deregulation and liberalization has been increased access to improved technology (including minor irrigation equipment, fertilizers, power tillers, pesticides and seeds, owing to a substantial decline in their prices) as well as large-scale private investment in agricultural machinery. The key element in enabling the shift from traditional rice varieties to HYVs has been the spectacular spurt in minor irrigation development (particularly low-cost shallow tubewells). The share of power-irrigated cropped land increased from 17 percent in 1979-81 to 31 percent in 1989-91 and again jumped to 40 percent of total crop-growing area by 1993/94. In the three-year period from 1989 to 1991, the irrigated area expanded by almost 700 000 ha, which was more than the total irrigated area added during the previous eight years. Between 1988/89 and 1994/95, 197 784 shallow tubewells were installed. The expansion of modern

ASIA AND THE PACIFIC

irrigation facilities has also contributed to employment opportunities in the rural areas.

While fertilizer liberalization has induced good progress in rice production, the present urea pricing policy is not consistent with the general orientation of trade and exchange rate liberalization. The manufacturing of urea has yet to be privatized. Urea is produced from subsidized gas and sold at below production cost by the public sector (Bangladesh Chemical Industries Corporation) directly to the dealers. Its cheap market price therefore remains lower than triple superphosphate (TSP) and muriate of potash (MP). It is reported that, as a result, farmers are not using TSP and MP in the required quantities, while they are overusing urea to the detriment of soil fertility. The artificially low price of urea has also given rise to its scarcity and to rent seeking by those with access to rationed supplies. This, in fact, was the cause of the urea crisis in 1995 and the early part of 1996. Despite the lowering of the issue price of urea, interference and hoarding of rationed supplies by entrepreneurs caused the retail price to increase to such an extent that fertilizer application decreased significantly. This ultimately caused substantial losses in rice production during that year, which led to severe food shortages, escalated food prices and rising inflation. This resulted in backtracking with respect to fertilizer policies; the government has reintervened in fertilizer distribution by controlling the appointment of dealers, allocating their fertilizer quotas and delineating their command area.

In line with the government seed policy approved in late 1992, responsibility for the multiplication, processing and marketing of improved seeds was transferred from the Bangladesh Agriculture Development Corporation (BADC) to the private sector. Although the BADC is still involved in seed distribution, the private sector is now permitted to import any improved germplasm for research and development and to develop its own facilities for producing foundation seeds. It is also allowed to import seeds, except for the five "notified" crops (rice, wheat, jute, sugar cane and potatoes). The private sector has now been importing hybrid seeds of maize, vegetables, sunflower, sorghum and rapeseed for the last few years. It is also now producing potato seeds in limited quantities from the foundation seeds provided by the BADC. It is not,

ASIA AND THE PACIFIC

however, interested in the production of foundation seeds of any crops because of the high investment requirement.

With the privatization of seed distribution, Bangladesh still faces a current problem with seed quality and varietal replacement. The genetic and physical quality of seeds has been deteriorating. The physical quality of seeds can be maintained through effective processing, quality control, chemical dressing, handling and storage.[37] However, it is very difficult to maintain the physical quality of seed at the farm level, since farmers retain 95 percent of seeds from earlier harvests rather than renew their seed stock by buying certified seeds. The production and distribution of quality seeds are insufficient to meet the demand. The BADC currently has a 3 percent seed replacement ratio but, according to national experts, a 10 percent ratio is needed as a basic minimum if Bangladesh is to continue on its agricultural growth path towards self-sufficiency.

The government has moved away from its previous intervention in the foodgrain market. In August 1992, it removed import restrictions on foodgrains for the first time. Private traders responded immediately by importing more than 300 000 tonnes of wheat by the end of that year. The private sector imported more than one-third of total foodgrain imports in 1995 to 1996. The government has also substantially downsized its food distribution system by eliminating the highly subsidized rural rationing channels and drastically reducing the total volume of distributed food. The rural rationing programme had cost the government $60 million in subsidies each year, and it is estimated that 70 percent of the foodgrains did not reach the intended beneficiaries of the programme. Because of the partial privatization of grain trading and the partial dismantling of the Public Food Grain Distribution System, the government has reduced public spending for food subsidies and has significantly reduced domestic procurement of foodgrains. It has been giving higher priority to the non-monetized targeted programmes such as food for work, vulnerable group development, rural maintenance and food for education, the first two of which are largely supported by international food aid.

All in all, the macroeconomic and sectoral policy reforms have reduced several price distortions and made allocative decisions in the agricultural sector more

[37] Z. Karim, op. cit., footnote 33, p. 135.

sensitive to price signals in external markets. The role of the private sector in agricultural inputs and the provision of services has been substantially enlarged. While, on the whole, most privatization policies have been successful, there are still short-term hurdles that need to be overcome, as evidenced by both the fertilizer crisis and the seed replacement issue. Even if market forces eventually stabilize the situation, it is the poorer farmers who are likely to be the hardest hit by the short- to medium-term impacts.

Challenges faced by Bangladeshi agriculture

Being an agriculture-dependent economy with a growing population and one of the world's lowest land areas per caput, the most important issue in Bangladeshi agriculture is to enhance and sustain growth in crop production. The most pressing problem is therefore the current state of stagnating yields and declining productivity in a range of food and non-food crops. Projections of foodgrain supply and demand are consistent in their conclusions that there is a widening foodgrain supply gap.

With negligible scope for area expansion, as most of the arable lands of Bangladesh are already under cultivation, future growth will have to continue to rely on raising productivity per unit of land. For this reason, continuous efforts are being made towards developing new improved seed varieties. It is also felt that the agricultural sector has by no means exploited its full potential for crop production and that there are various opportunities for substantially increasing cropping intensities. Currently only 40 percent of the potential irrigated area is actually irrigated, while only 55 percent of cultivated area is covered by modern varieties and, most important, there are wide gaps between the potential and the realized yields for all crops in the country.

Narrowing gaps between actual and potential yields, however, is easier said than done, for there are various underlying issues and constraints in terms of productivity that are beyond the bounds of technology and another green revolution. To think that the growth of crop production and the goal of self-sufficiency depend almost entirely on technological progress is not only deceiving but also detrimental to the long-term sustainable development of the country. Aside from the

fact that Bangladesh is prone to frequent natural disasters, there are other significant factors, both institutional and socio-economic, that play a part in determining the productivity of the agricultural sector and food security situation of the country. These include:

- landownership;
- environmental degradation;
- crop diversification;
- social and physical infrastructure and support services.

Landownership. The core problem facing Bangladesh is the scarcity of land. With a high and increasing rural population, farm sizes are declining rapidly and landlessness is rising. According to inheritance laws, land is divided equally among siblings and such fragmentation of landholdings is beginning to have serious repercussions. In general, fragmented landownership acts as an obstruction to modernization by reducing efficiency and deliverability of services. Smaller farms have less access to credit, machinery and other productivity-enhancing inputs. They also have less marketing flexibility. The dwindling per caput land resource is, as a result, one of the causes of persisting poverty and food insecurity in the country.

While most farms are becoming smaller in Bangladesh, about 10 percent of farm households own and operate 51 percent of agricultural land, while the bottom 40 percent own only 2 percent.[38] The category of larger landowners has been increasing in size and power. The majority of farmers in Bangladesh are sharecroppers or work the land as labourers for large landowners. There are various tenancy arrangements, sharecropping being the most prevalent, under which the tenant agrees to bear all costs and pay 50 percent (and in some cases two-thirds) of the gross produce to the landowner. In some parts of the country, landowners and tenants share the fertilizer and irrigation costs for growing HYV rice; in some cases, the tenancy arrangement is changing from sharecropping to a fixed rent, which is more conducive to the introduction of HYVs. Owing to the insecurity of tenure for most farmers, however, there is little incentive for farmers to think in terms of long-term sustainability of the land. As

[38] M. Hossain. 1996. Rural income and poverty trends. *In* H.Z. Rahman, M. Hossain and B. Sen, eds.*1987-1994: Dynamics of rural poverty in Bangladesh.* Dhaka, Bangladesh Institute of Development Studies.

ASIA AND THE PACIFIC

a result, investments in the long-term productivity of the land are not made, and short-term inputs and practices lacking environmental concern prevail.

Environmental degradation. Bangladesh's land resources are showing signs of fatigue which is resulting in the stagnation of yields of important crops. Although the adoption of modern varieties has increased, their yields have fallen in recent years. During the green revolution, for example, 1 kg of added nitrogen fertilizer produced 20 kg of grain, while now it only produces 8 to 10 kg. Declining productivity as a result of soil degradation is now a key constraint. The organic matter of more than 50 percent of cultivated soils in Bangladesh is said to be below the critical level of 1.5 percent and still declining at an alarming rate.[39] A number of soil-related problems have emerged, owing particularly to current agricultural practices such as the insufficient and unbalanced application of fertilizers and the monocultural cropping practice used in rice production. Salinity, soil erosion, micronutrient deficiency, waterlogging and alkalinity are just a few of the soil-related problems. Unless the use of balanced fertilizers and organic matter in soils are seriously considered, increased and sustained productivity cannot be achieved.

Many are beginning to worry about the exploitation of groundwater and the long-term future of tubewell irrigation, which provides more than 60 percent of irrigated area and has been the main catalyst of growth in rice production. The intensive and increasing use of shallow tubewell irrigation has led to a lowering of the water table in many areas of the country's north and northwestern parts. In periods of drought, many tubewells have begun to dry up totally. The quality of groundwater is also deteriorating because of the excessive use of chemical pesticides. Increased pest populations have been a direct result of crop intensification through HYVs, and this has had direct and disturbing implications on human health.

In some cases, for example in the coastal areas, land conflict exists between shrimp and rice cultivation. Saline water needed for shrimp cultivation pollutes adjacent paddy (rice) fields and degrades the soils, making them unfit for crop production. One particularly significant and difficult issue is how to deal with the

---

[39] **Z. Karim, op. cit., footnote 33, p. 135.**

ASIA AND THE PACIFIC

problem of entrepreneurs who are known to come in, rent the land, produce shrimp for export and then move on, leaving behind the problem of salinization.

The need for ecosystem management, i.e. plant nutrient and water management, has been generally recognized in Bangladesh and is currently being pushed wholeheartedly by NGOs such as Proshika. The difficulty lies in trying to convert people's agricultural practices, which were dramatically changed by the green revolution, to ecological agricultural practices. Since time is required to convert properly from old to new practices and actually to see increases in yields (because of the time the soil needs to rejuvenate), it is difficult to convince farmers to change their habits. For the large majority who do not actually farm their own land, there is not much incentive for them to adopt new practices. Until farmers convert to ecological practices, if indeed they do at all, they will continue to spend an increasing amount of resources on agricultural inputs, as more and more of these are required, and they will continue to receive less in net returns.

Crop diversification. With rice occupying almost 75 percent of the cropped area, followed by wheat which occupies approximately 4 percent and jute which occupies approximately 3 percent, less than 20 percent of the cropped area is devoted to a range of other crops. It appears that the benefits of crop diversification in the country are well known and have been recognized for a long time. However, all efforts seem to have been consumed by the domination of rice production and, as a result, the area under non-cereal crops has continued to diminish. The government has now recognized the urgent need for agricultural diversification, and a shift towards this end is beginning to take place, although – some would argue – at an unprogressive pace.

There are several immediate reasons why the focus of agricultural growth should incorporate more than the emphasis on foodgrain production alone and include several non-rice crops such as maize, pulses, oilseeds, potatoes and other vegetables as well as poultry, livestock and even sericulture production:
i) Bangladesh's serious nutrition predicament needs immediate attention. While the diet of the average Bangladeshi meets carbohydrate requirements, it is grossly deficient in proteins, vitamins and minerals.

ASIA AND THE PACIFIC

ii) Enlarging the cropping possibilities for Bangladeshi farmers will enable them to allocate their productive resources optimally and maximize their income. There are many opportunities to diversify farm products and by-products in support of agro-industries. iii) As already mentioned, the current cropping system, with its overdependence on rice production throughout the year, is detrimental to soil fertility. It also makes the crops easily susceptible to pest attacks. Crop diversification can help maintain a better soil structure for long-term sustainability. iv) A good proportion of the crops that are currently imported could be substituted through domestic production. Wheat is such an example; while the issue of taste was a constraint to increased wheat production and consumption in the mid-1970s, wheat has gradually become part of the rural diet. Not only does it require four times less irrigation than rice, making it ultimately less costly to produce, but it is also far less damaging to the environment. On the other hand, climatological constraints limit prospects for increasing wheat yields significantly. v) With the significant decline in jute production, together with the limited opportunities and intense overseas competition for rice exports, diversification is essential for agriculture to break into export markets and continue to make a significant contribution to GDP.

There are some obvious obstacles to agricultural diversification which need to be addressed. The development of modern technology for rice and wheat has impeded the development of seeds for other crops and reduced the competitiveness of pulses and oilseeds, which are important sources of protein for the poor. Additional research is needed to develop suitable HYVs and to make them competitive with modern varieties of rice and wheat. There is also an inherent difficulty associated with intercrop conflicts arising from competition for limited land area. Potatoes, vegetables, bananas, onions and spices are all easily produced in Bangladesh. However, up to now, storage and transport infrastructures have not been substantive enough to inspire the adoption of these crops on a large scale. Farmers have been discouraged by the high price risks associated with the marketing of these crops. Moreover, there has been inadequate extension of on-farm water management technology for non-rice crops. For a crop

ASIA AND THE PACIFIC

diversification programme to be successful, it will be necessary to create effective demand for the output through price support policies, education and consumer motivation and by ensuring a viable market with appropriate import and export policies.

Social and physical infrastructure and support services. The rural areas of Bangladesh suffer from severe constraints in terms of inadequate social and physical infrastructure and public support services. Government extension services, for example, are very weak and bureaucratic. They are also technology-driven (pushing rice production) as opposed to people-driven (responding to the interests of the farmers). The fact that the yield difference between demonstration plots and farmers' plots is significantly high in favour of demonstration plots is in part indicative of weaknesses in extension activities concerning management practices.

It is very difficult to disseminate information in the rural areas, especially with respect to technological options, as the vast majority of farmers are illiterate and have limited means of communication available to them. Cooperatives are slowly beginning to emerge but, on the whole, there is currently very little sharing of knowledge or best practices.

Access to financial services is limited in the rural areas, especially for the vast majority of smallholders. Small and marginal farmers generally have no access to bank credit, as they lack the required collateral. NGOs such as the Grameen Bank and Bangladesh Rural Advancement Committee (BRAC) try to make up for this by providing targeted credit to poor rural households, but the actual beneficiaries are still a small minority.

Lack of access to organized markets is another common constraint as well as the lack of physical infrastructure such as feeder roads, a riverine transport network, bridges, stores and refrigeration units, to name a few. In good production years, farmers have been victims of distress sales, since they have been forced to sell at extremely low prices in order to get rid of their produce because of a lack of storage facilities.

New phase of agricultural development
Although Bangladesh has approached foodgrain self-sufficiency at a national level, food security[40] has yet to be concretized, especially at the household level.

[40] Food security exists when all people, at all times, have physical and economic access to sufficient, safe and nutritious food to meet their dietary needs and food preferences for an active and healthy life. (FAO. 1996. *World Food Summit Plan of Action.* Rome.)

ASIA AND THE PACIFIC

Access to food remains a significant problem, with a sizeable proportion of the rural population still suffering from chronic and transitory food insecurity. Food insecurity in Bangladesh is closely linked to poverty; nearly half the population is simply too poor to obtain a reasonable share of the food that is available in the marketplace. The alleviation of widespread poverty is therefore a major challenge to the Government of Bangladesh.

The agricultural sector in Bangladesh clearly has major potential for contributing to overall GDP growth and poverty alleviation, especially considering that 62 percent of household income is spent on food. However, increasing rice production is not enough. Bangladesh is now entering a new and challenging phase of agricultural development; as has been seen, the opportunities and constraints facing the agricultural sector over the coming years are different from those of the past two decades. Many of the factors currently constraining growth in farm yields, incomes, diversification and exports could be ameliorated through changes in the policy environment, investments in rural infrastructure and technological change.

The food self-sufficiency objective must be viewed in terms of compatibility with other needs of the people and the economy, including foreign trade. It is time for a departure from rice-led growth to a more diversified production base that includes several non-rice crops, such as vegetable and horticulture crops. The diversification of agriculture, based on a better exploitation of international markets, is essential for broad-based growth in agriculture. Agricultural research and the identification of comparative advantages of agricultural products have to be re-examined in light of the need for diversification.

An agricultural development strategy based on the abolition of subsidies, the privatization of the delivery system of inputs, and an emphasis on the need for further development in high-quality seed and irrigation technologies is not enough to yield the desired results. Accelerating improvements in rural infrastructure is essential not only for the intensification of foodgrain production but also for facilitating diversification and expanding off-farm activities. Transport infrastructure will not only help in terms of employment generation but also by linking rural areas to major markets. "The key to

BOX 8
THE FISHERIES SECTOR IN BANGLADESH

Bangladesh is one of the richest countries in the world as far as inland fishery resources are concerned. The fisheries sector contributes to the national economy in a number of significant ways, playing a major role as a source of nutrition, income, employment and foreign exchange earnings.

The fisheries sector contributes around 8 percent of agricultural GDP, roughly 5 percent of total GDP and 12 percent of export earnings. Marine and inland fisheries provide full-time jobs to approximately 1.5 million rural people and part-time work for more than 11 million. Despite a decline in fish consumption since the 1970s, 71 percent of the daily per caput animal protein intake still comes from fish. The fisheries sector has been growing at approximately 2.3 percent per annum over the past decade.

Much of Bangladesh is a vast delta dissected by three major rivers and more than 700 other rivers and streams. The floodplain is rich in fish, and about one-third of the country is under water for six months each year. Fish ponds, which account for about 85 percent of the total aquaculture-based fish production, and tanks are also extensively spread over the countryside. Such freshwater resources explain why inland fisheries (capture and culture fisheries) account for just over three-fourths (77 percent) of the country's total fish production. The remainder comes from marine fisheries.

Despite the recognized importance of this resource base, the fisheries sector is under severe stress as a result of overfishing, environmental and habitat degradation and the uncoordinated, multiple use of water bodies. Capture fisheries production has been disrupted and seriously threatened by a proliferation of flood control interventions, drainage, road embankments, irrigation systems, pesticides and fertilizers. For example, major carps such as, *katla*, *mrigal* and *rui*, which used to account for up to 20 percent of the open water fish catches, now constitute less than 1 percent. The failure to maintain the wetlands in the face of radical engineering interventions is undermining natural fish production and canals and estuaries are silted up. It is estimated that, within the next ten years, the annual loss in fish production could be equivalent to 12 to 18 percent of today's catches if this process continues at the present rate.

Ironically, the same agricultural policies and projects that allowed rice farmers to increase their productivity and helped some landless to find more work often did so at the expense of open access capture fisheries. Water control projects, intended to create favourable conditions for rice production, frequently decrease flood duration and area. Embankments and regulators, for example, prevent fish from successfully carrying out breeding migrations, while structures to stop bank overtopping and lateral flooding lead to sedimentation further downstream, thereby adversely affecting fish production in river channels.

The resulting decline in inland capture fisheries is especially threatening for those Bangladeshis who depend on this open access resource as their only source of animal protein. The intensification of lease holding has also had profound effects on access by the rural poor to inland fisheries. Fisheries development projects that impose leasing systems are depriving the poor of their traditional fishing rights and heritage. The government's new fisheries management policy, however, has recognized the problem of the poor's access to common property resources and aims to bypass entrepreneurs and give licences directly to the genuine fishermen.

While the fisheries sector is facing infrastructural, environmental and socio-economic hurdles, there have been some recent positive developments: although inland capture and marine industrial fisheries have declined, there has been steady growth in aquaculture technology in shrimp farms and ponds; considerable efforts have been made to introduce rice-fish culture technology (the NGO CARE is currently doing extensive work in this area); private sector activities such as hatchery development, processing, preservation and export have expanded substantially in recent times, and the government is gradually implementing measures to mitigate environmental damage to fisheries. While there is still much to be done, these and many other planned improvements may expand Bangladesh's opportunities for both domestic and export production and contribute further to the country's social and economic development.

ASIA AND THE PACIFIC

agricultural development in Bangladesh lies in transforming the traditional peasantry of Bangladesh into agricultural entrepreneurs. The cultivators do not lack motivation, they lack expertise and resources."[41] As such, human resource development and the spread of education are essential. Efforts should also be made to ensure the availability of credit at reasonable rates of interest and with greater access for small farmers and the marginalized, including women. The strengthening of extension services for both food and non-food crops is a key concern. The marketing system, currently one of the weakest links in the development of Bangladeshi agriculture, needs to be developed. Linkages with NGOs, which currently have the closest contact with rural farmers, especially the marginalized ones, would facilitate the development of all these areas. Of equal importance is the need for support services to facilitate private sector investments in rural areas.

The development of rural infrastructure can contribute enormously to raising agricultural production but thought must also be given to the development of a more sustainable rural economy. Considering the very small size of the average landholding and the large number of landless poor, opportunities in other sources of sustenance should be expanded. Adequate farm and off-farm employment and income-earning opportunities (supported by technical, infrastructural and financial services) are essential for supplementing small farmers' income and enabling landless labourers to earn their livelihoods. Furthermore, the production potential from integrated homestead development should not be underestimated.

Investment should therefore be geared towards activities with the greatest potential for creating a dynamic and efficient economy in line with the country's comparative advantage and for alleviating poverty. In this respect, export-based and labour-intensive growth is crucial for achieving sustained increases in growth and employment opportunities and consequent poverty alleviation. In addition to enhancing the contribution of agriculture to economic growth, fostering significant growth in potentially very dynamic manufacturing industries, such as the garments industry, should be viewed as a mutually supportive objective.

[41] M. Hossain. Food aid, food security and development. Paper 7 of the Seminar on Food Strategies in Bangladesh, organized by the Government of Bangladesh and the European Economic Community. October 1988. Dhaka.

LATIN AMERICA AND THE CARIBBEAN

REGIONAL OVERVIEW

Recent economic and financial trends indicate an overall marked improvement in Latin America and the Caribbean's economic situation and prospects. At an estimated 3.5 percent in 1996, economic growth rebounded significantly from the depressed 1.3 growth the previous year, and is expected to accelerate to 4.4 percent in 1997 and further to more than 5 percent in 1998. However, performances varied across countries and subregions. The largest economies – Argentina, Brazil, Colombia and Mexico – expanded at rates of 3 to 4.5 percent, although in Argentina and Mexico such rates only represented a partial recovery from the decline in economic activity the previous year.[42] Among Andean countries, the Bolivian economy continued to expand at sustained rates of around 4 percent, while growth in Ecuador and Peru was only about 2 percent, a marked downturn in relation to previous years in the latter country. Chile's economy remained buoyant, expanding by more than 6 percent for the fifth time in the past six years and by an average 7 percent over the period 1991-96. Growth slowed down in most countries in Central America, while still remaining at fairly healthy rates of 3 to 3.5 percent in Costa Rica, El Salvador and Honduras.

Within the Caribbean area, performances appeared to have improved overall, despite wide variations across countries. The Dominican Republic and Cuba achieved growth rates of more than 7 percent, resulting chiefly from dynamic performances of the communications, construction and agricultural sectors in the former, and of sugar and tourism in the latter. The economies of Barbados, Guyana and Santa Lucia also expanded at very fast rates, while Haiti returned to positive growth after three years of catastrophic recession, but Jamaica continued to stagnate.

The region continued to achieve encouraging progress towards price stability. Average regional inflation fell to 25.5 percent in 1996 and was expected to fall to 19.3 percent in 1997 and further in 1998. Most remarkable was the performance of Brazil, where consumer prices only rose by about 10 percent in 1996, down from

[42] Country data and estimates in this section are from the Economic Commission for Latin America and the Caribbean (ECLAC).

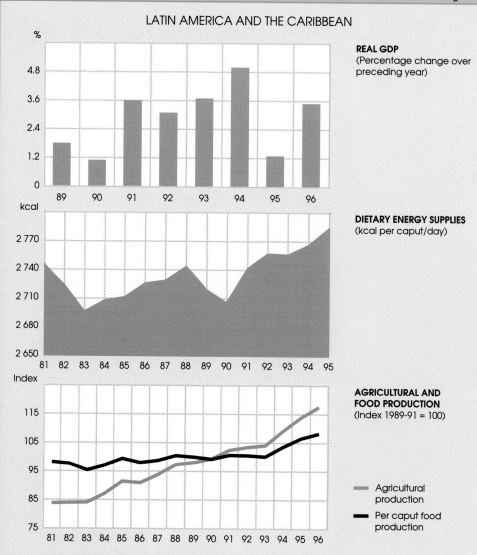

LATIN AMERICA AND THE CARIBBEAN

REAL GDP
(Percentage change over preceding year)

DIETARY ENERGY SUPPLIES
(kcal per caput/day)

AGRICULTURAL AND FOOD PRODUCTION
(Index 1989-91 = 100)

Agricultural production

Per caput food production

Source: FAO and IMF

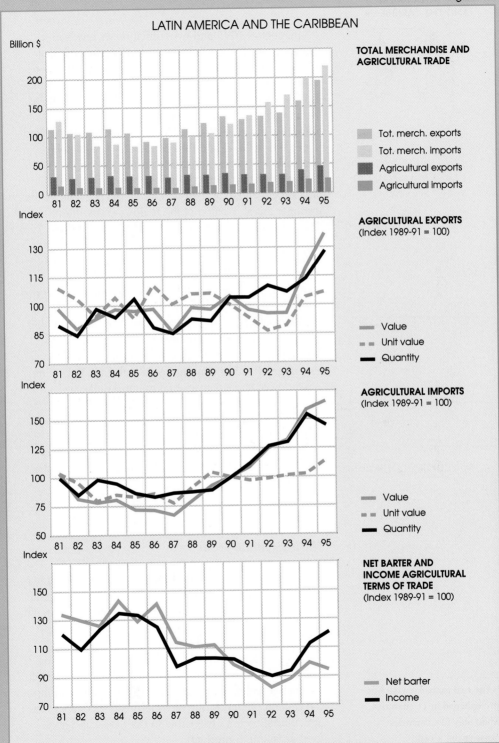

LATIN AMERICA AND THE CARIBBEAN

Billion $

TOTAL MERCHANDISE AND AGRICULTURAL TRADE

Tot. merch. exports
Tot. merch. imports
Agricultural exports
Agricultural imports

Index

AGRICULTURAL EXPORTS
(Index 1989-91 = 100)

Value
Unit value
Quantity

Index

AGRICULTURAL IMPORTS
(Index 1989-91 = 100)

Value
Unit value
Quantity

Index

NET BARTER AND INCOME AGRICULTURAL TERMS OF TRADE
(Index 1989-91 = 100)

Net barter
Income

Source: FAO

22 percent in 1995 and hyperinflationary levels in earlier years. Capital inflows, including a large FDI component, increased significantly, as investor confidence was boosted by the continuity in economic policy since the Mexican crisis. Indeed, capital inflows rose to an estimated $50 billion in 1996, more than offsetting the current account deficit (which represented 2 percent of GDP) and thus enabling a considerable increase in foreign exchange reserves. The rapid recovery since the crisis stemmed from strong investment and export growth, rendered possible by the stronger initial position of the region's economies following economic reform. Within this generally favourable picture, a number of latent problems and uncertainties persist. The revival of economic activity has not translated as yet into any reduction in unemployment which, on the contrary, continued to rise throughout the first three quarters of 1996, after having also increased considerably in 1995. The strengthening of the exchange rate in many countries of the region[43] has helped to check inflation but has also inhibited export growth. The continuing difficulties in balancing government budgets in several countries may be accentuated by the tendency of governments to overspend during favourable periods. The international trade climate also presents negative aspects and uncertainties for the region. In particular, the terms of trade of non-oil exporters deteriorated markedly as the net result of declining prices of basic commodities, higher oil prices and lower inflation rates in industrialized countries.

The agricultural sector

The agricultural sector of the region continued to expand at a relatively robust rate in 1996, following two years of above-average growth. Total regional food and agricultural production rose by an estimated 3.2 percent in 1996, less strongly than in 1994 and 1995 (4.9 and 4.4 percent, respectively) but still significantly above longer-term trends (about 1.9 percent annually during 1981-1990 and 1.4 percent during 1990-1994). Despite significant variations across countries and commodities, the general picture is one of widespread recovery of the agricultural sector, observable in both food and non-food agricultural products.

The relatively strong performances of regional

---

[43] The real exchange rate was strengthened in 11 countries, while only five countries experienced a real devaluation.

agricultural production for three consecutive years, after a long period of mediocre growth, have raised expectations for the possible emergence of a more favourable trend. However, such a short time span of recovery does not allow any conclusive assessment of the importance of transient market and climatic factors *vis-à-vis* progress of a more structural nature, associated in particular with economic and agricultural reform. Such an assessment is also difficult in view of the wide variations in performance and policy factors affecting such performances. Behind the relatively strong growth in 1996 were bountiful harvests in Mexico and Argentina, relatively good ones in Brazil, a marked slowdown in production growth in Chile and shortfalls in Colombia and a number of smaller producer countries. Among the main commodities, cereals and sugar cane showed vigorous growth and coffee staged a strong recovery, while cocoa bean production fell for the second consecutive year and that of roots and tubers also declined. Finally, while the process of liberalization is widespread across countries, there are significant differences in the pace and depth of this process as well as in the mechanisms of support to agricultural and rural development, as reviewed in the following section.

Developments in agricultural policies
Food security has been a recurrent theme in the policy formulation and implementation of Latin American and Caribbean countries. The recent past has seen the introduction and strengthening of numerous concrete initiatives addressing various dimensions of the problem. These range from measures focusing on specific aspects – such as the efforts in El Salvador to bring large idle areas in the eastern region back to grain production – to integrated food security programmes such as those found in Venezuela and Honduras, where national food councils have been created. In line with the general policy framework provided by the World Food Summit Plan of Action, these councils are in charge of formulating national food security plans which define strategies, objectives and programmes for the public sector organizations concerned, with the participation of national NGOs. In addition, a bill on agricultural development and food security, covering all sectors of society, has been elaborated in Venezuela by a presidential commission with FAO expert advice. This

legal instrument is to be submitted for approval to the Congress of the Republic in order to be converted into law.

National food security was also addressed through a variety of policy measures put into place to stimulate food and agricultural production. Despite the general move towards market liberalization, many countries have continued to implement price support programmes in favour of crops considered to be of importance for food security. Milk, rice and sugar benefit from the highest levels of protection, particularly in the Andean countries, while wheat, maize and soybeans are also widely protected in these and other countries in the region. The degree of such intervention, however, varies considerably. While countries such as Colombia, Venezuela and Ecuador have maintained a relatively active sectoral policy, Bolivia and Peru take a more liberal approach and Argentina no longer intervenes in any direct agricultural support programme, except in the case of tobacco producers who benefit from a special fund collected through taxes on cigarettes. In Mexico, support is provided through the rural alliance programme *Alianza para el Campo*, which encompasses action carried out under PROCAMPO and PRODUCE (programmes of direct and productive support for the rural areas) as well as other support service programmes. *Alianza para el Campo* was introduced in the context of a decentralization drive that allows better cooperation between the federal and state governments and the private sector to create income opportunities in rural areas and reduce income disparities. The Colombian Government has continued to implement agricultural support programmes in the form of minimum guaranteed prices for white maize, paddy rice, dried beans, soybeans and sesame seed. The objective remains, however, to align domestic prices gradually with international prices so that farmers' decisions are based on market realities.

Similar concerns are found in other countries where the objectives of agricultural support and liberalization require, in many cases, difficult policy choices. The Costa Rican Government has been facing pressure to slow down the pace of reform or provide more compensatory assistance to those negatively affected by liberalization. Several associations and groups of producers have been campaigning for the promotion of

basic foodstuffs production, including rice, beans and white maize, in response to the country's growing dependence on food imports and the high prices for several of these products. In the Dominican Republic, price support programmes have been reduced reflecting the overall liberalization drive, budget constraints and management problems and indebtedness on the part of the price stabilization authorities. Direct support to the small farm sector has also been reduced and confined to emergency programmes in case of severe price declines. Small farmers also benefit from a limited distribution of seeds and some access to mechanized equipment.

In Brazil, a new round of deregulation for the crop year 1996/97 included the phasing out of minimum prices, henceforth restricted to small farmers. The government is devising legislation to allow the privatization of government-owned storage facilities. The abandonment of commodity purchasing and selling under price support is expected to result in considerable savings for the Treasury as well as the elimination of the complex problems and disputes that surfaced when dealing with warehouse and transport operators. The reform of agricultural finance has involved the elimination of cheap credit and farmers will now have to base their production decisions more on market expectations.

The progressive reduction of direct support interventions has shifted the focus of policy-makers towards alternative ways of favouring agriculture that emphasize modernization and competitiveness. Argentina has been able to gain competitiveness in international markets following the virtual elimination of export taxes and major improvements in rail service and port facilities. Current policies in Chile aim at modernizing traditional sectors that have shown lagging performances (grain, oilseeds, beef, sugar beet) and expanding and diversifying export products and markets. This is to be achieved through a set of programmes that were announced by the President of the Republic in May 1996, and that include improving rural infrastructures, emphasizing research and technology transfer, the further refining of marketing systems, lowering duties on farm inputs and modernizing credit and financing systems in favour of small farmers. The promotion of high-value products with great market opportunity remains a key element in

the country's strategies. According to estimates quoted by the Minister of Agriculture, Chile's agricultural and forest product exports could double in 15 years to $12 billion. In Paraguay, there is serious concern for the crucial cotton industry, which faces problems of low productivity, falling competitiveness in world markets and vulnerability to shocks and depressed conditions in international markets. As a measure to promote productivity, the government has introduced a programme to modernize production, with the stated goal of mechanizing 10 000 ha per year. Major difficulties have been encountered in trying to meet this target, however, given the poor topology of large areas cultivated with cotton. In El Salvador, significant increases in the budget for research and technology dissemination through the National Agricultural Technology Centre (CENTA) are expected to provide long-term impetus to food and agricultural development. In Cuba, efforts are being made to improve management systems and efficiency in the Basic Units of Cooperative Production that are replacing state farms.

A major limiting factor to modernization of the sector has been, however, the lack of adequate financing for agricultural investment, accentuated in many cases by the withdrawal of the public sector from agricultural credit operations. This is the case in Colombia, where private investment continues to be hindered by high interest rates, farmers' indebtedness and difficulties for many farmers in gaining access to commercial bank credit. Similarly, while interests on commercial credit in the Dominican Republic declined in 1996 in relation to the previous year, they remained unaffordable for most farmers. In Brazil, private credit at high interest rates has represented a considerable financial problem for the large number of highly indebted farmers as well as those dependent on production loans. As a measure to alleviate these problems at the farm household level, a national credit scheme to strengthen family farming (PRONAF) was instituted in May 1996. In Honduras, the National Complementary Guarantee Fund was established in 1996 to guarantee financing for agricultural production and marketing activities. About 70 percent of the guarantees will be geared towards basic grain production. In Cuba, a shortage of finance continued to be a major constraint affecting agriculture

as well as other economic activities, although some agrifood sectors, such as the depressed dairy industry, have recently attracted badly needed FDI.

Credit shortages have affected farmers even in Argentina and Uruguay, despite favourable market conditions for the main traded products of these countries and widespread optimism over their agricultural outlook. In Uruguay, the record level of farmers' requests for loans from the Banco de la República in 1996 is an indicator of farmers' optimism regarding the country's agricultural prospects and their willingness to invest in a broad range of agricultural activities. In the case of Argentina, record crops of cereals in 1996 and unprecedented earnings enabled many farmers to expand their use of inputs and modern machinery, improve infrastructure and restructure debt. However, many medium and small farmers and producers of crops other than cereals and oilseeds continued to face serious indebtedness. Although no comprehensive scheme of debt refinancing is being contemplated, the Argentine Government is examining the problem of farm indebtedness on a case by case basis. The situation in Peru, discussed in the following section, illustrates a problem faced by many other countries, that of inadequate financing for agriculture and poor access to credit, particularly for small farmers, in the new context of liberalized capital markets.

As regards the external sector, policies have continued to emphasize trade openness, although a degree of protection continues to be granted to crucial agricultural activities, and trade restrictions are still applied in various forms. As a means to reduce external account imbalances, the Brazilian Government has slowed down import licences and eliminated the export tax on raw and semi-processed agricultural products. In Colombia, interventions continue to be applied through price bands, or variable duties, and import licensing. A sharp reduction in the production of many crops in 1996, contributing to an estimated 1 percent decline in overall agricultural production, was largely attributed to competition from imports and declining profitability of crop production which caused the diversion of land use towards alternative activities. In the Dominican Republic, despite some relaxation in the trade regime, restrictions continue to be imposed in the form of import certificates and high tariffs to protect a number of

commodities, such as maize, sugar, poultry, potatoes, swine and rice, considered critical to the country's economy.

El Salvador has continued its liberalization policies: the harmonization of tariffs with other countries within the Central American Common Market (to a range of 5 to 20 percent) and the elimination of all import and export permits have been important steps in this direction. Current plans are for a gradual reduction of tariffs to a range of 1 to 6 percent by 1999. A flat 20 percent tariff has been imposed on all basic grains except maize, for which a seasonal tariff mechanism is applied to safeguard domestic producers. In order to counter the decline in coffee prices and the formation of excess volumes of coffee in the market, producers of this commodity introduced a plan to install sales on a quarterly basis, and quarterly exports are being regulated by a Coffee Council. Moves are under way to privatize the remaining government-controlled sugar mills which operate less efficiently than private ones. Government action has strongly emphasized the development of non-traditional agricultural exports such as fresh fruits, flowers, organic coffee and sesame seeds, particularly through cooperative work between the private sector and the Foundation of Salvadoran Economic Development (FUSADES).

In Ecuador, WTO membership is expected to enable greater access for agro-industrial products and thus boost the agricultural sector overall. Lower tariffs on imported inputs and machinery are also likely to lower costs and promote competitiveness.

Following the signature by Central American countries of a Tariff and Customs Regime Agreement in December 1995, a number of duty reductions for selected capital and raw materials were implemented in the course of 1996. The agreement authorized the reduction of tariffs for capital and raw material products, at the discretion of the countries concerned, from 5 to 1 percent as of 1 January 1996. For intermediate and finished goods, the reduction may be from 20 to 15 percent. The agreement is part of a liberalization process accelerated by the strong reduction of tariffs which El Salvador implemented unilaterally in 1994 and which raised the issue of the extent to which other Central American countries should follow suit.

As of 1 January 1995, with some exceptions, customs

**LATIN AMERICA
AND THE CARIBBEAN**

duties among Argentina, Brazil, Paraguay and Uruguay, the member countries of the Southern Common Market (MERCOSUR) were eliminated, and a common tariff for most products was implemented. The exceptions to the agreed tariffs are expected to disappear by 2006. Following negotiations that were successfully concluded in the course of 1996, Chile (1 October 1996) and Bolivia (1 January 1997) became Associate Members of MERCOSUR. Negotiations are also under way with other Andean Pact countries to develop a duty-free trade relationship. For Chile, association with MERCOSUR means assured access to a market of 200 million consumers, and hence major opportunities for market diversification and export expansion. While the modern agro-industrial sector is likely to benefit considerably from this association, some sensitive traditional production sectors will need to adjust to trade competition with Argentina. Such adjustment is to be facilitated by the extended periods, 10 to 18 years, that were allowed for duty reduction as well as by the new programmes of investment in rural infrastructure.

Under Chile's price band system, intended as a mechanism for price stabilization, tariffs on wheat, sugar and vegetable oils had been raised in 1995 in line with the decline in prices of these products below predefined levels. With the subsequent strengthening in prices, however, no tariffs were applied to these products in 1996.

In Uruguay, dairy and livestock products have expanded significantly in recent years owing to strong demand in the United States and other developed countries and preferential access to Brazilian markets in the context of MERCOSUR. Argentina's agricultural exports have also benefited from trade intensification in the context of MERCOSUR.

Another important issue addressed by regional policy-makers has been that of environmental conservation, including the preservation of biodiversity and reforestation. Recent initiatives in this area include a long-term forestry action plan, introduced in Honduras in 1996 and comprising strategic programmes in ten different areas of the country. About 1 million ha of forest area are affected by the management plan. The Forestation and Reforestation Incentives Law provides for fiscal and other incentives for such activities.

With annual exports in the order of $2 billion, the

forestry sector in Chile is the country's third largest source of foreign exchange. Plantations of fast-growing species cover 1.95 million ha and natural forests an estimated 12 million ha. The annual rate of reforestation (more than 100 000 ha) largely exceeds that of forest exploitation (about 50 000 ha). About 85 percent of cuts for industrial purposes (estimated to be 25 million m³ annually) are made in plantations, and the conversion of natural forest into plantation area has only affected 132 000 ha over the past 30 years. The national norms for forest exploitation have been increasingly severe. Under a provision recently incorporated in national legislation, any intervention for industrial purposes that affects forest resources will be subject to a specific environmental impact study.

In Mexico, soil erosion (about 80 percent of farmland is sensitive to soil erosion), depletion of water resources and biodiversity losses are serious problems that are largely associated with agricultural activities. These problems have given rise to discussions concerning the establishment of a comprehensive scheme that ensures agro-environmental sustainability. At present, only isolated regulations exists in this direction, such as the registration of pesticide toxicity.

PERU
General characteristics

Peru is divided topographically into three regions: an arid coastal plain, the Andean highlands and the eastern lowlands consisting of subtropical forest. This means that almost any crop can be cultivated in the country. Around 3.4 million ha are estimated to be arable and permanent crop land, of which almost 40 percent is irrigated. The area actually sown has fluctuated in recent years around 1.5 million ha, falling to a low of 1.1 million ha in 1992, a year of particularly severe drought. Agriculture contributes about 13 percent of GDP. Nearly 40 percent of the economically active population is employed in agriculture.

Peru's 1993 census gave a mid-year population of just over 22.5 million inhabitants, including an estimated 532 000 not contacted by census officials and an estimated 60 000 forest-dwelling Indians. The population growth rate averaged 1.8 percent between 1990 and 1995.

Seventy percent of the Peruvian population now resides in urban areas, up from 65 percent ten years ago. A large percentage of Peruvians were forced to abandon their homes in the rural areas owing to the serious threat of guerrilla movements and the low standard of health care and educational facilities that are usually lacking in the rural communities. This trend towards urbanization is expected to continue, but at a reduced rate, since more peaceful conditions prevail and the overcrowded shanty towns are now less attractive to potential migrants.

The proportion of the population living in poverty (defined as those living on $65 per month or less and unable to cover basic food, clothing, housing and transport requirements) dropped from 54 percent in 1990 to 50 percent in 1994 and again to 49 percent by mid-1995. This was primarily due to rapid economic growth and the government's social development projects. However, progress in reducing poverty is likely to have stalled owing to slow economic growth in 1996.

There have been some advances in health care over the past few decades. Life expectancy at birth, for example, rose from 47 years in 1960 to 69 years in 1995 (71.1 years for women and 66.2 years for men). Improvements in health care have reduced the infant mortality rate from 109 per 1 000 in 1972 to 48 per

1 000 by the end of 1996. Nutrition levels, however, remain low for large segments of population. In 1995, one-fifth of all Peruvians (4.7 million) were unable to meet basic nutritional needs. Child malnutrition, measured by height and weight statistics, remains a serious problem, especially in the remote rural districts.

Public education standards are among the worst in Latin America. This is especially seen in the rural areas where terrorism and a lack of discipline among poorly paid teachers have cut teaching hours drastically. According to the 1993 census, 7.8 percent of the population (1.78 million) were illiterate, of which 1.3 million were women. The overall illiteracy rate was 29.8 percent in rural areas, compared with 6.7 percent in urban areas. Now that the Peruvian economy has opened up and companies have been forced to compete in the international marketplace, improving education – particularly primary education – has become a priority. In 1995, the budget allocation for education was 3.9 percent of GDP, up from 2.1 percent in 1990.

Economic developments and policies
The Government of Peru is confronting the difficult task of consolidating economic stabilization and recovery after the disastrous experience of the 1980s, a period marked by deep economic recession, civil unrest and terrorist activity. This period was also one of poor agricultural supply performances which, added to the declining food import and consumers' purchasing capacity, resulted in a marked deterioration in the country's food security situation. Although the economic and food security conditions have improved significantly in recent years, full recovery to pre-crisis levels remains to be achieved. Indeed, the strong economic growth of recent years must be considered against the background of a 29 percent fall in per caput GDP during the 1980s (ECLAC estimate).

The immediate causes of the economic crisis of the 1980s were a series of unusually adverse events in the early part of the decade. A steep decline in world prices of the country's main export commodities and rising interest rates for its burgeoning foreign debt coincided with a devastating El Niño in 1982-1983[44] and a rise in guerrilla movements that required the diversion of ever-increasing resources towards military and reconstruction operations. Although the government aimed at market

[44] **The El Niño phenomenon, manifested in a rise in temperature of the ocean off Ecuador and Peru, occurs at intervals of several years. However, in 1982 El Niño started in October and continued throughout 1983. Through ocean-atmosphere interaction, it was associated with major natural disasters across the world and, in Peru, agricultural production shortfalls, devastating mud slides and a fall in fish stocks.** *Note:* **By mid-1997, there were signs that a particularly severe El Niño, perhaps the worst in the century, would occur late in the year.**

liberalization, its reform programme was frustrated by the need to place priority on short-term objectives of economic stabilization and the control of violence and civil unrest. Popular resentment over austerity measures led to the defeat of the governing party in the 1985 presidential elections.

With the rise to power of the American Popular Revolutionary Alliance (APRA) in 1985, a radical policy shift took place. The government adopted a heterodox approach to macroeconomic management in which income redistribution and social equity considerations played a major role. Economic policy was based on the premise that inflation was primarily a "cost push" problem, as ample margins existed for boosting demand-led growth by expanding expenditure capacity, particularly among the poor. It was also considered that the costs of adjustment – not the least the huge debt-servicing obligations – were not only socially unacceptable but were the primary obstacles to sustained recovery. Thus, fiscal and monetary policies became markedly expansive and wages initially rose significantly in real terms. In the agricultural sector, considered a priority area, abundant credit in addition to remunerative farm prices was made available under extremely favourable conditions. In order to contain production costs and ensure an adequate supply response, a stable exchange rate was maintained while a number of input prices were controlled. The financial costs of such a programme were to be covered by a unilateral decision to devote no more than 10 percent of the export earnings for servicing the foreign debt of $14 billion – a decision that shocked the international financial community, making Peru ineligible for future loans and credits – and by drawing from what were, at the time, relatively large international reserves.

These policies were initially successful to the extent that GDP growth rose from 2.3 percent in 1985 to 9.2 percent in 1986 and 8.5 percent in 1987 while the inflation rate fell from 158 percent in 1985 to 63 percent in 1986. The agricultural sector also benefited from a gain in domestic terms of trade, since controlled prices rose by 25 percent while non-controlled prices (mainly those of agricultural products) rose to nearly 100 percent.

However, as the utilization of productive areas reached full capacity, the unsustainability of such

demand-led growth policies became evident. GDP fell by 8.3 percent in 1988 and by a further 11.7 percent in 1989, more than offsetting the gains of the previous two years. Prices entered an accelerating spiral that turned progressively hyperinflationary: consumer prices rose by 114 percent in 1987, 2 775 percent in 1988 and more than 5 300 percent annually during the last six months of the APRA administration. The public sector deficit more than doubled from 3 percent of GDP in 1985 to about 8 percent in 1987-89; international reserves were depleted and fiscal expenditure was increasingly financed by primary monetary emission. As low-income groups and wage earners were hardest hit by recession and hyperinflation, the process ended up negating the very distributional equity objectives of the government. The end of the APRA term was marked by political confrontations (even within the ruling party itself), a series of crippling general strikes and a widespread call for "change".

The new administration that entered into force in the 1990s introduced another radical policy shift towards stabilization and market-oriented reform. The reform programme entailed the privatization of state-owned companies, drastic reductions in public sector employment, the elimination of price controls and state subsidies and financial and monetary restraint. While these measures initially exacerbated inflation and economic recession, some months later positive results began to emerge. After having fallen by nearly 5.4 percent in 1990, GDP rose by about 3 percent in 1991, fell again in 1992 but expanded vigorously by, respectively, 6, 13 and 7 percent in the following three years, thus producing the highest growth rates in the region. A marked slowdown to 2.8 percent was recorded in 1996, reflecting measures to contain the current account deficit, maintain the fiscal equilibrium and cool an overheating economy. The government forecasts 4 to 5 percent annual growth for the rest of the decade, which would be a less spectacular but more sustained performance than in 1993-95.

Particularly dramatic results have been achieved in price stabilization. Consumer price growth fell from the 40 percent monthly rates of the early 1990s to yearly rates of about 15 percent in 1994 and about 10 to 12 percent in 1995 and 1996. The official target for 1997 is 9 percent.

As regards external accounts, trade liberalization resulted in a strong upsurge in imports of capital and consumption goods which, together with depressed prices of Peru's commodity exports, caused a strong deterioration in the trade balances in 1990-93. Although the commodity boom of 1994-95 enabled a significant expansion in exports, both the trade and current account deficits continued to widen. On the other hand, stabilization and better prospects for recovery prompted a return of investors' confidence and consequently induced a turnaround in net capital inflows, which went from a negative $6.14 billion in 1991 to a positive $1.92 billion in 1994.

Peru's external debt was estimated to be $22.6 billion in 1994 (about 50 percent of GDP), of which $17.9 billion was long-term public and publicly guaranteed debt. Short-term debt amounted to $3.5 billion. After having defaulted in its external debt servicing from 1985 to 1990, Peru resumed payments to official creditors in 1991. Debt servicing represented around one-fourth of exports in both 1991 and 1992, 60 percent in 1993 and 20 percent in 1994. A number of rescheduling agreements have been negotiated in recent years, bringing welcome relief.

In particular, an important agreement in December 1996 along the lines of the Brady Plan was expected to reschedule debt in highly favourable terms, settle all remaining debt disputes and allow Peru to gain access to world commercial credit markets. Nevertheless, debt repayment obligations are still a major financial burden.

The dismantling of guerrilla and terrorist organizations in recent years has been an important factor contributing to economic stabilization and recovery – the recent retention of hostages at the Japanese Embassy in Lima being a dramatic but isolated, episode of organized terrorism. The outlook remains fraught with uncertainties, however. Social hardship associated with reform has so far been tolerated as the unavoidable cost of overcoming economic disorder and setting the basis for recovery. Nevertheless, the economic slowdown in 1996 and prospects for moderate medium-term growth are raising concern about the country's capacity to reduce unemployment and poverty to the extent and speed needed for maintaining political and social stability.

Agricultural sector performances and policies prior to 1990

Despite the importance of agriculture as a contributor to economic growth and employment, the long-term performances of the sector have been generally poor. Agricultural GDP increased at an average annual rate of 2.1 percent in 1950-89, well below the growth rates of manufactures (3.8 percent), mining (3.8 percent), services (3.5 percent) and population (2.6 percent). Food production barely kept pace with population growth, and some periods, particularly 1971-80, brought pronounced declines in per caput food production. Inadequate domestic supplies required growing recourse to food imports, which increased in volume by about 4, 9 and 3 percent annually during the 1960s, 1970s and 1980s, respectively – the lower growth rate in the latter period reflected somewhat better production performances and foreign exchange constraints. Overall, however, food imports were unable to prevent a deterioration in the population's food consumption levels. Indeed, per caput food intake fell from 2 317 kcal per day in 1969-71 to around 2 200 in 1979-81 and less than 2 000 in 1990-92. Consequently, the proportion of undernourished people increased from 20 to 49 percent of the population between 1969-71 and 1990-92 (FAO estimate).

While the poor agricultural performances prior to 1990 reflected many developmental and natural resource constraints as well as external shocks and influences, the policy factor played a major role. The pronounced interventionism that characterized government policies until the early 1990s often had a marked anti-agricultural bias which was only partially compensated by direct farm support. This neglect of the sector explains, to a large extent, the high degree of productive inefficiency and poverty still prevailing in rural areas.

The distortions affecting the sector were accentuated during the second half of the 1980s, a period of particularly strong public sector involvement in markets, prices and credit. Current attempts to redress the anti-agricultural bias implicit in previous development models and to place agriculture in an undistorted economic and market environment must be assessed against such a historic background.[45]

---

[45] The following section largely draws from: J. Escobal D'Angelo. 1992. *Impacto de la política de precios y de crédito agrícola sobre la distribución del ingreso en el Perú: 1985-1990.* Lima, GRADE.

**LATIN AMERICA
AND THE CARIBBEAN**

[46] The volumes of production purchased by the government at guaranteed prices represented in some cases a significant share of total production, but then tended to diminish markedly by the late 1980s. For instance, the shares at their peak levels in 1986-87 were around 50 percent for sorghum, 66 percent for soybeans, 25 percent for maize and 15 percent for wheat.

[47] Subsidies through agricultural support credit by the Agrarian Bank have been estimated to have increased from $99 million in 1980 to a peak $495 in 1987. A. Gonzáles. 1989. Los subsidios financieros a la agricultura en el Perú, 1980-88. *Debate Agrario*, 6 (April-June).

The 1985-1990 period

Government action from 1985 to 1990 had actively sought to stimulate farm incomes, investment and productivity through various price, credit and other support mechanisms. Price support, the fundamental instrument for promoting production, was provided through the agricultural and food security programme, the Programa de Reactivación Agropecuaria y Seguridad Alimentaria (PRESA). The main elements of PRESA were: the purchase of staples (maize, potatoes, wheat, barley, quinua, beans and peas) at guaranteed prices in targeted regions;[46] the creation of strategic stocks of potatoes, maize and other Andean products subject to wide price fluctuations; monopoly importation of wheat, maize, sorghum, dairy products and vegetable oils by a national marketing enterprise; the elimination of food import subsidies and the introduction in 1986 of a 15 percent additional tariff on imports of these products. Price control was exerted on a number of basic foodstuffs.

The high costs of market regulation were to be "internalized", i.e. covered by revenues obtained from importing food at preferential exchange rates and the tariffs charged to such imports. However, as such forms of revenue proved insufficient, intervention was required on the part of the Treasury.

An essential means for reducing production costs was the strong subsidization of imported fertilizers and pesticides. Between 1986 and 1987 the implicit subsidy to fertilizer imports through preferential exchange rates doubled in real terms, coming to represent an estimated 0.7 percent of the agricultural GDP. In addition, the direct subsidy to urea and other fertilizers was estimated to be 0.6 percent of the agricultural GDP.

Considerable amounts of agricultural credit were made available at interest rates below inflation rates, implying again heavy and growing subsidization.[47] The main source of credit was the Agrarian Bank, with the private banking sector playing a minor role. Loans by the Agrarian Bank between 1985 and 1990 amounted to a total of $2 950 million, about 27 percent above the levels of the previous five years. At their peak in 1987, loans by the Agrarian Bank totalled $1 576, out of a total agricultural credit of $1 824 million. About 2.4 million people were employed in agriculture during the period 1985-1990. As a result, each of them received on average $250 per year and as much as $760 in 1987 –

the latter figure being above the average farm wage. The distribution of these loans, however, was far from even. Most went to medium-sized and large farms located in the coastal region which were richer in resources and technology and better integrated in domestic and international markets. Small producers had virtually no access to credit, except the onerous loans they could get from informal sources. A major impediment to creditworthiness was the inability of farmers to use land as collateral for loans, owing to regulations under the Agrarian Reform Law of 1969. Indeed, a survey found that only 16 percent of rural households were able to obtain some form of credit, and the formal sector was the source of such credit in only 50 percent of cases.[48] Furthermore, large amounts of credit were utilized outside agriculture, and frequent cases of non-payment and cancellation of debt obligations required ever-increasing transfers from the Central Reserve Bank.

In summary, it appears that the Agrarian Bank was largely unsuccessful in its attempts to promote agricultural production cost-efficiently and self-sustainably, and it may in fact have contributed significantly to accentuating disparity in rural incomes.

The market, price and credit policies had varied degrees of success but, on the whole, do not appear to have contributed much to improving conditions in the farm sector. A comparison between prices received by producers and import prices, including transport costs, between 1985 and 1990 suggests that a considerable negative subsidy (tax) was in fact paid by producers of the main agricultural products. In other words, direct price support was unable to compensate farmers for the gains they would have achieved from unprotected markets.

Domestic agricultural terms of trade (price relationship between overall wholesale and farm prices) showed significant variations by product, region and period. The general trend was, however, a marked improvement until 1987-88, followed by an even more marked deterioration so that, by the early 1990s, agricultural terms of trade were below the levels of 1985. Real farm incomes (farm product value deflated by wholesale prices) reveal a similar pattern: strong gains were recorded between end-1985 and end-1987 and, again, the subsequent fall brought income levels down below those of 1985.

[48] Government of Peru. *Encuesta nacional sobre niveles de vida, 1985-86.* Lima.

LATIN AMERICA
AND THE CARIBBEAN

Agricultural performances and policies since 1990

Following a period of sluggish growth (1 percent annually during 1981-90) agricultural GDP rose by an accumulated 20.7 percent between 1990 and 1995 (4.8 percent annual average). After a sharp contraction in 1991-93, when bad weather[49] added to the first impact of stabilization and structural reform, a vigorous rebound in agricultural production took place in 1994-96. Improved weather was a major reason for this recovery, but other market and policy factors also played a role. The most significant production increases were recorded for exportables, chiefly coffee and cotton, which benefited from better market conditions and prices. However, the production of non-traded food staples (maize, potatoes, sheep) also showed a robust growth. Agricultural trade also gained dynamism in recent years, on the side of both exports and imports.

It is difficult to assess the extent to which the favourable performances of the past three years constituted a cyclical recovery caused by weather and transient market factors, or the beginning of a new trend made possible by the new economic environment and policy framework. The present administration has repeatedly emphasized the need to extend free market principles to agriculture on the grounds that, in the long term, free markets and improved marketing infrastructure and services, together with a propitious environment for private investment, will do more for agriculture than direct credit, price and market support.

The reforms undertaken to liberalize input and product markets have included the reduction and harmonization of duties, the relaxation of price controls on inputs and food and agricultural products and the end of state marketing monopolies. Thus, the national input marketing board, Empresa Nacional de Comercialización de Insumos (ENCI), is in the course of privatization and the food marketing board, Empresa de Comercialización de Alimentos (ECASA), has been abolished altogether.

The government considers, nonetheless, that agriculture requires more active protection from international competition than any other sector, given the fragility of domestic farming after decades of neglect and unfair competition from highly subsidized sectors in many exporter countries. The main instrument of border protection is a system, introduced in 1991, of flexible

[49] **The lowest rainfall for 70 years was recorded in 1992.**

import duties (*sobretasas*) on rice, wheat and flour, sugar, yellow hard maize and whole and skim milk powder. In April 1997 tariffs were increased from 15 to 25 percent on most imported food items and, at the same time, tariffs on agricultural machinery, equipment, genetic material and other inputs were reduced from 15 to 12 percent. While not explicitly designed to protect domestic markets, a number of sanitary and phytosanitary regulations also have the effect of restricting imports.

Contrasting with the maintenance of external protection, interventions in domestic markets have been virtually eliminated. Only occasional purchases of rice and potatoes are made in years of overproduction (as in 1993/94) under the national food assistance programme, Programa Nacional de Ayuda a la Alimentación (PRONAA). The objectives of PRONAA are of a primarily social nature, as the agency provides short-term relief to producers in periods of exceptionally poor price conditions, while also making indigenous foods available to very poor consumers. While PRONAA's purchases are sometimes made at well above market prices, the volume of such purchases, and hence their overall impact on markets and prices, is very limited.

With the end of credit subsidization, a new system for agricultural financing has been established, comprising the Development Financial Corporation, a commercial bank that addresses the financial requirements of the modern agricultural sector, and the Cajas Rurales de Ahorro y Crédito (Rural Saving and Credit Funds), which provide credit to small farmers and rural workers. In addition, a transitory system of agrarian development funds, organized at regional government levels, provides credit to organized peasant farmer groups. Finally, the poorest peasant farmers in marginal areas benefit from rotating funds, which provide loans in the form of seeds, fertilizers, pesticides and production equipment.

An important development, with major implications for agricultural financing, has been the Law on Investment Promotion in the Agrarian Sector. This law marked the end of the restrictions to private landownership and enabled landowners to sell, loan or transfer their land. It is expected that the ability of landowners to use their land as collateral for loans will remove one major obstacle to investment in agriculture.

BOX 9
THE FISHERIES SECTOR IN PERU

Despite having lost ground relative to other sectors over the past two decades, fisheries remains an important economic sector in Peru, with its contribution to GDP fluctuating around 1 percent in recent years, down from about 1.9 percent in 1970. In 1994 the sector contributed about 19 percent ($856.4 million) of total export earnings, with fishmeal ranking as Peru's second most important export earner behind copper. The fisheries sector provides direct employment to an estimated 50 000 to 60 000 people, three-quarters of whom work in the fish capture sector and one-quarter in the processing sector.

The Peruvian stretch of the Pacific Ocean is one of the world's richest fishing grounds. With an estimated catch of 12 million tonnes in 1994 and 8.9 million tonnes in 1995, Peru's fisheries production is the second largest in the world, after China. The fishmeal processing and canning industry became a large foreign exchange earner in the 1960s and then experienced a sharp decline from 1970 to 1973. Sluggish performances ensued until the mid-1980s owing to a combination of overfishing and periodic appearances of the warm El Niño current. Production staged a recovery in the late 1980s, however, with catches returning to the levels of the late 1960s. The sector enjoyed two of its best years ever in 1993 and 1994.

Anchovies and sardines constitute the bulk of Peru's catch, most of which is delivered to the fishmeal industry. Anchovies, in particular, account for about 80 percent of total production and are the largest single source of fish for reduction to fishmeal and fish oil. Traditional fisheries such as those for anchovy and sardine are excessive while others, such as those fisheries targeting horse mackerel and squid stocks (also abundant), still have potential for expansion.

Fishing and the production of fishmeal and fish oil came under government control in 1973. By 1990, however, the private sector had gradually worked its way back to producing half of Peru's fishmeal. This process of liberalization has since continued and, by the end of 1996, ten of the state-owned fishmeal plants had been auctioned to the private sector.

The oil and fishmeal industry processes 90 percent of the national landings; it has an excess capacity despite the fact that some factories still use outdated technology and operate below their optimum capacity. In view of the limited potential for sustainably expanding the volume of catches, there is no justification to increase the total processing capacity, and future investments would be better aimed at improving and modernizing factories and processes by updating and replacing obsolete equipment. This would involve placing emphasis on the sanitary and hygienic aspects, improvements in handling and preservation of raw material, better yields and more efficient processes. Some enterprises are starting to produce special high-quality fishmeal, and this should be encouraged by paying due attention to market limitations.

As can be seen by the fish-oil and fishmeal industry alone, Peru's fleet and plant capacity is considerably oversized, with around three times the necessary capacity of a bumper year such as that experienced in 1994. Any decision to increase the size of Peru's fishing fleet needs first to take into account the availability of fish resources and the capacity to land, receive and market the catches. In fact, improving current facilities and processes should be the fishing sector's first priority. In order to enter more developed and demanding markets, the canning industry, for example, which currently only uses 7 percent of its capacity, needs more modern technology and infrastructure to be able to produce low-cost products. The frozen fish industry, also with a large non-utilized capacity, has good prospects of expansion, since some products are well accepted in international markets. Improvements in the facilities for handling and treating fish, on-board and on land, will be needed to increase fresh fish production.

The last five years have actually witnessed somewhat of a revival in the fishing industry in Peru. Efforts have been made towards modernizing the poorly equipped and antiquated artisanal fishing fleet. Investments have included new fishing boats as well as high-technology plants for the production of prime-quality fishmeal used for fish farming and aquaculture.

There seem to be no major problems for increasing the internal trade of traditional industrial products, such as frozen and canned fish, but this is not the case for fresh fish or non-traditional products, which so far have not entered commercial marketing channels. There are good development prospects for the internal market, judging from population growth projections and the government's intention to increase fish consumption, although this will require an improvement in landing, reception, storage, off-vessel sales, transport and marketing capacities and, consequently, heavy investment and state participation and support.

The export of a product that is of a higher quality and price and has a greater added value is an interesting alternative for the country. Expansion prospects for the international marketing of national fish products are generally good but, to a great extent, will depend on the improvements and modernization needed in several aspects of the capture and processing of fish as well as on better promotion of national fish products abroad.

In an attempt to work towards the

sustainability of both the resource and the industry and to match FAO's Code of Conduct for Responsible Fisheries, Peru's Ministry of Fisheries has drawn up a new management and development plan. One important recent development has been the adoption of a licence scheme requiring payment for the right to fish. The proceeds from this scheme are intended to be used for monitoring fishing access rules and procedures as well as for research, the conservation and rational exploitation of the fishery resources and benefits granted to licence holders.

**LATIN AMERICA
AND THE CARIBBEAN**

---

[50] Between 1969 and 1992, the number of ownership titles issued totalled 123 000, of which fewer than 10 000, or 8 percent, were officially registered. Between 1993 and 1996, 160 000 titles were issued, of which 90 000 were officially registered. It is estimated that 17 percent of the 5.7 million land parcels recorded in the National Agricultural Census of 1994 have been officially titled.

[51] Agricultural exports currently account for 14 percent of the value of total merchandise exports, compared with 21 percent in 1979-81 and 16 percent in the late 1980s. The value of agricultural exports is currently barely 30 percent of that of agricultural imports, down from 68 percent in 1979-81 and 49 percent in 1989-91.

[52] A limiting factor to the expansion of trade in Andean animal products is the need to preserve the genetic resources. Because of this concern, an export quota has recently been introduced, limiting exports of llamas to 600 and alpacas to 1 700 units per year.

However, while the process of formalizing land titles has significantly accelerated in recent years, much remains to be done.[50] Another significant institutional development has been the issuance of the Water Law which no longer relates the use of water to land area and introduces provisions governing payment for water used by farmers.

Despite all existing credit schemes and improvements in the economic and institutional environment, inadequate financing remains a limiting factor to agricultural modernization. The dismantling of the Agrarian Bank has created a vacuum that the government expects will eventually be filled by private financing sources. Private financing has been slow to develop, however, particularly owing to low profits from agricultural investment, relative to other sectors, and slow progress in land titling.

In the trade sector, current policies seek to stimulate an agricultural export sector that has been rapidly losing relative economic importance and to contain the deterioration of agricultural trade balances.[51] The government has set the objective of increasing the value of agricultural exports to $1 billion by the year 2000, from levels of $400 million to $600 million in the mid-1990s. Much of this increase would be achieved through the liberalization of trade, investment and foreign exchange regulations, with the private sector leading the way. Other than traditional export products – coffee, cotton, vegetables and sugar – products with market potential such as fresh fruits, asparagus, flowers and Andean animal products are expected to gain a progressive market share.[52] Although there is no direct state support for agricultural exports, a number of government programmes indirectly favour external competitiveness. In particular, the strengthening of the health authority, Servicio Nacional de Sanidad Agraria (SENASA), enables the promotion of exports through numerous phytosanitary and animal health activities.

Concluding remarks
The Peruvian Government can be credited with remarkable achievements in redressing what was, at the beginning of the 1990s, a chaotic economic, political and social situation. Its success in combating terrorism and violence has been an important factor in enabling

LATIN AMERICA AND THE CARIBBEAN

[53] The role of organized resistance groups in rural areas (*rondas campesinas*) was as determinant as government and military action in the elimination of terrorism. Despite their peaceful nature and limited armament, many peasants became committed anti-guerrilla fighters after years of harassment and violence that claimed 25 000 to 30 000 lives in rural areas.

[54] The poor state of roads had made land transport so onerous that rice from the Tarapoto zone 700 km north of Lima would have cost Lima consumers more than twice the price of rice imported from Thailand. About 10 000 km of road have been reconstructed since the early 1990s, greatly contributing to restore competitiveness to, *inter alia*, local rice.

[55] Agricultural public investment fell from about $400 million in 1985-90 to $325 million in 1990-93 (annual averages in constant 1993 dollars), although its share in total public investment tended to rise (to about 28 percent in 1990-93, from 16 percent in 1980 and 24 percent in 1985-89).

[56] Much of the public investment in agriculture in

(continued)

these achievements.[53] Government action has also created a less distortive basis for agricultural growth, while maintaining a degree of protection for the sector and for less-favoured segments of agro-rural society. By emphasizing infrastructural improvement, it has promoted marketing efficiency in a more effective way than previous mechanisms of direct intervention.[54]

Much remains to be done, nonetheless, to turn agriculture into a modern and competitive sector. Overcoming the complex natural, developmental and social problems involved will require, in the first place, the continuation of political stability that enables consolidating macroeconomic stabilization and reform. Pursuing reform that involves financial and monetary discipline is a particularly difficult policy option in a country afflicted by mass poverty and unemployment, as is Peru. This was recently illustrated by the set of measures implemented to cool down the overheated economy in 1996: regardless of their economic justification, these measures risked popular opposition owing to their short-term negative effects on growth, wages and employment.

Modernizing agriculture will also involve a reactivation of investment from both the public and private sectors. Public investment in agriculture has been declining[55] and is likely to remain depressed until stabilization has been consolidated. Thus, the future of agricultural financing will much depend on the success of current public investment policies that emphasize the quality rather than the volume of public investment. Even more crucially, it will depend on the government's ability to attract domestic and international private capital for financing, not only physical infrastructure, in particular irrigation projects and transport and marketing facilities,[56] but also activities related to credit, research, extension and technology transfer. Such involvement of the private sector will require confidence in the overall political and economic environment as well as confidence in the agricultural sector's potential as a profitable and competitive investment option.

Given the likelihood of continuing financial restraint and selectiveness in resource allocation, what should be the priority areas for agricultural financing? Perhaps the most authoritative opinion on this issue is that of farmers themselves. A recent survey explores what a

recent years has been absorbed by large irrigation projects initiated under previous administrations. Current policies emphasize the need to reconsider the approach to irrigation in the light of the failure of these projects to meet their economic and social objectives.

[57] The survey was carried out in December 1995 by the Inter-American Institute for Cooperation on Agriculture (IICA) and the Asociación de Promoción Agraria (ASPA) under the auspices of the Konrad Adenauer Foundation. It involved 100 farmers from different parts of the country, selected on the basis of their successful production and economic performances.

representative group of successful Peruvian farmers consider to be basic ingredients for modernizing agriculture and gaining competitiveness.[57] The following are seen as top-priority areas: extension, technology dissemination, entrepreneurial organization, credit and clear agricultural incentives. As second priorities, technical assistance, marketing efficiency and prices are mentioned. All these elements are, in the farmers' opinion, still inadequately addressed by government policies, although it is recognized that, overall, the policy framework has created better conditions for agriculture.

That farmers place extension, technology and organizational issues at the top of their list of concerns is very interesting, since it suggests a shift in farmers' perceptions of what is best for them, away from top-down direct state support. Such a new perception indicates awareness of the primary importance of human development and willingness by farmers to "help themselves" by acquiring technological and managerial expertise. This is an important message for policy-makers. There is ample evidence to confirm that agricultural extension can be, in many countries' circumstances, the best way to achieve long-term development in both its economic growth and human resource components. Peru has a variety of public and private institutions that provide different forms of extension, technology transfer and technical assistance. Nevertheless, the system suffers from old inadequacies, and new uncertainties are emerging. Despite an abundance of extension personnel, very few are technically well trained and experienced. Key aspects such as post-harvest management, marketing information and linkages between extension and research are often inadequately addressed in extension programmes. Extension services fail to reach small-scale subsistence farmers, especially female-headed farm households and young farm families. Here, as in many other developmental problems, a common denominator is financial constraint. This raises two fundamental issues: i) the importance that should be assigned to agricultural extension compared with other areas that may give more visible and immediate returns on expenditures; and ii) what the role of the state should be vis-à-vis the private sector in the financing of extension, research and technology. While current policies

emphasize a greater role of the private sector and NGOs and the creation of self-sustainable extension services, the viability of such an approach is contingent on the existence of profitable market opportunities. Indeed, the private sector has shown remarkable dynamism in importing technology and developing competitiveness, for instance for asparagus, broccoli, other vegetables and fruit. However, it is important that the reduced involvement of the state and the consideration of financial sustainability and cost-efficiency do not translate into reduced access to technological innovation and training for the vast majority of agricultural producers. These issues are particularly relevant in the context of the institutional reform under way and the efforts to develop a national plan for research and technology transfer.

NEAR EAST AND NORTH AFRICA

REGIONAL OVERVIEW
Economic developments

Economic growth in most of the countries of the Near East and North Africa gained momentum in 1996. For the region as a whole, GDP growth in 1996 was estimated to be 4.5 percent, up from an average 3.5 percent during the previous five years. Factors contributing to the above-average economic growth were: higher oil prices, which led to larger than expected revenue flows for the oil-producing countries; timely rainfall in many countries of the region; progress in stabilization, leading to lower inflation rates (following from an average 34 percent in 1995 to 24.5 percent in 1996) and reduced current account imbalances; and the deepening of structural reforms, which created a better environment for trade and private sector investment. Political tensions, however, continued to dampen progress in several countries in the region while some others faced overheating problems, with accelerating inflation and a growing fiscal deficit.

The rise in oil prices in 1996, undisturbed by the entry of Iraq in the oil market, contributed to the increase in the rate of GDP growth in the oil-producing countries. The GDP increased by 9.9 and 4.2 percent in the United Arab Emirates and Iran, respectively, and by 2.5 percent in Saudi Arabia, the latter modest expansion representing, however, an improvement from the zero growth of the previous year. Gradual fiscal consolidation has been the centrepiece of Saudi Arabia's reform efforts. Although public expenditure restraint exerted a depressing effect in this country, it also contributed to increased private sector confidence and a revival of economic activity. The impetus towards higher growth in Egypt, at 4.3 percent in 1996 compared with 3.2 percent in 1995, was as much due to an increase in oil revenue earnings as to substantial progress in structural reforms. Egypt also displayed declining internal and external imbalances and lower inflation rates of 7.2 percent in 1996, down from 9.4 percent in 1995. In Turkey the economy maintained high growth for the second consecutive year in 1996, at about 6.4 percent following the 7.5 percent of 1995, recovering from the effects of

**NEAR EAST
AND NORTH AFRICA**

the strong contractionary economic adjustment measures adopted in 1994. Despite stringent demand management measures, however, the fiscal deficit climbed to more than 9 percent of GDP in Turkey, and interest rates reached more than 120 percent. Although attempts at curbing the triple-digit inflation, which peaked at 106.3 percent in 1994, showed some success, inflation still remained high at 82.3 percent in 1996. These inflationary pressures also spilled over to the Turkish-Cypriot zone, which is linked with the Turkish economy. Such pressures, combined with political uncertainty affecting revenues from tourism, led to a slowdown in the economy of Cyprus.

Economic adjustment measures continued in a majority of countries in the region, but progress remained mixed. Some countries such as Egypt, Jordan and Tunisia advanced considerably in privatization, while in others, such as the Syrian Arab Republic and Yemen, much remains to be done. Reform was impeded by political tension in several countries. In the Sudan, civil strife led to economic depression, high inflation of 85 percent and disruptions in trade flows and domestic marketing, leading *inter alia* to acute food shortages. Towards the end of 1996, the Sudan suspended payments on its arrears to IMF, and this had strong negative repercussions on the country's creditworthiness. In Algeria, while most macroeconomic targets under the adjustment reform programme were achieved or surpassed thanks to strong performances in the oil and the agricultural sectors, recessionary trends persisted, with unemployment at 28 percent for example. In Lebanon, a rising external debt made debt management and fiscal consolidation the priority for government efforts over the next few years. Export diversification, a central objective of structural reform in Oman, remained elusive as the non-oil economy stagnated.

Prospects for the short and medium term appear generally promising. The price of oil is expected to come down, but only moderately, and it is expected to help sustain economic growth in oil-producing countries while having spillover effects in other countries of the region. Ongoing efforts at strengthening economic and trade links with the EU by many of the countries in the region, such as Turkey, Jordan, Morocco and Cyprus, are likely to lead to improved trade and growth prospects.

Uncertainty about peace prospects and the regional

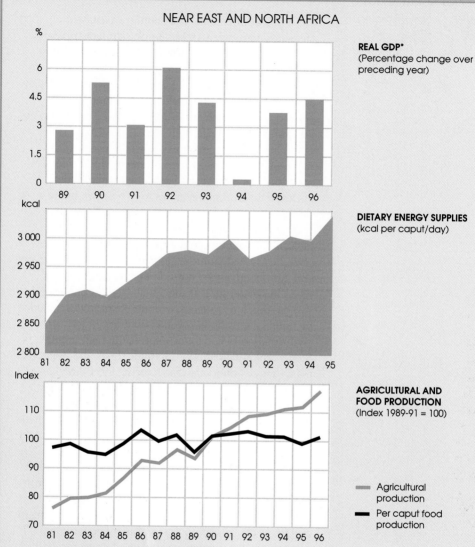

Figure 12A

NEAR EAST AND NORTH AFRICA

REAL GDP*
(Percentage change over preceding year)

DIETARY ENERGY SUPPLIES
(kcal per caput/day)

AGRICULTURAL AND FOOD PRODUCTION
(Index 1989-91 = 100)

Agricultural production

Per caput food production

Source: FAO and IMF

*Excludes Algeria, Morocco and Tunisia (according to IMF country classification)

Figure 12B

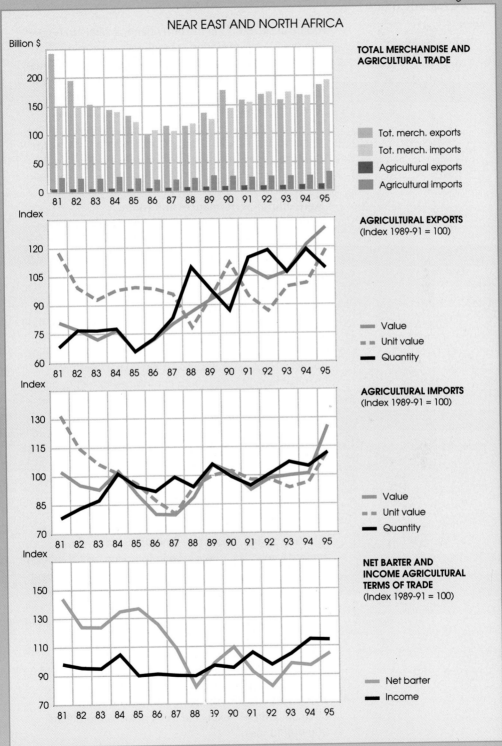

NEAR EAST AND NORTH AFRICA

Billion $

TOTAL MERCHANDISE AND AGRICULTURAL TRADE

- Tot. merch. exports
- Tot. merch. imports
- Agricultural exports
- Agricultural imports

Index

AGRICULTURAL EXPORTS
(Index 1989-91 = 100)

- Value
- Unit value
- Quantity

Index

AGRICULTURAL IMPORTS
(Index 1989-91 = 100)

- Value
- Unit value
- Quantity

Index

NET BARTER AND INCOME AGRICULTURAL TERMS OF TRADE
(Index 1989-91 = 100)

- Net barter
- Income

Source: FAO

political situation, on the other hand, is likely to hinder the previous expectations of regional economic integration, especially in Jordan, Palestine and, to some extent, Egypt. The stalemate regarding peace between Israel and the Syrian Arab Republic is likely to retard economic progress further in the region as a whole. Planned or potential regional projects, especially in the water sector, may take longer to materialize, owing to political uncertainty and internal strife in some North African countries.

Agricultural performances and issues
Growth in the agricultural sector was higher in 1996 than in the previous year in most North African countries, in particular Tunisia, Morocco, Algeria, and in the Sudan, which contributed in turn to a higher rate of economic growth. In 1996, production of wheat in North Africa increased by 7.5 percent to a record 16.5 million tonnes as a result of above-average production in all countries. The production of coarse grains in 1996 increased in the subregion by 60 percent to 13.6 million tonnes. Above-average and timely rainfall and better management practices both contributed to higher output in the production of cereal and barley as well as other crops such as citrus, olives and lentils.

Emerging from a severe drought in 1995, Morocco in 1996 benefited from the highest rainfall levels in the past 30 years. As a result, wheat production in 1996, estimated to be 5.9 million tonnes, was more than five times larger than the previous year's crop of only 1.1 million tonnes. The output of barley increased by 3.2 million to 3.8 million tonnes and that of maize to 235 000 tonnes, about five times higher than the previous year. The citrus crop in Morocco, at 1.4 million tonnes in 1996, also registered a large increase of about 35 percent. As a result, citrus exports are estimated to have expanded by about 50 percent.

In Tunisia, good farming conditions during the year led to an estimated increase of 18 percent in overall agricultural production, up from the 9.7 percent recorded in 1995. Cereal production reached a record high of 2.8 million tonnes – a threefold increase over 1995. This was also the case with the production of olive oil, which is expected to increase to more than 200 000 tonnes.

In the Syrian Arab Republic, investment and better

FOOD INSECURITY IN IRAQ

Large groups of Iraq's population are suffering from severe problems of food insecurity. Whereas per caput calorie intake levels in the Near East and North Africa region remained broadly unchanged between 1988 and 1994, they decreased by 34 percent in Iraq during the same period. At 43 percent, the decline in protein intake was even more severe. More recent years have seen a further serious deterioration of the population's nutritional and health situation.

Important relief is expected from an agreement, reached in December 1996 between Iraq and the United Nations, on the implementation of the oil-for-food deal, which allows Iraqi oil exports of up to $1 billion during each 90-day period in exchange for the importation of humanitarian goods such as food, health supplies and medicines and other basic necessities. Initially set for a six-month period, the oil-for-food deal was extended for another six months by the United Nations Security Council on 4 June 1997.

Under the oil-for-food deal, $804.63 million (out of a total of $1.3 billion for humanitarian assistance) were allocated to the procurement of food commodities to help ensure a daily energy intake of 2 030 kcal and daily protein intake of 47 g per caput. By the end of May, the country had received 692 000 tonnes of food, about one-third of the 2.2 million tonnes expected under the deal. The first commodities started arriving in late March, and the distribution of wheat flour started in April. In May, food distribution included rations of wheat flour, rice, pulses and oil. As for salt, sugar and tea, deliveries had not been sufficient for a monthly distribution. The distribution of the full ration quota is expected to start in July. An emergency feeding operation, targeted at vulnerable groups whose special food needs will not be covered by the distribution of food under the deal, has been jointly approved by FAO and WFP for the period 1 April to 31 December 1997. It is estimated, however, that the allocation of $804.63 million for food will only cover slightly more than 50 percent of the estimated food import requirements.

Although the food-for-oil deal will undoubtedly alleviate the present serious food shortages (as total monthly ration quotas will increase by 20 percent with the arrival of food under the deal) and ameliorate somewhat the nutritional and health situation of the affected population, food security remains precarious. The scarcity of basic agricultural inputs such as seeds, spare parts, vaccines and agrochemicals, together with the wide-spread incidence of pests, weeds and animal diseases, has resulted in low yields and productivity. The general performance of the agricultural sector, particularly in the 1996/97 season, is cause for concern. The output of wheat and barley for the 1996/97 winter crop season is forecast to be significantly below normal.

With expectations of continued sanctions, an increased domestic production of food remains vitally important and the government is making strong efforts in this direction. As part of these efforts, attention is currently focused on land reclamation and irrigation in the south. The reclaimed areas are also provided with services, including electricity, education and health. Research is under way in Iraq to develop new agricultural strains and increase seed production and to maximize the use of livestock resources. Iraqi authorities are reportedly considering ways of ensuring that farmers have a financial stake in these projects in order to ensure that they are fully involved.

NEAR EAST
AND NORTH AFRICA

irrigation management, coupled with higher international prices, helped spur domestic agricultural crop production. Having achieved self-sufficiency in wheat in 1992, the Syrian Arab Republic produced more than 4.2 million tonnes of wheat in 1996 – about 2 million tonnes more than domestic requirements. In the first three quarters of the year, about 850 000 tonnes of cereals were exported, compared with 600 000 tonnes for the whole of 1995. Further increases in cereal exports are anticipated in the near future, as investments are being made to expand storage capacity, in particular with the assistance of the Islamic Development Bank. Among the country's non-food crops, a record cotton harvest was recorded in 1996, about 11.5 percent over 1995 levels and approximately 20 percent above the average for 1991-95. Assisted by timely rainfall, the major factor behind increased output was the jump in yields to 3.4 tonnes/ha in 1996 from 3.1 tonnes/ha in 1995 and only 1.6 tonnes/ha in 1991.

Favourable climatic conditions in the Sudan resulted in increased wheat production in 1996 compared with the previous year. The production of other commodities, such as sesame seed, also increased. Timely rainfall also led to an increase in cotton production of more than 12 percent over last year, although yields have been tendentially declining and compare poorly with world averages. A major reason for the declining yields is a lack of maintenance and the consequent sedimentation of canals, which impedes an adequate flow of water, especially important for the cotton crop. There is cause for concern, as cotton is the Sudan's largest single export earner and a major contributor to economic growth.

In Saudi Arabia, budgetary constraints over the last few years required a reconsideration of the policies in support of agriculture. Reforms begun in 1991, with the aim of reducing the production of highly subsidized wheat in harsh desert conditions, have continued and led to further reductions in the subsidies. As a result, wheat production, which reached a peak of 4.1 million tonnes in 1991/92, was down to between 1 million and 2 million tonnes by 1996. With an estimated local consumption of 1.8 million tonnes, the gap is expected to be met by existing stocks. Barley production, estimated to be 450 000 tonnes, also declined to half its previous level. Cereal production, which is mostly dependent on groundwater sources, has led to the rapid

**NEAR EAST
AND NORTH AFRICA**

depletion of this non-renewable resource. Since the agricultural sector uses about 80 percent of available water in Saudi Arabia, efficient management of water resources is now a government priority, which has implications for grain production. Diversification from grain to crops that consume less water, such as fruits and vegetables, is being encouraged.

EGYPT

Economic overview

The economic adjustment programme initiated in 1991 in Egypt has marked a turning point in the country's macroeconomic and sectoral policy orientation. Until the early 1970s, inward-looking, state-sponsored economic growth policies were the cornerstone of Egypt's development strategy, with an emphasis on social welfare and state subsidization of basic needs. Although this approach did lead to improvements in living conditions for the majority of Egyptians in the 1960s and the 1970s, it nevertheless laid the basis for the economy's structural imbalances which, by the 1990s, had proved to be unsustainable in the long term.

Notwithstanding a few liberalization initiatives in the mid-1970s, the economy remained characterized by pervasive controls and a predominantly import-substitution regime. As a result of the high oil prices and the concomitant remittances from expatriate Egyptian labour in the Gulf Cooperation Council (GCC) countries, together with earnings from the Suez Canal, the economy still grew at a very rapid pace. Expansionary policies continued well into the 1980s when oil prices were declining and financial and external account disequilibria were beginning to emerge as a serious problem.

By the end of the 1980s, together with the concomitant decline in oil prices after 1982, the prolonged recessionary global economic climate had made evident the structural weaknesses in the economy. These weaknesses were exacerbated by mounting external debt and fiscal deficits. An overreliance on oil exports, declining non-oil exports and inefficiencies in resource use made the pattern of growth unsustainable. GDP growth decelerated significantly during the latter part of the 1980s, translating into a decline in GDP per caput from an average of $615 in 1980-86 to $588 by the end of the decade.[58] Budgetary deficits, financed primarily by the printing of money, led to double-digit inflation and contributed to the slowdown in growth. Mounting debt-service payments led to an accumulation of arrears.

In 1991, Egypt adopted an Economic Reform and Structural Adjustment Programme (ERSAP), aimed at stabilizing and restructuring the economy to achieve greater efficiency in resource use, and at restoring

[58] UN. 1995. *Impact of selected macroeconomic and social policies on poverty: The case of Egypt, Jordan and the Republic of Yemen*, p. 14. E/ESCWA/ED/1995/6. New York.

NEAR EAST AND NORTH AFRICA

macroeconomic growth. The comprehensive policy agenda included liberalization of the foreign exchange market; trade liberalization; financial sector reforms; reform of public enterprises and their eventual sale; elimination of price controls, tax reform; and the institution of an effective regulatory framework. As part of the initial phase of the programme, key reforms undertaken in Egypt were the alignment of the exchange rate; the deregulation of agricultural, food and industrial prices; a gradual reduction in consumer food subsidies; and a move towards greater privatization in an effort to establish a more market-based economy.

The 1991 ERSAP was followed in 1993 by another economic reform programme, ERSAP Phase II. Reforms under the second phase helped to stabilize macroeconomic balances further and, after a difficult start, revive the economy. Economic growth remained weak during the early 1990s, averaging just over 1 percent during 1992-94, but it gained strength in 1995 (+3.2 percent) and again in 1996 (an estimated +4 percent). For the fiscal year 1997/98, the first year of the next five-year plan, targets include GDP growth of 6.2 percent. Underlying the improved growth performances in recent years were major advances in economic stabilization. Despite a reduction in fiscal revenues from duties, the budget deficit, which stood at around 8 percent in the late 1980s, is projected to decline to a remarkably low 1.1 percent of GDP in 1996/97. The rationalization of government expenditures and tight monetary policy brought the current account almost in balance in 1996, while inflation declined from about 20 percent in 1991 to an estimated 7.2 percent in 1996. This is a considerable achievement in the face of the substantial decontrol of prices for basic food commodities, electricity, petroleum and transport, among other things. A further reduction in subsidies on petroleum products, natural gas and electricity is expected in the coming years. After a devaluation of more than 300 percent between 1988 and 1991, the liberalization of the foreign exchange markets stabilized the currency, which has now become convertible.

Although it got off to a slow start, the privatization programme has since made some progress. More than 90 state enterprises are expected to be privatized by mid-1998, although company valuations could be a

contentious issue. In addition, one of the four major public sector banks is expected to be put up for sale in the course of 1997. Debt restructuring of public enterprises is also expected to generate income. It is expected that privatization in 1997 alone will generate revenues equivalent to about 5 percent of GDP, some of which could go towards servicing the external debt which currently stands at about $37 billion. Private sector involvement is also being encouraged in energy projects. An investment law to streamline investment regulations as well as an anti-trust law are expected to be passed in 1997.

In late 1996, Egypt concluded another $391 million standby agreement with IMF in anticipation of the meeting of the Paris Club to facilitate the third and last $4 billion of a total $10 billion Paris Club debt write-off, contingent on the successful completion of an IMF programme. However, this is associated with stringent criteria requiring further macroeconomic, financial, trade and privatization reforms in the coming months. The debt relief is expected to save more than about $290 million per year in debt servicing and reduce external debt to around $28 billion, or a little more than half the total debt of $50 billion at the time the programme was adopted in 1991.

Agricultural resources and prospects

An overall scarcity of water is a constraint to the expansion of agricultural land in Egypt. Furthermore, rapid population increases in the last two decades have put additional pressure on domestic food production while, at the same time, urbanization has encroached on potentially viable agricultural land.

Cultivable area in Egypt is limited. Of the total land area of about 1 million km², less than 4 percent is habitable, mainly along the Nile where most of the country's population of more than 60 million people is concentrated. With the Nile providing almost the only source of water, owing to the very limited rainfall, the 3.7 million ha of arable land base is limited primarily to the irrigated area. At 0.06 ha per caput, Egypt's per caput cultivable land area is therefore among the lowest in the world. The major crops in Egypt are cotton, rice, wheat, maize, sugar, berseem, beans and fruits and vegetables.

With an improved climate for investment and an economy on the road to recovery, large development

schemes are being considered. A highly ambitious project recently launched is the Nile Irrigation Plan, aimed at diverting one-tenth of the flow of the Nile to irrigate the western desert. The project, which is expected to extend over 20 years, aims to pump water 5 km through a tunnel into a canal and then raise it to a height of 55 m, requiring the world's largest pumping station. Only 20 percent of the cost of the project should be covered by the government, with the rest being financed by private investors who should be attracted by such incentives as cheap land. According to some analysts, however, the very high costs involved are not justified on economic grounds. Moreover, since the Sudan and Ethiopia are also building dams on the same river, the flow of water could be less than expected in Egypt. In the past, attempts at irrigating deserts in Egypt through long-haul canals have not been very successful, not least owing to huge evaporation losses and the problem of moving dunes. Since the proposed site is also in a depression, waterlogging is a potential drawback.

Agricultural performances and policies
Although agriculture remains an important sector in the Egyptian economy, its share in GDP has markedly declined, from more than 38 percent in 1975 to 25.6 percent in 1985 and 16 percent in 1994-95. The declining economic importance of agriculture reflected the greater dynamism of other sectors and, in particular, the rise in oil and Suez Canal revenues. However, the decline also reflects lacklustre performances in the agricultural sector, constrained as it is by natural resource limitations in addition to having been severely encumbered by controls during the past decades. Amid pronounced fluctuations, food and agricultural output has risen only slowly, particularly between the late 1960s and early 1980s when it actually declined by about 10 percent in per caput terms. Production growth subsequently accelerated to a fairly sustained rate, although with some temporary setbacks, particularly in 1988-89 and 1994. Overall, however, domestic production has been inadequate to cover the needs of a rapidly expanding population, thus requiring massive volumes of food imports, both commercial and in the form of food aid. The value of cereal imports, which account for more than one-third of total agricultural imports, rose steeply during the 1970s, peaking in 1982

NEAR EAST AND NORTH AFRICA

at $1.7 billion, but declining since the late 1980s to about $900 million in recent years. In certain periods, particularly 1987-90, the value of food imports significantly exceeded the total value of merchandise exports. This was explained to a large extent by the important concessional or grant component of food imports. Indeed, after 1975-76, Egypt received considerable volumes of food aid in cereals which, in some years, largely exceeded 2 million tonnes or about one-third of the country's total cereal imports. In those peak years, Egypt was receiving 15 to 20 percent of the world's total food aid in cereals. Since 1991, however, cereal food aid to Egypt has sharply declined, reaching about 200 000 tonnes in recent years.

Social welfare considerations have traditionally been at the centre of the policy concerns of the Government of Egypt. Agricultural and food policies have aimed at ensuring the availability of basic food at cheap and affordable prices for the vast majority of the population. To the extent that they contributed to raising the average food intake and reducing poverty, these policies may be considered successful. However, they also had the effect of depressing the economic climate for agricultural development. To achieve "cheap food" objectives, interventions by the government in both food production and consumption were implemented through direct price controls as well as indirectly, through exchange rate policies. Until the alignment of the exchange rate in 1991, valuation of the agricultural food or non-food commodities at the official (overvalued) exchange rate led to artificially low prices both for imported agricultural products and domestically produced tradables. This resulted in a heavy tax on domestic producers; the implicit tax on wheat increased from 42 percent in 1973-79 to 55 percent in 1980-85, the same trend as exhibited for rice and maize.

At the same time, production was subsidized through the public provision of agricultural services and the granting of low rates or exemptions for the recovery of operation and maintenance costs on public sector investment. Direct subsidies to agricultural inputs, such as fertilizers, pesticides, seeds and animal feeds, started in the early 1970s. Socialist policies included land redistribution, the formation of agricultural cooperatives and state controls on cultivable area and cropping patterns. The government implemented large irrigation

investment schemes to reclaim marginal lands, which contributed to increasing the effective cultivable land area. State intervention also included the nationalization of cotton trade, government monopolies and a mandatory delivery system for export crops.

Since the inception of the reform programme, both direct and indirect interventions in agriculture have generally been removed and most subsidies have been abolished. While economic reforms in the agriculture sector have no doubt contributed to a better environment for farm activity, the extent to which they have translated into output and productivity gains is difficult to assess. Overall, agricultural output growth averaged 2.7 percent yearly during 1991-96, close to the population growth rate, suggesting an improvement from the performances of previous decades. The picture varies significantly depending on the various crops, however, and agricultural production has remained subject to pronounced fluctuations. Indeed, behind the average growth of the 1990s, yearly variations ranged from -3.3 percent in 1994 to 7.4 percent in 1995. As regards individual crops, wheat production rose by a significant 34 percent between 1990 and 1996, thanks in particular to better extension and land reclamation programmes which started in the mid 1980s, but maize only rose by 14 percent during the same period. After two bad crop years that brought cotton production to the lowest levels in several decades, cotton output rose by almost 50 percent in 1996 (from the 1995 level), reflecting a 40 percent increase in the land area under this commodity as well as better pest control and improved market prices. Similarly, price liberalization over the years contributed to an increase in rice production to a record high of an estimated 2.8 million tonnes in 1996, with a projected export surplus of 600 000 tonnes. However, the large quantities of water required for this crop, together with its high production costs and considerable domestic demand, may not allow for large exportable surpluses in the future.

Consumer subsidies and food security
Despite the inadequacies of the domestic food supply system and the financial difficulties posed by the need to import large quantities of food, Egypt has achieved remarkable success in improving the nutritional status of its population. Calorie supplies rose steeply from about

2 500 kcal per day during the early 1970s to more than 3 200 kcal per day in the early 1980s and subsequently remained at a high level. The current level of 3 340 kcal per day is about 15 percent above the average for the Near East and North Africa region, and 25 percent above the average for the developing countries as a whole.

Improvements in the food consumption levels of a vast majority of the population have been achieved to a large extent through social welfare measures, including consumer food subsidies that have been generously provided during the expansionary fiscal policies of the last two decades.

By the 1980s, Egypt had one of the most extensive consumer subsidy systems in the world. Quotas of rice, oil, sugar, tea and soap were guaranteed by the government to each individual through a ration card system. In addition, state cooperative stores sold food items such as macaroni, eggs, oil, cheese, sugar and tea at below market prices. Bread was, and still is, available at subsidized prices in unlimited quantities.

In addition to the ration card schemes, the consumer prices of food commodities were officially controlled. From 1975 to 1979, the price to the consumer of locally produced wheat was about half its cost to the government, while that of imported wheat was one-third of the international cost. Similar policies were applied for sugar, wheat flour and beans.

Largely as a result of food subsidy policies, during the period of rapid economic growth, the percentage of urban poor, estimated to be approximately 37 percent of the population in 1974/75, declined to about 23 percent in 1981/82, and the decline was even more pronounced in the rural areas.

The high level of consumer protection, however, contributed to unsustainable budgetary deficits which reached a peak of about 10 percent of GDP in 1980-82. About half of the total subsidies went towards meeting the costs of highly subsidized wheat while another third went towards sugar.

With the global and regional recession that lasted throughout the better part of the 1980s, which for Egypt translated into macroeconomic imbalances and a slowdown in economic growth, the gains made towards increased food security and reduced poverty were reversed. Food production performances were particularly poor during the early part of the 1980s, and

the cost of cereal imports more than doubled between 1978 and 1981. The financial burden of general and indefinite subsidies on food production and consumption went well beyond the means of the government. It became increasingly accepted that the short-term welfare gains created by these subsidies were largely outweighed by the losses involved in the ensuing financial disequilibria and long-term distortions arising from the extensively protected systems.

Thus, an important element of the economic reform programme in 1991 was the reduction in consumer subsidies, which declined to 2.3 percent of GDP in 1990-93. On a per caput basis, the real value of the average subsidy declined from 108.4 Egyptian pounds (LE) during 1980-89 to less than half that level, at LE 41.8, during 1990-93. By 1993, most subsidies were removed but those on wheat, oil and oil products and sugar remained. Since then, the selling price of most of these subsidized commodities has been gradually increased, with the price for wheat approaching its actual cost.

After an initial drop in welfare during the initial phase of the economic reform programme, food supply and access now seems to be on the increase in Egypt. Self-sufficiency rates in wheat have increased from about 20 percent in the mid-1980s to about 45 percent in 1996. Policies aimed at greater investments in extension services, land reclamation, research and development for HYVs and population planning since the 1980s, combined with the liberalization of prices in particular and the removal of controls on the agricultural sector as a whole, have led to increases in wheat yields and production. Egypt's production and availability of fruits and vegetables has also improved. The liberalization of the economy has brought dividends in terms of stabilization and a decline in food prices, especially in the last couple of years.

CENTRAL AND EASTERN EUROPE AND THE COMMONWEALTH OF INDEPENDENT STATES

CENTRAL AND EASTERN EUROPE
Decelerating economic growth and weaker agricultural performance

Following encouraging developments during the previous year, 1996 proved to be a difficult year for the transition process as a whole in Central and Eastern European countries.[59] While still standing out as the fastest growing area in Europe, GDP growth decelerated from 5.6 to 4 percent in the subregion. However, this lower aggregate growth covered sharply contrasting economic trends between countries. Except for Hungary, where GDP growth fell to 1 percent in 1996 as a consequence of a tough but successful stabilization programme, the core group of countries forming the Central European Free Trade Agreement (CEFTA)[60] achieved significant expansion. Poland and Slovakia stood out with the highest growth rates of 6 and 7 percent, respectively. On the other hand, several countries in southeastern Europe experienced major reversals, with Bulgaria in particular recording a dramatic 10 percent fall in GDP in 1996. In Bulgaria as well as in Albania and Romania inflation rates increased two- to tenfold. These developments seemed to confirm earlier signs of the existence of a "two speed" transformation process towards a market-based economy in the subregion, the "fast reforming" countries being those in CEFTA.

The slowdown in overall economic development of the subregion was the combined effect of several factors. An important influence was the economic slowdown in some of Central and Eastern Europe's main trading partners in Western Europe. Furthermore, countries at a more advanced stage of transformation could no longer resort to cheap labour and strong devaluation as a means to maintain competitiveness. In addition, high inflation in several fast-reforming countries (e.g. 24 percent in Hungary and 19 percent in Poland) hindered domestic capital formation.

Increases in real wages generally outpaced those in productivity, consequently accelerating unit labour costs

---

[59] For the purposes of this subregional overview, the Central and Eastern European countries include: Albania, Bosnia and Herzegovina, Bulgaria, the Czech Republic, Croatia, Hungary, Poland, Romania, Slovakia, Slovenia, The Former Yugoslav Republic of Macedonia and the Federal Republic of Yugoslavia.

[60] CEFTA includes the Czech Republic, Hungary, Poland, Slovakia and Slovenia.

CENTRAL AND EASTERN EUROPE

and fuelling inflation in most Central and Eastern European countries.

Hit by adverse weather, the subregion's agricultural production declined by about 4.6 percent in 1996,[61] returning close to the levels of 1994. Encouraging exceptions were Hungary, Slovakia and Croatia, with the latter two showing particularly high growth rates of 6 and 8 percent, respectively. The most dramatic decline in agricultural output (-30 percent) was recorded in Bulgaria, where total crop and livestock production in 1996 was down to only about half of the 1989 level. The overall weaker agricultural performance of the subregion chiefly reflected a decline of more than 12 percent in grain production. The decline was relatively moderate in Poland and Hungary but dramatic in Bulgaria, Romania and Yugoslavia (of 46, 28 and 19 percent, respectively, with yields per hectare falling by 35, 21 and 14 percent). The shortfall generally reflected poor climatic conditions and financial constraints which limited the use of inputs in the latter countries. During the past difficult years of transition, a reduced use of industrial inputs, particularly fertilizers and pesticides, has made the subregion's grain sector much more vulnerable to weather conditions. Benefiting from the favourable crop harvest of the previous year, the output of livestock products in 1996 suffered a less dramatic decline. Thus, meat production in the subregion as a whole fell by around 2 percent in 1996, with occasional short-term increases caused by distress slaughterings in southeastern Europe.

The setback in agricultural output, particularly grain, combined with high international cereal prices, resulted in pronounced rises in producer prices all over the subregion. Grain producer prices rose by about 40 percent in the Czech Republic and Poland in 1996, while the futures price for wheat in Hungary doubled within a year. In Romania, the procurement price offered by the state for the 1996 harvest was 40 percent higher than in 1995, while still falling far behind the free market price.

Higher producer prices for grain had strong transmission effects on prices of other products such as rapeseed in Poland, milk and dairy products in Romania and livestock for slaughter in several countries. As the increase in producer prices outpaced the overall rate of inflation, domestic agricultural terms of trade tended to improve, notably in Slovakia, Hungary and the Czech

[61] The average excludes Albania and Bosnia and Herzegovina.

CENTRAL AND EASTERN EUROPE

Republic. In the latter, the improvement was also due to a better organization of producers in some subsectors.

Price rises at the farmgate also resulted in increasing consumer food prices in 1996, although the full effect was expected to develop only in the course of 1997. Consumer food prices increased by 19 to 20 percent in Poland and Hungary in 1996, well below the producer price increases. On the other hand, consumers in some countries of southeastern Europe were confronted with exploding food prices (57 percent in Romania and 311 percent in Bulgaria in 1996), reflecting high consumer price inflation overall as well as tight domestic supply for some basic food items.

Central and Eastern Europe's agricultural policies were further aligned with those of the EU. Limited but still growing support to producers and agricultural markets was granted through production quotas and guaranteed floor prices (e.g. for milk in Hungary and Slovakia). While still significantly below EU levels, the producer subsidy equivalent (PSE) indicator[62] tended to increase in some countries (e.g. in Hungary from 11 to more than 20 percent between 1992 and 1996). The new agricultural programme of the Czech Republic included provisions for the protection of agriculture and rural regions in a broad sense, with over half of the growing state aid to agriculture to be provided as direct payments to farms.

Facing disruptions in their agricultural production and domestic supplies, some countries of southeastern Europe introduced ad hoc or emergency policy measures in 1996 (such as sharp increases in regulated prices, export bans, recourse to food aid) which brought short-term relief. However, at the root of the acute problems of these countries were the half-hearted structural reforms of past years and the institutional vacuum left after the dismantling of the former system of economic organization in the agrifood sector. The sustainability of the new market-based agrifood system in southeastern European countries will hinge on their capacity to build institutional and policy delivery mechanisms that are both operational and supportive of structural changes.

Developments in agrifood trade

As economic transformation and trade liberalization were progressing, the overall trade balances of all Central and Eastern European countries slipped into

---

[62] **The PSE percentage measures total support to producers for a given product or group of products as a percentage of the overall value of production of that (those) product(s).**

deficit in the mid-1990s. This deficit deteriorated substantially from $20 billion to $32 billion during 1996, while the net capital inflows were reduced from $24 billion to $15.4 billion during the same year. The agrifood sector contributed significantly to the overall trade deficit. While agrifood trade showed great dynamism between 1993 and 1995, the growth of imports (+20 percent) outpaced that of exports (+17 percent). In 1995 and 1996, only Bulgaria and Hungary maintained a surplus in their trade of agricultural and food products.

The agrifood trade balances turned increasingly negative, reflecting in particular the economic slowdown in Western Europe and growing imports resulting from demand for high-quality and high-value food products on the part of a minority of affluent consumers in Central and Eastern Europe. From mid-1996, the reduced agricultural output also put a brake on exports in some countries.

Internal pressure to increase protection (to compensate for low competitiveness) and, on the other hand, external pressure to comply with international (WTO and CEFTA) commitments imposed difficult choices on policy-makers in Central and Eastern Europe. As a consequence, policies were often characterized by variability. Many countries used trade policies as short-term means for addressing domestic market problems. While import surcharges that had been introduced earlier were being reduced (e.g. in Hungary, Poland and Slovakia), several countries (sometimes the same ones) applied new import tariffs to specific products for limited periods in order to protect domestic producers. This certainly did not help stablilize business conditions or build investors' and traders' confidence.

As a positive development, trade liberalization among CEFTA countries helped intensify trade flows within the group, with trade in food and agricultural products expanding at a faster rate than total intra-CEFTA trade. The dynamic expansion of intra-CEFTA trade had varying effects on the agrifood trade balances of the various member countries (e.g. a positive impact in Slovakia but a negative impact in Poland in 1995). One reason for the asymmetric trade performances of the various countries was that they entered CEFTA with different initial levels of tariff protection. A recent significant step towards further intra-CEFTA trade

CENTRAL AND EASTERN EUROPE

liberalization was the decision taken in 1996 to apply a zero tariff rate to more than half of all agrifood products traded among the member countries. It was further decided to abolish all border restrictions by 1999.

Implementation of the CEFTA treaty in the future will require further efforts to reduce market protection to a minimum and eliminate the existing differences in market and trade policies. Such growing convergences in policies will no doubt add further momentum to agrifood trade within the area.

Agricultural trade relations between Central and Eastern Europe and the EU were strengthened further in 1996, with annual increases in the EU import quotas granted under preferential trade agreements, although the rate of utilization of such quotas varied, in extreme cases remaining under 50 percent. The countries in Central and Eastern Europe have experienced a gradual deterioration of their agrifood trade balance with the EU since 1993. This phenomenon resulted from the subregion's lower competitiveness and greater demand for high-quality food products, but other factors related to the system of quotas also played a role.

The EU import quotas under the Europe Agreements were established on the basis of pre-reform trade patterns of the Central and Eastern European countries. The fact that much trade is occurring outside the quotas shows that the system no longer fully corresponds to the present, more market-oriented, export structure of the eastern partners. Furthermore, past experience has shown that EU importing agents captured the bulk of the economic benefits through the use of quotas. In other words, the Europe Agreements did not guarantee improved export prices for the supplier countries of the East. This was a consequence of the current system of administration of the preferential EU quotas. Central and Eastern Europe could derive economic gains from a modification of the system in a way that ensures a better sharing of the preference margin as well as from an expansion in the volumes of export quotas.

From policy negotiations and discussions throughout 1996, it appeared that the enlargement of the EU towards the East would not take place before the year 2003. By that time, the EU's common agricultural policy (CAP) is likely to have undergone important changes. In this sense, the goal of adjusting to a future CAP presented itself very much as a moving target for the

Central and Eastern European countries which, by 1996, had announced their wish to join the EU. Moreover, both in the EU and the WTO member countries of the subregion, the Uruguay Round Agreement on Agriculture is expected to have an important impact on future agricultural policies. On the one hand, agricultural tariff bindings for Central and Eastern Europe have in many cases been set so high that their reduction during the lifetime of the present WTO agreement would bring little real liberalization of imports. On the other hand, WTO commitments involve increasing pressure for more liberal agricultural policies in the subregion.

Market-oriented reform and food security
In the pre-reform era, countries in the subregion had generally enjoyed a more than adequate average per caput dietary energy supply (DES), except Albania, as well as a relatively diversified diet. An abundant supply of food, affordable by all, had been a major policy objective of communist governments and had been achieved through extremely low consumer prices supported by heavy subsidization.

The process of market-oriented reform and the discontinuation of consumer subsidies, together with reduced real incomes for large segments of the population, had a profound negative impact on food demand and nutrition patterns in all countries. Average per caput dietary energy and protein supplies declined in most countries. In Bulgaria, the per caput DES declined from 3 620 to 3 160 kcal/day between 1979-81 and 1990-92, and developments in more recent years may have brought a further deterioration. In Hungary, a surplus producer of food, per caput daily protein supplies were reduced from 96 to 89 g between 1979-81 and 1992-94. In the fast-reforming CEFTA countries, food supply at the national level was not seriously affected by the reform but localized food access problems emerged, causing household food insecurity among the poorer population groups. According to some estimates, 20 to 40 percent of people in those countries were affected by poverty in the early 1990s. Their nutritional and health standards deteriorated and they received minimal attention in the form of very limited social schemes. With the generally declining trend in output, agrifood trade gained importance for the food security of countries in CEFTA.

Particularly for southeastern Europe, serious problems emerged with regard to the other fundamental dimensions of food security, i.e. the availability and stability of food supplies. In order to meet domestic food requirements, Romania had to more than double food imports during the 1990s (while its exports declined sharply). Even more serious were the experiences of Bulgaria and Albania where economic disruptions, along with failures of stockholding and trade policies, brought about grave food crises in the course of the 1990s. Since financial means for importing food on a commercial basis were not always available, Bulgaria had to resort to food aid in 1991, 1993, 1994 and 1997, as did Albania in 1997. These developments suggest that failure to deepen and consolidate economic transformation can negatively affect all dimensions of food security, even in those countries of the subregion that are best endowed with natural resources for food production.

Reduced production intensity and its environmental implications

The transition process in Central and Eastern Europe occurred along with a dramatic decline in industrial input use and investments in agriculture, thereby entailing a less intense production process. This raised the interesting question of whether such developments increased prospects for a more sustainable pattern of agricultural development in the subregion.

The reduction in the intensity of production manifested itself in drastic declines (by 55 to 75 percent) in fertilizer and pesticide use between 1989/90 and 1994/95; widespread declines in crop yields, ranging from 25 to 35 percent in grains; and important reductions in livestock density and productivity. Related aspects included a widespread appearance of subsistence farming, a reduced rate of utilization of cultivable land and an increase in agriculture's share in total employment in southeastern Europe (e.g. from 18 to 22 percent in Bulgaria and from 28 to 36 percent in Romania). In the fast-reforming countries, a declining agricultural output was accompanied by a sharp reduction in agricultural employment (e.g. by about two-thirds in Hungary and the Czech Republic from 1990 to 1996). Such declines were less accentuated in countries relying traditionally on a small-scale farm structure, i.e. in Poland and Slovenia.

CENTRAL AND EASTERN EUROPE

Although the reduced production intensity reflected changed farm input and price structures following reductions in subsidies, it was a major factor contributing to the general fall in agricultural output, investment, real agricultural incomes and profitability in the subregion. This factor was also associated with declining national food self-sufficiency rates and the deteriorating net trade position of several countries and subsectors. A positive aspect of this process was, as mentioned above, the reduced pressure on the environment.

The experience of Western Europe provides a comparative reference for examining this issue. In 1996, intensity levels of Central and Eastern European agriculture (measured by its output patterns, yields and the use of fertilizers, pesticides and machinery) lagged far behind those in Western Europe; in fact, they had been lower even before the onset of the transition process. However, already then, they had sometimes entailed very severe environmental pollution problems. Such problems were caused by unprofessional and environmentally damaging practices (such as improper storage and application of industrial inputs, high concentrations of livestock and policies exclusively oriented towards increasing physical output) rather than by very high levels of industrial inputs. The resulting ecological damage required environmental relief measures in many areas of the subregion.

In the case of Western Europe, environmentally unsound side-effects of certain agricultural practices (impacting on water, soil, natural flora and fauna as well as on produce quality) became increasingly visible during the late 1980s and early 1990s. In response, efforts were made to integrate individual agro-environmental measures into an overall policy framework. Economic incentives and administrative measures were introduced to reduce the use of fertilizers and pesticides and improve application techniques and farming practices as a means of reducing nitrate leaching, phosphorus emissions and pesticide residues. Combined with environmental conservation programmes, such measures resulted in a gradual extensification of agricultural production in several countries. In several subsectors, however, the important reduction of fertilizer and pesticide application that took place did not result in lower yields, but rather in slower

progress in land productivity. Successful results were achieved in organic farming in some EU countries (e.g. Austria, Finland and Germany), from both ecological and economic viewpoints.

What differentiates the process of extensification in Central and Eastern European countries *vis-à-vis* countries in Western Europe is that, in the former, it was a spontaneous process brought about by economic and financial difficulties at the farm level, while in Western Europe it was the result of deliberate policies aiming at a better balance of agricultural supply and demand as well as achieving sustainable agricultural and rural development.

Although some countries did introduce a number of laws and regulations with regard to the use of pesticides and the problem of residues in food, sustainable agriculture has yet to be placed in an integrated policy framework and treated as a major development objective in the subregion. With a few exceptions, such as those of Slovenia and the Czech Republic, the approach that puts output growth first, still prevailing in Central and Eastern Europe, does not yet adequately address sustainability concerns. However, such neglect of sustainability aspects could be expected to change slowly with the progressive alignment of policy-thinking with that of the EU.

With recovering economic development and hence the growing demand for food, production intensity can be expected to increase again in the years to come. Agriculture in the subregion could then take a more sustainable route. Some of the essential conditions for this to take place include:

- The elaboration of comprehensive national policies for sustainable agriculture and rural development, relying on the latest scientific research and on practical experience of environmentally sound practices, gained in particular in Western European countries and also in some Central and Eastern European countries.
- The creation of an institutional and legal framework for the planning and implementation of incentive, disincentive or punitive measures aimed at ensuring sustainability in agricultural production practices.
- The promotion of human resource development for sustainable food production. Sustainable agriculture

and rural development is a rather recent and evolving concept in the subregion. New systems of agricultural professional education, extension services, training and retraining should widely disseminate the concept of sustainable resource use and practices in agriculture. Awareness of the fundamental importance of ensuring environmental sustainability needs to be created among farm managers, whose perceptions of agricultural activity are mostly limited to productivity and profitability. In all these areas, international cooperation can provide an important contribution to the benefit of the subregion.

RUSSIAN FEDERATION

This year's subregional review of the Commonwealth of Independent States (CIS) focuses on the Russian Federation, which is continuing its transformation into a political democracy and market economy. Its macroeconomic performance has continued to improve, particularly in the area of monetary and price stabilization and, although official GDP fell in 1995 and 1996 by 4.2 and 6 percent, respectively, these declines compare favourably with the 8.7 and 12.6 percent decreases in 1993 and 1994. Further, the drops are probably overstated, given the likely understating in official statistics of new private economic activity. The decline in output can be viewed as part of the Russian Federation's vast reallocation of resources and restructuring of output as consumers' preferences replace those of state planners as the driving force of production and the country is integrated into the world economy. The country's stricter stabilization policies in 1996 paid off well, as inflation fell to 22 percent, compared with 215 and 130 percent in the two previous years, and the exchange rate stopped plummeting. In 1996, the rouble depreciated against the United States dollar in nominal terms by only 16 percent, after a total depreciation in the two previous years of 73 percent. Yet major problems remain, the most immediate being a breakdown in tax collection and economy-wide payment arrears.

The reform-induced restructuring of Russian output has strongly affected agriculture. From 1990 to 1996, total agricultural production fell by 38 percent, with the sector's share in GDP dropping from 22 to 12 percent (according to official figures, with shares in GDP measured in current prices). While production of both crops and livestock products has declined, the share of the latter in total agricultural output decreased over the period from 63 to about 45 percent. Whereas the contraction of Russian agriculture, particularly the livestock subsector, is considered to be a disaster within the sector, it can probably be more realistically assessed as an inevitable part of long-term market reform and the result of an irrational use of resources previously.

Institutional reform

Two main elements can be distinguished in Russian agricultural reform: institutional reform and economic

restructuring. Institutional reform involves privatization, land reform and the creation of market infrastructure, such as systems of commercial law, rural banking and finance. Economic restructuring, on the other hand, involves changes in the flow and use of real resources and goods in the agricultural and food economy, as indicated by changes in the volume and mix of production, consumption and trade.

Since economic reform began in early 1992, institutional reform of Russian agriculture has been slow. The state and collective farms inherited from the Soviet period continue to dominate the sector, having changed in nature and function only cosmetically. In 1996, these farms accounted for about 63 percent of the total output of livestock products and 47 percent of that of crops (including 95 percent of grain production). In 1992-93, the central government required all state and collective farms to reorganize. Their main options were to become joint stock companies (the most common choice made), partnerships, associations or cooperatives, to break up into private farms or to retain their current status. However, the official reorganization of farms has done little to change their real organization, managerial behaviour or internal incentive structure. The decline of the planned command economy in agriculture has strengthened farm managers, who resist fundamental reform in agriculture, especially to the extent that it affects their farms.

Early in the reform period, the federal government encouraged the development of private farming. The number of private farms hit its peak in 1994 at about 280 000 (although not all were functioning) and has declined slightly since then. In 1996 the share of private farms in total agricultural land was a meagre 6 percent.

A major impediment to private farming has been the absence of a meaningful land reform that establishes secure property rights in land. Land reform to date has been based mainly on a presidential decree of October 1993 (*The Regulation of Land Relations and the Development of Agrarian Reform in Russia*), buttressed by another presidential decree of March 1996. According to the 1993 decree, the (former) state and collective farms take initial possession of the land they hold and then give each farm member a land share. The share entitles the holder to a plot of land within the farm. Shareholders may farm the land obtained, rent it either

to another farmer or to their parent farm, or invest their share in the parent farm. The land can only be used for agricultural purposes and cannot be sold outside the parent farm.

Although the presidential decrees have established certain rights for potential landholders, effective land reform requires enabling legislation (specifically a land code) that establishes secure property rights in land, allowing landholders to inherit, buy, sell, lease or mortgage land freely. In summer 1995, a land code cleared its first hurdles for passage in the Russian legislature (Duma), but the Federation Council (the upper house) has rejected the code. The proposed code would recast land shares as shares in the enterprise and would no longer entitle holders to an automatic claim to land. Unanimous consent by all farm stockholders would be required to allow people either to sell their stock share or use it to establish an independent farm. Such a law would not only fail to create property rights in land, but could also block the distribution of land to aspiring private farmers. Thus, without a legislative code, land reform in the Russian Federation remains in limbo.

Another obstacle facing private farmers is the underdevelopment of the Russian Federation's commercial infrastructure, support services and credit in the rural economy. Farmers need a system for quick and inexpensive dissemination of market information, a financial system that allows fast and affordable access to capital and a strong system of commercial law that upholds contract rights. A commercial credit system for agriculture is particularly necessary. However, the lack of private property in land is retarding its development, since land cannot be used as collateral for loans. Although vulnerable private farmers are the most in need, all enterprises within the agricultural and food economy would benefit from a more developed commercial market infrastructure.

Although private farming has hardly flourished during the reform period, the share of agricultural output produced on private plots has grown to about 46 percent (while still comprising only about 6 percent of total farmland). These plots produce the bulk of the country's potatoes and vegetables and about half of its meat and milk. Most of the output is either consumed by the plot holders or sold directly to consumers in farmers' markets.

The main reform-induced institutional change in Russian agriculture has been the erosion of the state procurement system, as a growing share of output is being sold through private channels. In 1996, state procurement of grain equalled only 12 percent of production, with the bulk of purchases being made by regional rather than federal authorities. Although commodity exchanges were the first private marketing channel for grain, private traders have since eclipsed them. Compared with the state, private traders have offered producers higher prices and prompt payment.

Economic restructuring

Although institutional reform in Russian agriculture has been slight, economic reform has triggered major economic restructuring. The policy changes that have spurred the restructuring most have been price liberalization and the reduction of subsidies to the agricultural and food economy. Although price liberalization and decreases in subsidies have been imposed on agriculture mainly as part of the government's larger macroeconomic stabilization programme, the policy changes have substantially affected farms' decisions concerning input use and output.

The price liberalization begun in early 1992 has freed prices for almost all agricultural inputs and output. The exceptions are: continued (although diminished) state procurement, resulting in some de facto fixing of producer prices; controlled energy prices kept below world prices (although they are rising); and regional and local governments' continued regulation (to a certain degree) of consumer prices for foodstuffs. In 1990, Soviet subsidies to the agricultural and food economy equalled 10 percent of GDP, while in 1995 and 1996 Russian agricultural subsidies represented only about 4 percent of GDP. Furthermore, the nature of subsidies has changed: explicit budget subsidies (especially for inputs) have fallen while indirect subsidies have increased, the two main types being tax exemptions and the writing-off of debts to the state.

The main development in the economic restructuring of Russian agriculture has been the severe contraction of the livestock sector. From 1990 to 1996, inventories of cattle, hogs and poultry dropped by 32, 43 and 33 percent, respectively. Output of meat decreased over the

CENTRAL
AND EASTERN EUROPE

period from 10.1 to 5.4 million tonnes, milk from 55.7 to 36 million tonnes and eggs from 47.5 to 31.5 billion pieces.

By the late 1980s, Soviet per caput consumption of most livestock products equalled that of many OECD countries. Since real per caput Soviet GDP was at most only half the OECD average, the former USSR was producing and consuming high-value livestock goods at a much greater level than one would have expected, given the country's real wealth and income.

When economic reform liberalized prices and reduced subsidies, consumer prices jumped in response to the high costs of production, not only for foodstuffs but for all consumer goods. With prices rising more than wages, consumers' real incomes fell. As a result, demand for foods with a high income elasticity,[63] such as meat and other livestock products, dropped. Demand for food with a low income elasticity did not fall by much, and in the case of such staples as bread and potatoes it actually increased.

Price liberalization also had the negative supply side-effect of worsening producers' terms of trade, not only for the livestock sector, but for agriculture as a whole. From 1991 to 1996, the percentage increase in agricultural input prices was four times that for output prices. The deterioration in terms of trade following price liberalization was a result of the fact that, during the Soviet period, agriculture was not only subsidized through direct subsidies but also indirectly through the price system.

Another way in which reform has hurt the livestock sector is by opening the country up to foreign competition. From 1992 to 1996, total Russian meat imports increased from 700 000 to 2.2 million tonnes. Poultry led the surge, with imports soaring over the period from 55 000 to 950 000 tonnes. The growth of meat imports is part of a more general shift in Russian agricultural and food imports towards high-value products, especially in trade with countries that were not part of the former USSR. In 1996, high-value products accounted for about 90 percent of Russian agricultural and food imports from these nations.

The main reason why meat imports have grown, despite falling consumer demand for livestock goods in general, is that the Russian Federation is a high-cost producer of meat. During the 1980s, the USSR had a

[63] **High income elasticity indicates that a change in consumers' income will lead to a large change in their demand for a given good; low income elasticity, on the other hand, implies that consumers' demand for a good is less sensitive to their level of income. This will typically be the case for staple foods.**

[64] R. Koopman. 1991.
Agriculture's role during the
transition from plan to
market: real prices, real
incentives, and potential
equilibrium. In *Economic
Statistics for Economies in
Transition: Eastern Europe in
the 1990s*, p. 127-156.
Washington, DC, US Bureau
of Labor Statistics and
Eurostat; W. Liefert, R.
Koopman and E. Cook. 1993.
Agricultural reform in the
former USSR. *Comparative
Economic Studies*, 35: 49-68;
R. Tyers. 1994. *Economic
reform in Europe and the
former Soviet Union:
implications for international
food markets.* Research
Report No. 99. Washington,
DC, IFPRI.

greater comparative disadvantage in the production of meat than in machinery and equipment, and also a greater disadvantage in meat compared with grain.[64] Since the Russian Federation is a higher-cost producer of meat than Ukraine or Belarus, if the former USSR in the aggregate had a comparative disadvantage in meat, this is particularly so for the Russian Federation.

The price of Russian meat is uncompetitive, not only because of the high costs of primary production but also because of the considerable expense of transporting output from production sites to the locations in the Federation (mainly the large cities) where domestic output competes with imports. These distribution costs are high largely because of deficiencies in the physical and institutional infrastructure for interregional movement of agricultural output. Another advantage of imported meat over domestic output is its superior quality, not necessarily in terms of the pure product but for its variety, packaging, shelf-life and ease of preparation. The growing inequality of income distribution resulting from reform has created an upper-income class of Russian consumers who particularly value higher-quality Western foods.

The crop sector has also been restructuring. Although production of vegetables has remained stable, that of potatoes has increased, while output of grain and sugarbeet has dropped substantially. Average annual grain production fell from 104 million tonnes in 1986-90 to 71 million tonnes in 1994-96, while the corresponding drop for sugar beet was from 33 million to 16 million tonnes.

The contraction of the livestock sector has strongly affected the grain economy, by reducing the demand for animal feed. Production of grain, as well as that of other crops, has also suffered the shock of worsening terms of trade following price liberalization. For some years now, Russian fertilizer producers have been exporting the bulk of their output for hard currency, and energy producers can also obtain higher prices by selling on the world market than to domestic farms. With the state no longer guaranteeing input supplies and farms facing much higher real prices for resources, crop producers have severely reduced their use of inputs – machinery, fertilizer, pesticides and fuel. Yet for most crops, yields have dropped by a much lower percentage than input use. In fact, the average annual grain yield of 1.44

tonnes per hectare during the 1990s is almost unchanged from the 1980s. This suggests that higher prices and reduced input availability have motivated farms to use their limited resources more productively.

The downsizing of the livestock sector has also substantially reduced Russian imports of grain and virtually eliminated imports of soybeans and soybean meal. In 1994/95 (July/June) and 1995/96, Russian net grain imports equalled only 0.2 and 5 million tonnes, respectively, compared with an average annual figure for 1987-92 of 22 million tonnes. Net annual imports of soybeans and soybean meal in 1995-96 averaged only 8 000 and 57 000 tonnes.

Trade policy

Since the beginning of reforms, Russian agricultural trade policy has switched from controls on exports to restrictions on imports. In 1992, the government closely controlled agricultural exports, using quotas, licences, taxes and even complete bans on exports. By 1994, almost all export controls at the national level had been lifted and import restrictions began to be imposed. There are two main reasons for the shift in trade policy. The first is that reform is forcing farms to become more self-financing and more responsible for marketing their output, i.e. to function like competitive, market-oriented producers. The new overriding concern to sell their output (and at the highest possible price) has motivated farms to lobby for the type of state support that is more common to market than planned economies – for instance measures restricting foreign competition.

The second reason is that the substantial appreciation of the rouble in real terms during the reform period has hurt the competitiveness of producers (not only in agriculture, but throughout the economy) by making imports less expensive relative to domestic output. Indeed, although the rouble has depreciated in nominal terms, the inflation rate has exceeded the rate of nominal depreciation, thereby leading to an appreciation of the currency in real terms. Thus, since the end of 1992, the rouble has appreciated in real terms *vis-à-vis* the United States dollar by about 600 percent.

Russian import restrictions are nevertheless moderate. Tariffs range from 2 to 10 percent for most crops and 10 to 30 percent for livestock products. There are no quotas or other quantitative restrictions on imports. However,

pressure for greater protectionism from the agricultural establishment is growing. Although attempts in 1996 to create import quotas for sugar, ethyl alcohol and vodka failed, licensing has been established for imports of the latter two products.

Two factors which should check the pressure for agricultural protection are opposition from the main import-consuming areas (mainly the large cities) and the Russian Federation's desire to join WTO (the country applied for accession to the General Agreement on Tariffs and Trade in 1993, which WTO replaced as an organization in 1995). The Agreement on Agriculture, negotiated during the recently completed Uruguay Round, forbids import quotas and any other quantitative import restrictions (although it allows tariff rate quotas). As a condition of WTO membership, the Russian Federation must also accept negotiated maximum allowable tariffs for agricultural products.

Long-term outlook and policy issues

The Russian livestock sector will probably continue to contract for another two to three years, and any subsequent growth is unlikely to be rapid. The country is also likely to remain a major importer of meat and high-value products in general for a long time to come.

Budget stringency and opposition from reform liberals should preclude any return to the generous subsidies on livestock production in previous years. A substantial strengthening of trade protection for the industry is also unlikely, for the reasons mentioned above. One development that could conceivably help the sector would be increasing consumer demand stemming from rising real incomes. Some experts consider that the country's real GDP will probably begin to grow within one to two years, and evidence indicates that real incomes are already increasing. However, given that the Russian Federation is currently uncompetitive in livestock production *vis-à-vis* the world market, in terms of both costs and quality, the bulk of any rise in consumer demand would probably be met by an increase in imports rather than domestic output.

For these reasons, any major increase in livestock output and drop in imports would require a reduction in domestic production and marketing costs. Lowering production costs involves input prices and productivity. Although livestock producers' terms of trade improved

**CENTRAL
AND EASTERN EUROPE**

slightly in 1995, they appear to have worsened again in 1996. Since Russian energy prices are still below world levels, although they are steadily approaching them, aggregate real input prices are likely to rise rather than fall in the near to medium term. Nor are the prospects for farm productivity growth encouraging, as no major institutional reforms are foreseen that could significantly improve incentives to use inputs more efficiently. The unreformed former state and collective farms continue to dominate production, private farming is stillborn and private plots, where livestock output has been growing, cannot serve as the basis for modern competitive agriculture. In addition, commercial market infrastructure, which is necessary to lower domestic transaction costs, is likely to continue developing only slowly.

If the Russian meat industry fails to cut its costs of production and distribution, the country's comparative disadvantage in meat will persist. The industry is also unlikely in the near future to improve the quality and appeal of output relative to imports. For these reasons, Russian annual net meat imports for the next ten years could well remain at about 2 million tonnes, with poultry perhaps accounting for about half that volume.

A bright spot, however, is that in 1996 the rouble stopped appreciating in real terms against Western currencies, thereby eliminating the exchange rate as a cause of worsening trade competitiveness. If prices and the nominal exchange rate continue to stabilize, which appears likely, the rouble will also remain generally stable in real terms.

In the early 1990s, a number of studies forecast that successful economic reform in the Russian Federation could turn the country into a non-trivial exporter of grain, with possible net exports of 10 million to 20 million tonnes.[65] A major assumption behind the forecasts is that agricultural reform would improve productivity in the grain economy. After five years of reform, however, the country is still a net grain importer (5 million tonnes in 1995/96).

The studies did not anticipate the worsening of agriculture's cost structure as input prices move towards world market levels following price and trade liberalization. Although higher input prices and a reduced use of inputs have motivated grain producers to use resources more efficiently and waste less, the deeper

[65] See footnote 64, p. 212.

institutional reform that could improve productivity even more has not yet occurred. Without the cost reduction that would follow from this productivity growth, Russian grain will probably not be sufficiently competitive on world markets to result in major exports. Yet the Russian Federation is also unlikely to return to being a major grain importer. The contraction of the livestock sector has ended its large demand for imported feedgrain for the long term. Also, in contrast to meat, the country does not appear to be such a high-cost producer of grain *vis-à-vis* the world market; grain is a more homogeneous product, which lowers the potential quality difference between foreign and domestic output, and it is also less perishable than meat, which means the costs and risks in internal transport are relatively lower.

Thus, in the absence of major institutional reform, the Russian Federation is likely to be either a small net importer or exporter of grain, with its trade balance probably not exceeding 5 million tonnes either way.[66] If it does export, the most likely products are barley and other coarse grains. The large imports of soybeans and soybean meal are also unlikely to return, although annual soybean meal imports of a couple of hundred thousand tonnes are possible.

The only feasible reform-consistent way by which agriculture can rebound and improve its competitiveness *vis-à-vis* the world market appears to be through institutional reform that improves productivity and lowers production and distribution costs. Regardless of how primary production is organized, the sector needs a stronger system of supportive commercial infrastructure, in particular a system of rural finance, and a land code that establishes secure property rights in land. These two supports are particularly important for the growth of private farming.

Some observers of Russian agriculture argue that institutional reform of the sector can proceed only if the government breaks up the former state and collective farms. One development, however, that would help these farms function in the new market-oriented environment would be to relieve them of the burden of providing for their workers' social welfare needs (housing, health, education, entertainment). Although, in some areas, local governments have begun to take over these responsibilities, the process could be accelerated.

Effective agricultural policy must also be consistent

---

[66] The studies previously identified (footnote 64, p. 212) predict that, in the absence of productivity gains stemming from agricultural reform, the Russian Federation would be a small net importer of grain. In addition, the studies forecast that, with less than strong reform, the country would remain a net importer of meat.

CENTRAL AND EASTERN EUROPE

with the general policy goals of economic reform. The main reform objectives are likely to remain macroeconomic stabilization, privatization and development of the institutional base of a market economy, and integration into the world economy (with admission to WTO as a top priority). The implications of these goals for the agricultural and food economy are that markets must be the fundamental determinant of prices for inputs and output, subsidies to agriculture must continue to fall, trade barriers must remain mild and privatization must be reinvigorated.

The policy goals of the conservative Russian agricultural establishment differ from those of the more reformist federal government. The main stated objective of the former is to achieve as high a level of agricultural self-sufficiency as possible. The identified means to this end, for which agricultural interest groups lobby strongly, are increased state subsidies, "price parity" (which would require the government to fix prices for inputs and output to agriculture's advantage) and protection against imports. The conservative agricultural establishment fails to provide inspiration for, and often blocks, reform within the sector. Pushing reform forward without the support of the country's main agricultural interests remains one of the government's top challenges.

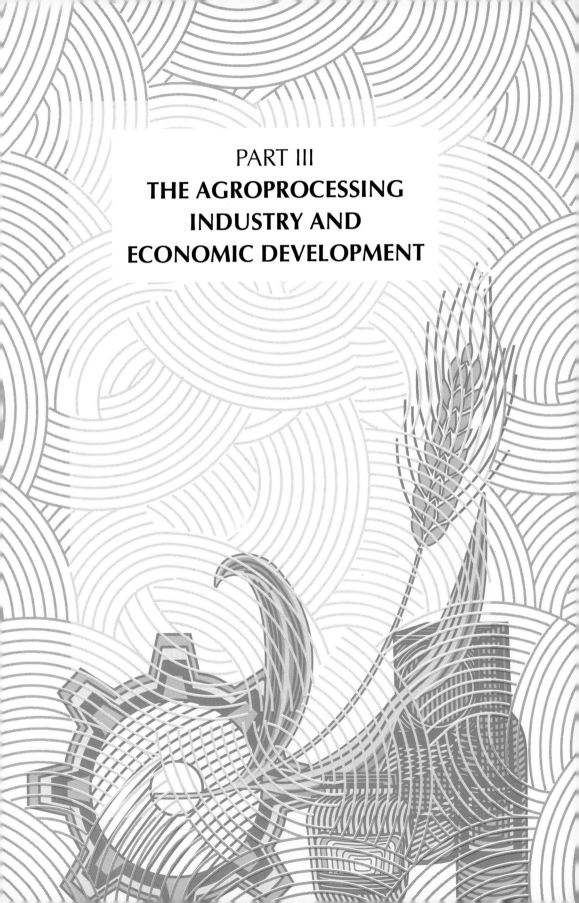

PART III
THE AGROPROCESSING INDUSTRY AND ECONOMIC DEVELOPMENT

THE AGROPROCESSING INDUSTRY AND ECONOMIC DEVELOPMENT

INTRODUCTION

Agriculture and industry have traditionally been viewed as two separate sectors both in terms of their characteristics and their role in economic growth. Agriculture has been considered the hallmark of the first stage of development, while the degree of industrialization has been taken to be the most relevant indicator of a country's progress along the development path. Moreover, the proper strategy for growth has often been conceived as one of a more or less gradual shift from agriculture to industry, with the onus on agriculture to finance the shift in the first stage.

This view, however, no longer appears to be appropriate. On the one hand, the role of agriculture in the process of development has been reappraised and revalued from the point of view of its contribution to industrialization and its importance for harmonious development and political and economic stability. On the other hand, agriculture itself has become a form of industry, as technology, vertical integration, marketing and consumer preferences have evolved along lines that closely follow the profile of comparable industrial sectors, often of notable complexity and richness of variety and scope. This has meant that the deployment of resources in agriculture has become increasingly responsive to market forces and increasingly integrated in the network of industrial interdependencies. Agricultural products are shaped by technologies of growing complexity, and they incorporate the results of major research and development efforts as well as increasingly sophisticated individual and collective preferences regarding nutrition, health and the environment. While one can still distinguish the phase of production of raw materials from the processing and transformation phase, often this distinction is blurred by the complexity of technology and the extent of vertical integration: the industrialization of agriculture and development of agroprocessing industries is thus a joint process which is generating an entirely new type of industrial sector.

This chapter attempts to review some of these issues and assess the actual and potential role of the agroprocessing industry in economic development. It starts by discussing the definition of the sector and reviewing some of the statistical evidence of its economic importance worldwide. It then moves on to a discussion of the role that the agroprocessing industry can play in economic development in the developing countries, before reviewing how conditions for agro-industrial development are currently changing worldwide as a result of changing trade policies and regimes and the evolution of both technology and food consumption patterns. The chapter then underlines the growing internationalization of agroprocessing activities, in particular through the increasing importance of international capital activities, and the role played by multinational corporations in this process. Finally, it discusses elements of a conducive policy environment for promoting the agroprocessing industry and for ensuring that the sector can provide the optimum contribution to economic development.

AGROPROCESSING INDUSTRY: DEFINITION AND DIMENSIONS
Types of agroprocessing

A common and traditional definition of agroprocessing industry refers to the subset of manufacturing that processes raw materials and intermediate products derived from the agricultural sector. Agroprocessing industry thus means transforming products originating from agriculture, forestry and fisheries.

Indeed, a very large part of agricultural production undergoes some degree of transformation between harvesting and final use. The industries that use agricultural, fishery and forest products as raw materials comprise a very varied group. They range from simple preservation (such as sun drying) and operations closely related to harvesting to the production, by modern, capital-intensive methods, of such articles as textiles, pulp and paper.

The food industries are much more homogeneous and are easier to classify than the non-food industries since their products all have the same end use. Most preservation techniques, for example, are basically similar over a whole range of perishable food products, whether they be fruit, vegetables, milk, meat or fish. In fact, the processing of the more perishable food products is to a large extent for the purpose of preservation.

Non-food industries, in contrast to the food industries, have a wide variety of end uses. Almost all non-food agricultural products require a high degree of processing. Much more markedly than with the food industries, there is usually a definite sequence of operations, leading through various intermediate products before reaching the final product. Because of the value added at each of these successive stages of processing, the proportion of the total cost represented by the original raw material diminishes steadily. A further feature of the non-food industries is that many of them now increasingly use synthetics and other artificial substitutes (especially fibres) in combination with natural raw materials.

Another useful classification of agroprocessing industry is in upstream and downstream industries. Upstream industries are engaged in the initial processing of agricultural commodities. Examples are rice and flour milling, leather tanning, cotton ginning, oil pressing, saw milling and fish canning. Downstream industries undertake further manufacturing operations on intermediate products made from agricultural materials. Examples are bread, biscuit and noodle making, textile spinning and weaving; paper production; clothing and footwear manufacturing; and rubber manufactures.

A further specification is related to the nature of the production process which, in many cases, can range from craft to industrial organization. For example, in some developing countries the same good may be produced both by handloom weavers working in their own home and by large textile factories that have sophisticated machinery and complex systems of organization and that produce a range of industrial products for the domestic and external markets. In such cases, it can be misleading to define agroprocessing industry just on the basis of the goods produced because only the second method of production mentioned has industrial characteristics.

Today, however, it is becoming even more difficult to provide a precise demarcation of what should be considered an agro-industrial activity: the impact of innovation processes and new technologies suggests a widening of the range of agro-industry[1] inputs that could

be considered, including biotechnological and synthetic products, for example. This implies that agro-industry today continues to process simple agricultural goods while also transforming highly sophisticated industrial inputs that are often the result of considerable investments in research, technology and innovation. Corresponding to this growing complexity of inputs is an increasing range of transformation processes, characterized by physical and chemical alteration and aimed at improving the marketability of raw materials according to the final end use.

All these factors – the growing complexity of inputs, the impact of innovation processes and new technologies, the sophistication and the growing range of the transformation processes – makes it increasingly difficult to draw a clear distinction between what should be considered strictly industry and what can be classified as agro-industry.

According to the traditional classification of the UN International Standard Industrial Classification of All Economic Activities (ISIC), which is quite rigid but useful for statistical purposes, agro-industrial production is present in many manufacturing sectors: 3.1 Manufacture of Food, Beverages and Tobacco; 3.2 Textile, Wearing Apparel and Leather Industries; 3.3 Manufacture of Wood and Wood Products, Including Furniture; 3.4 Manufacture of Paper and Paper products, Printing and Publishing;

---

[1] The term "agro-industry", sometimes used in this chapter as a convenient abbreviation of "agroprocessing industry", should not be understood to comprise industries supplying agriculture with industrial machinery, inputs and tools.

TABLE 3

Share of agro-industries in total manufacturing value added[1] in selected country groups, 1980 and 1994[2]

Country groups	Food, beverages, tobacco (3.1)		Textiles, clothing, leather, footwear (3.2)		Wood products, furniture (3.3)		Paper & products, printing (3.4)		Rubber products (3.5.5)		All agro-industry (3.1-3.4, 3.5.5)	
	1980	1994	1980	1994	1980	1994	1980	1994	1980	1994	1980	1994
Industrialized countries	13.3	12.6	8.3	5.7	3.6	3.1	7.9	8.9	1.2	1.1	34.3	31.4
EC	11.9	13.5	8.5	6.0	3.7	3.4	6.8	7.6	1.3	1.1	32.2	31.6
Japan	11.3	9.4	7.2	4.3	4.4	2.3	8.8	9.2	1.4	1.2	33.1	26.4
North America	13.7	11.9	6.4	4.8	2.8	3.0	11.4	11.3	1.0	1.1	35.3	32.1
Eastern Europe and CIS	20.8	20.5	14.4	13.7	2.7	3.2	2.2	1.8	1.4	1.1	41.5	40.3
Developing countries	18.2	17.7	15.2	11.4	2.8	2.2	4.3	4.6	1.5	1.7	42.0	37.6
NIEs[3]	15.1	14.5	15.0	10.8	2.4	1.6	4.5	5.0	1.6	1.8	38.6	33.7
Second-generation NIEs[4]	23.5	19.7	16.2	13.0	3.2	3.8	3.3	3.8	2.0	2.2	48.2	42.5

Note: ISIC classifications in parentheses.
[1] At constant 1990 prices.
[2] 1993 for developing countries.
[3] NIEs = Argentina, Brazil, Mexico, former Yugoslavia, Hong Kong, India, the Republic of Korea, Singapore and Taiwan Province of China.
[4] Second-generation NIEs = Morocco, Tunisia, Chile, Turkey, Indonesia, Malaysia, the Philippines and Thailand.
Source: UNIDO. 1997. International Yearbook of Industrial Statistics 1997. Vienna.

3.5.5 Manufacture of rubber products. Although this chapter is about all these areas of agro-industry, it often focuses on the particularly important group of food, beverages and tobacco.

Agroprocessing industry in figures
Table 3 shows the contribution of agro-industries to total manufacturing value added (MVA) in selected country groups in 1980 and 1993-94, based on the broad ISIC classification outlined above. Even in the most advanced economies, these industries represent a large part of total industrial activity. In industrialized countries, while primary agriculture

accounts for a very small proportion of total output, the various industries derived from agricultural transformation represented nearly one-third of total MVA in 1994. The share is even higher (37.6 percent) in developing countries, where agro-industry is often the main industrial activity and a major contributor to production, export earnings and employment. However, the share of agro-industries has dropped by around three to four percentage points in both developing and industrialized countries since 1980, slightly more in the former and slightly less in the latter.

The major component of agro-industrial activities in both industrialized and developing countries is composed of the food, beverages and tobacco industry, which accounted in 1994 for about 13 percent of total MVA in the industrialized countries and 18 percent in the developing countries, although the share has also been declining in both groups.

As regards the distribution of world value added in the various branches of agro-industry, the share of the developing countries has increased significantly in all branches, reaching close to one-third of the world total in tobacco, footwear and textiles and also rising considerably in the cases of beverages and leather between 1980 and 1994 (Table 4).

Among the industrialized countries, a strong advance was made by the European Community (EC) in food products, beverages, tobacco and leather which, however, went along with relative declines in most other agro-industrial branches. North America strengthened its market dominance in wood and paper products, and also increased significantly its share in the rubber and textile industries. By contrast, steep relative declines occurred in Eastern Europe and the CIS, where problems of economic transition imposed a heavy toll on, *inter alia*, agro-industrial activity. Shares in output in this region declined for all branches, from around three percentage points for footwear, wood products and tobacco, to up to nine or ten points for food, beverages, textiles and leather.

The overall gains in contribution to output by the developing countries were reflected in the faster rates of expansion of their industries compared with those of the industrialized countries during 1980-94 (Table 5). Their rate of growth exceeded those of industrial and transition economies for all branches of industrial activity during the 1980s, and again in 1990-94. Rubber and paper were particularly buoyant throughout the period, as was the beverage industry in 1990-94.

The food, beverages and tobacco industries combined are by far the most important component of agro-industrial activities in both developed and developing countries, and also account for a sizeable share of their overall economic output. In the case of the developing countries, food, beverages and tobacco manufacturing account for about 3 to 4 percent of GDP, the share in the various regions showing a remarkable convergence over the past decades (Figure 13).

Latin America and the Caribbean stands apart from the other regions, however. While the economic weight of the subsector has been historically greater in this region, it has tended to lose relative importance since the mid-1980s, in contrast to the other regions where it has tended to increase. Most notable is the steady rise in Asia and the Pacific throughout much of the 1970s and 1980s, a trend which has continued also in the 1990s.

TABLE 4

Distribution of world[1] value added by branch of agro-industry, 1980 and 1993[2]

Branch (ISIC)	Year	Industrialized countries and economies in transition					Developing		World[1]
		All	EU	Japan	North America	Eastern Europe and CIS	All	NIEs	
Food	1980	85.5	28.0	14.8	22.3	16.3	14.5	7.4	100.0
(3.1.1/2)	1994	82.0	32.3	13.7	24.7	6.9	18.0	9.0	100.0
Beverages	1980	79.3	32.6	10.4	18.6	14.0	20.7	11.1	100.0
(3.1.3)	1994	73.2	36.3	8.8	19.2	4.8	26.8	13.6	100.0
Tobacco	1980	73.7	33.7	3.2	29.3	5.8	26.3	12.2	100.0
(3.1.4)	1994	66.8	35.9	2.8	23.4	2.8	33.2	14.7	100.0
Textiles	1980	78.1	29.3	14.4	14.0	17.9	21.9	13.2	100.0
(3.2.1)	1994	71.3	29.7	11.4	19.0	8.8	28.7	16.5	100.0
Wearing apparel	1980	81.5	34.2	11.1	21.7	11.6	18.5	10.9	100.0
(3.2.2)	1994	76.0	29.3	10.3	25.9	7.4	24.0	12.6	100.0
Leather	1980	76.7	34.6	9.9	12.0	18.9	23.3	15.3	100.0
(3.2.3)	1994	72.2	39.1	10.4	11.5	9.1	27.8	18.1	100.0
Footwear	1980	74.1	42.1	4.4	13.1	11.7	25.9	17.6	100.0
(3.2.4)	1994	69.3	41.8	6.4	8.5	9.2	30.7	20.0	100.0
Wood products	1980	89.6	33.5	22.1	19.4	7.6	10.4	4.9	100.0
(3.3.1)	1994	87.8	34.4	14.7	27.5	4.3	12.2	4.0	100.0
Paper	1980	90.4	33.1	12.7	35.0	6.1	9.6	6.3	100.0
(3.4.1)	1994	88.3	33.5	13.4	36.5	1.5	11.7	7.7	100.0
Rubber	1980	84.9	36.3	17.2	17.6	11.3	15.1	10.1	100.0
(3.5.5)	1994	78.2	31.7	16.2	24.3	3.7	21.8	14.2	100.0
All manufactures	1980	87.1	35.7	14.2	23.9	9.5	12.9	8.2	100.0
(3.1-3.9)	1994	83.5	33.0	17.1	25.9	4.2	16.5	9.8	100.0

[1] Excluding China, for which data were not available.
[2] At constant 1990 prices.
Source: UNIDO. 1997. *International Yearbook of Industrial Statistics 1997.* Vienna.

TABLE 5

Average annual growth of value added in agro-industries by country groups, 1980-90 and 1990-94[1]

Branch (ISIC)	Industrialized countries		Eastern Europe and CIS		Developing countries	
	1980-90	1990-94	1980-90	1990-94	1980-90	1990-94
Food (3.1.1/2)	1.8	1.4	1.7	..	2.6	3.4
Beverages (3.1.3)	1.8	1.2	-1.7	..	2.6	4.9
Tobacco (3.1.4)	0.0	-1.4	0.4	..	1.8	2.1
Textiles (3.2.1)	0.2	-1.5	1.1	..	2.2	0.8
Wearing apparel (3.2.2)	-0.6	-2.3	1.7	..	2.4	-1.7
Leather (3.2.3)	-1.4	-4.1	0.0	..	0.7	-3.6
Footwear (3.2.4)	-3.1	-3.5	2.4	..	-0.4	-2.4
Wood products (3.3.1)	1.6	-0.1	2.1	..	2.1	..
Paper (3.4.1)	3.4	1.8	1.2	..	4.3	4.5
Rubber (3.5.5)	2.6	-0.3	1.4	..	4.9	3.9
Total MVA	2.8	-0.4	2.5	-10.1	4.4	3.5

[1] At constant 1990 prices.
Source: UNIDO. 1997. *International Yearbook of Industrial Statistics 1997.* Vienna.

At the global level, the food, beverages and tobacco industries are dominated by the developed countries, which in 1994 accounted for about 80 percent of the world value added in the subsector, with western Europe and North America together accounting for nearly 60 percent (Figure 14).

In the developing countries, the lion's share of total production in the subsector is accounted for by Asia and the Pacific and Latin America and the Caribbean, each with approximately 45 percent of developing country production (Figure 15). Yet, while Latin America and the Caribbean, once dominant among the developing country regions, has seen its share decline significantly in the course of the 1980s from the 50 to 60 percent of the 1970s, the share of Asia and the Pacific has expanded rapidly over the same time span. The decline in the relative position of sub-Saharan Africa has

been dramatic: after peaking in 1983, its share in developing country production has contracted steadily, falling below that of the Near East and North Africa.

Expressed as a ratio to agricultural GDP, value added in food, beverages and tobacco provides a broad indicator of the importance of processing relative to primary agriculture (Figure 16). As emerges from the figure, processing has always been an important component of overall agrifood production in Latin America and the Caribbean, indicating a relatively greater sophistication of the whole food chain in that region. However, processing has tended to lose importance *vis-à-vis* total agricultural GDP since the early 1980s in this region.

In all the other developing regions, processing has gained in importance relative to primary agricultural production, most notably so in the case of Asia and the Pacific.

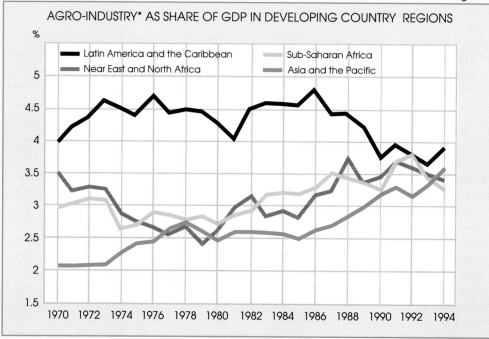

Figure 13

AGRO-INDUSTRY* AS SHARE OF GDP IN DEVELOPING COUNTRY REGIONS

Source: FAO, World Bank and UNIDO   *Food, beverages and tobacco value added

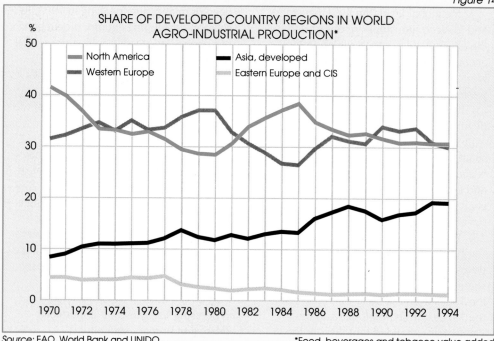

Figure 14

SHARE OF DEVELOPED COUNTRY REGIONS IN WORLD
AGRO-INDUSTRIAL PRODUCTION*

Source: FAO, World Bank and UNIDO   *Food, beverages and tobacco value added

Figure 15

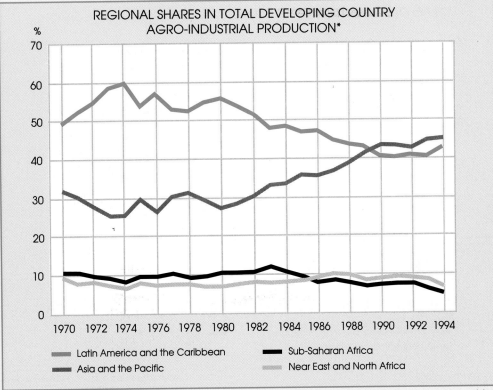

REGIONAL SHARES IN TOTAL DEVELOPING COUNTRY
AGRO-INDUSTRIAL PRODUCTION*

Legend:
- Latin America and the Caribbean
- Asia and the Pacific
- Sub-Saharan Africa
- Near East and North Africa

Source: FAO, World Bank and UNIDO   *Food, beverages and tobacco value added

Figure 16

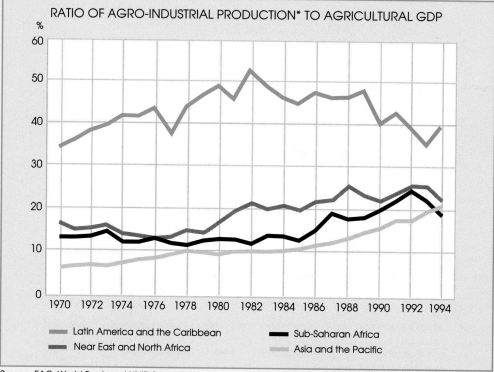

RATIO OF AGRO-INDUSTRIAL PRODUCTION* TO AGRICULTURAL GDP

Source: FAO, World Bank and UNIDO   *Food, beverages and tobacco value added

DEVELOPMENTAL ROLE OF THE AGROPROCESSING INDUSTRY

Theoretical and empirical studies of the structural changes that accompany the development process have revealed a number of constant patterns. The most basic is a secular decline in the relative weight of the agricultural sector *vis-à-vis* non-agriculture as per caput income increases. This relative decline is observed as a fall in the share of agriculture in value added, employment, trade and per caput consumption. This goes together with a drop in the share of primary agricultural production in the value of the final product, and with a parallel increase in the agroprocessing industry value added.

These observations have emanated the popular prescription that development necessarily involves a transfer of resources out of agriculture and that this is largely coterminous with industrial development. More recently, however, the development debate has increasingly focused on the far more relevant issue of whether and how the agricultural sector can be expected to make an optimum contribution to the overall process of economic growth. This question can be asked both regarding the size and functioning of the agricultural sector itself and regarding its links with the rest of the economy. More specifically, it can be argued that the development of agro-industry, for those countries with a comparative advantage in this sector, may contribute to achieving the proper balance between agriculture and industry.

A precise theoretical rationale for emphasizing the role of agro-industry during the process of development is provided by Hirschman's linkage hypothesis,[2] which postulates that the best development path lies in selecting those activities where progress will induce further progress elsewhere. Thus, an activity that shows a high degree of interdependence, as measured by the proportion of output sold to or purchased from other industries, can provide a strong stimulus to economic growth. While the issue of linkages will be discussed in some detail later, the general observation can be made here that, because of its high degree of interdependence with forward and backward activities, agro-industry can play a very important role in accelerating economic activity.

Potential for agro-industry in developing countries

The potential for agro-industrial development in the developing countries is largely linked to the relative abundance of agricultural raw materials and low-cost labour in most of them. The most suitable industries in such conditions are indeed those that make relatively intensive use of these abundant raw materials and unskilled labour and relatively less intensive use of presumably scarce capital and skilled labour.

Many of the industries using agricultural raw materials have in fact those characteristics that make them particularly suitable for the circumstances of many developing countries. Where the raw material represents a large proportion of total costs, its ready availability at a reasonable cost can often offset such disadvantages as a lack of infrastructure or skilled labour. Furthermore, for many agro-industries, a small plant may be economically efficient, which is another important factor in developing countries where the domestic market is limited by

[2] A.O. Hirschman. 1958. *The strategy of economic development*. New Haven, USA, Yale University Press.

BOX 11
LABOUR PRODUCTIVITY AND COST STRUCTURE IN AGRO-INDUSTRY

Value added per employee varies widely, both among countries and among different branches of agro-industry. The Table (column 1) shows value added per employee in food processing for selected countries, ranging from a high of $102 300 per worker in the United States to a low of $1 700 in India, among the countries covered. The disparities are also substantial – more than 10:1 – between NIEs (e.g. the Republic of Korea, Singapore and Hong Kong) and the low-income countries (e.g. China, Kenya and India), no doubt reflecting differences in the technologies used as well as in managerial and operative skills. The Table (column 2) also shows that, as expected, wage levels rise with

Selected indicators for the food industry[1] in various countries, 1991-93

Countries	Value added per employee ($'000)	Wages per employee ($'000)	Percentage in output		
			Materials and utilities (%)	Labour (%)	Operating surplus (%)
INDUSTRIALIZED					
United States	102.3	24.0	61.8	8.9	29.3
Germany	87.3	27.8	66.2	10.8	23.0
Japan	83.3	26.7	60.7	12.6	26.7
Italy	66.1	..	79.5	12.4	8.1
France	63.8	..	69.5	15.3	11.4
United Kingdom	56.0	20.9	64.8	13.2	22.0
Russian Federation	8.4	1.9	62.9	8.3	28.8
DEVELOPING					
Korea, Rep.	50.1	10.7	60.0	8.6	31.4
Singapore	37.5	14.6	68.2	12.4	19.4
Chile	25.7	5.1	62.1	7.6	30.3
Hong Kong	23.6	11.4	66.3	16.3	17.4
Malaysia	15.2	3.6	84.5	3.7	11.8
Thailand	12.3	2.0	72.8	4.5	22.7
Ghana	6.9	1.4	65.0	7.4	27.7
Indonesia	6.1	0.6	64.8	3.7	31.5
China	3.8	3.5	71.0	3.5	12.5
Kenya	2.8	0.7	93.1	1.6	5.3
India	1.7	0.7	89.7	4.2	6.1

[1] ISIC 3.1.1/1.2.

Source: UNIDO. 1996. *International Yearbook of Industrial Statistics 1996.* Vienna.

productivity. In food products, annual wages per employee range from a low of $600 in Indonesia to a high of $27 800 in Germany. Workers in the food industry in Singapore are paid 20 times as much on average as those in Kenya and India.

As for the cost structure, raw materials and utilities (water and power) account for well over half the total cost of production in food processing (column 3). In most countries the cost of these inputs represents between 60 and 90 percent of the gross value of production. The proportion tends to fall as productivity rises. Peak levels were found in Kenya and India, where the cost of raw materials and utilities constituted 93.1 and 87.7 percent, respectively, of the value of output in 1993. Labour costs, expressed as a percentage of the total value of output, fluctuates within a relatively narrow range, but the share tends to be higher in the industrialized than in the developing countries. Operating surplus (column 5) covers the returns to capital and entrepreneurship in the form of interest payments, profits and dividends. The data do not reveal any clear-cut pattern. The level of operating surplus seems to depend more on the market conditions and degree of competition prevailing in each country than on the nature of the technology used.

low purchasing power and sometimes by the small size of the market itself.

The factors actually determining the most economic location for an agro-industry are complex. Generally transport is a main factor. Most agricultural products either lose weight and bulk in processing, meaning they can be transported more cheaply after they have been processed, or they are perishable and so can be more easily transported in processed form. The situation is also affected by labour supplies and the availability of power and other infrastructure, but industries based on these products can often be set up economically in the area where the raw material is produced. They can therefore contribute to the relief of the rural underemployment which is characteristic of developing countries.

There are, however, exceptions. For most grains, shipment of the raw material in bulk is frequently easier, while many bakery products are highly perishable and thus require production to be located close to the market. Oilseeds (except for the more perishable ones such as olives and palm fruit) are also an exception and can be transported equally easily and cheaply in raw form or as oil, cake or meal, so there is more technical freedom of choice in the location of processing. The same is true for the later stages of processing of some commodities. For example, while raw cotton loses weight in ginning, which is consequently carried out in the producing area, yarn, textiles and clothing can all be transported equally easily and cheaply.

Where there is a high degree of technical freedom in the choice of location, industries have frequently tended to be located in proximity to the markets because of the more efficient labour supply, better infrastructure and lower distribution costs in the large market centres. With production for export, this factor has often tended to favour the location of processing in the importing country. This tendency has been reinforced by other factors, including the need for additional raw materials and auxiliary materials (particularly chemicals) that may not be readily available in the raw material-producing country; the greater flexibility in deciding the type of processing according to the end use for which the product is required; and the greater regularity of supply and continuity of operations that are possible when raw materials are drawn from several different parts of the world. However, with improved infrastructure, enhanced labour efficiency and growing domestic markets in the developing countries, there is increased potential for expanding such processing in the countries where the raw materials are produced. In addition, with growing liberalization of world trade, more developing countries will be able to take advantage of lower labour costs to expand their exports of agro-industrial products.

One further aspect of importance for the location of agro-industries would appear to be the possible existence of economies of scale. Where there are considerable economies of scale (as in the production of rubber tyres and pulp and paper), large markets are of course essential. The size of market needed for economic production in such cases may be far in excess of the domestic market in individual developing countries, where it is limited not only by the low level of per caput income but also by the frequently small size of the total population. However, although in most agro-industries average costs of production can be reduced as the scale of plant is increased, the importance of economies of scale should not be exaggerated. The lower cost of production with a large-scale plant results not only from the spreading of capital and other overhead costs, but also from the frequently smaller labour requirements per unit of output in the larger plant, an aspect which is of less importance in developing countries where labour costs are low.

The specificity of agro-industry

Processing is only one link in a continuous chain between raw material production and final consumption. The specificity of agro-industry *vis-à-vis* other industrial subsectors lies largely in the biological nature of the raw material. The raw materials used by agro-industry are generally characterized by the seasonal nature and the variability of their production as well as by their perishability. These aspects put particular demands both on the organization of agro-industrial activities and on the agricultural base producing the inputs, thereby adding to the need for a close integration of raw material production and processing.

Crop and livestock production cannot be controlled with great accuracy and tends to vary sharply from year to year owing to the effects of weather and pests and diseases. It is possible to some extent to reduce these fluctuations through the better use of soil and water resources and control of pests and diseases. It is generally in the interest of the processing enterprise, which requires as regular a supply of raw material as possible, to ensure or promote implementation of these measures by producers.

Furthermore, for most crops production tends to be concentrated in a particular season. It can therefore be advantageous for processing enterprises, particularly

those engaged in canning and freezing, to promote the production in a particular area of a suitable range of crops and varieties maturing in different seasons in order to keep processing facilities in operation for as long as possible. The perishable nature of many crop and livestock products also requires close contact between the producer and processor as well as advance planning to keep losses to a minimum.

However, the most impelling reason for the necessity of this close contact arises from the possibility of controlling the quality of the raw materials. Their quality can be influenced by such factors as the choice of seed; the application of fertilizers; the control of weeds, pests and diseases; and sorting and cleaning. Processors are interested not only in obtaining uniformity in the quality of their raw material supplies, but in some cases their needs are quite specific. Particular varieties of some crops (for example, of tomatoes, apples and pears for canning) have long been grown for processing, but the need for such varieties is increasing as food technology develops more advanced processes. Often there are specific requirements for such factors as shape, size, texture, colour, flavour, odour, acidity, viscosity, maturity, specific gravity, soluble solids, total solids and vitamin content.

The initiative for the introduction of different varieties and practices has usually come from the processing enterprises. As a result, for some commodities, especially fruit and vegetables for canning and freezing, raw material production and processing are increasingly "vertically integrated" in the developed countries through various forms of contract farming. In the developing countries, the large-scale plantation production of such crops and sugar, coffee, tea, sisal and rubber is based on the vertical integration of raw material production and processing.

Linkage effects

From the point of view of development strategy, one of the most important features of any industry is the degree to which it is able to generate demand for the products of other industries. This phenomenon is known as linkage. An industry may encourage investment both in subsequent stages of production by "forward linkage" and in earlier stages through "backward linkage".

The establishment of certain primary processing industries can lead, through forward linkage, to a number of more advanced industries. Forest industries are particularly valuable as a base on which other industries can be established in this way. Once paper and paperboard production has been started, a large number of conversion industries can emerge, such as the manufacture of paper bags, stationery, boxes and cartons, wooden containers, furniture and a wide range of timber products. There are many other examples: products such as vegetable oils and rubber are used in a wide variety of manufacturing industries; based on the preparation of hides and skins, tanning operations can be started, as can the manufacture of footwear and other leather goods.

The development of agro-industries also has many beneficial feedback effects on agriculture itself. The most direct one is, of course, the stimulus it provides for increased agricultural production through market expansion. Often, in fact, the establishment of processing facilities is itself an essential first step towards stimulating both consumer demand for the processed product and an adequate supply of the raw material. The provision of transport, power and other infra-structural facilities required for agro-industries also benefits agricultural production. The development of these and other industries provides a more favourable atmosphere for technical progress and the acceptance of new ideas in farming itself.

The capacity of agro-industry to generate demand and employment in other industries is also important because of its growing potential for activating "sideway linkages"; that is, linkages that derive from the use of by-products or waste products of the main industrial activity. For example, animal feed industries can utilize several agro-industrial by-products, such as whey, oilseed presscakes and blood, carcass and bone meal. In addition, many industries using agricultural raw materials produce waste that can be used as fuel, paper pulp or fertilizer. Recycling and biological agriculture are two activities that go together to respond to the idea of a sustainable form of exploitation of natural resources within an efficient industrial context.

An effect that is sometimes overlooked is the substantial increase in employment that may result from setting up an industry using a raw material. Even if the industrial process is itself capital-intensive, considerable employment may be generated in providing the raw material base. Finally, agro-industry gives rise to a demand for a wide variety of machinery, equipment, packaging materials and intermediate goods used in the processing itself.

The agroprocessing industry in the process of development

The role of agro-industry as a sector of the economy has multiple facets and changes in the course of development. In the early stages of growth, industrial processing of agricultural products tends to be limited to a few export crops, while the majority of agricultural products are consumed after minimal forms of processing that are performed entirely within the agricultural sector. Upstream processing industries prevail in their more primitive form, such as rice and flour milling, oil pressing and fish canning. An example of this stage would also be the plantation economy, where agro-industry and primary agriculture appear as a vertically integrated activity, with upstream processing taking over the agricultural base through a production system that is often founded on forms of disfranchisement of labourers and small cultivators.

Other cases of apparently more diversified agro-industrial activities, based on fruits and vegetables or livestock products, may be equally primitive in their organization, the low degree of value added produced and the lack of linkages both with the chemical and mechanical industries and with marketing and financial services. Such is the case for Egypt where, in spite of the growth of vegetable and fruit production and the related transformation industry, primary agriculture still accounts for almost 90 percent of the intermediate goods purchases of the industry, while a longer chain of links has developed only for livestock-related products. Similarly, a large share of agricultural raw products in total intermediate purchases characterizes most agro-industrial production of tropical beverages and other products originating from plantation crops, as well as vegetables, fruits, tobacco and livestock in the first stage of domestic industrial development.

Even in the case of limited backward linkages outside agriculture, food processing in the early stages of development can be an important direct complement to agriculture as a source of employment for seasonal labour. It requires very little investment and provides ample opportunities for expanding value added by using underemployed resources as well as for improving incomes and nutrition. Cottage industries of various forms are found in almost all areas where agriculture is sufficiently diversified, and there is scope for extending the range and timing of production both for dietary reasons and as a hedge against uncertainty. The off-farm employment opportunities provided by food processing may thus represent the first instrument of time-smoothing in the labour market and, as such, is an important factor of capital accumulation in rural areas.

Morocco provides an example of a more advanced stage of development of agro-industry, characterized by some more sophisticated downstream industrial activities, but where off-farm employment nevertheless remains the industry's main engine of growth. In this country, the presence of a well-developed food preserve industry for tomato sauce, fruit juices and other canned fruit ensures stronger links with sectors other than agriculture, both as providers of inputs (chemicals, glass, aluminium and paper) and as dependent sectors of further processing (marketing services). The food industry in Morocco is estimated to purchase only about 70 percent of its raw materials from agriculture, while the final product sold to the consumer and exported in increasing quantities contains more than 45 percent of non-agricultural products.

A further stage of development of agro-industry as a producer of food and beverages can be observed in a number of middle-income countries, such as Turkey, Argentina and Chile. This stage is characterized by full development of the forward linkage chain, with several marketing and other services incorporated in the final product, and product innovation prevailing over process innovation to provide a competitive advantage and sources of growth to the firms in the market. The linkage with the marketing chain tends to be well established, with both organizational and financial links between the producers and the retail outlets. The pace at which new products are introduced is extremely high, and this testifies to the importance of product innovation in this phase of the industry cycle.

Finally, for high-income areas such as the EU or the United States, the mature stage of the food industry still appears to be very dynamic. While the backward and forward links do not go much beyond what has already been achieved by third-stage firms in middle-income countries, a separate series of linkages develops through the production of specialized machinery and process innovation. Because of their size, market leadership and degree of internationalization, the food-producing companies located in the high-income countries are often instrumental in setting the base for a whole technology of processed food production. The areas involved range from the planning and quality control of agricultural products and other raw materials, to the design and manufacture of machinery, specification and monitoring of the production cycle and the provision of specialized financial and other services.

Thus, the multiplicative power of the agroprocessing industry throughout the economy through the linkage effects appears to be an important factor of growth both for developing and developed countries. An additional reason why agro-industries are especially effective in activating demand from the upstream and downstream sectors lies in the position of food in the consumption chain. Thus, even at a relatively low level of sophistication with limited backward and forward linkages, agro-industries may still be particularly effective in channelling increased global demand into increased output. This is so because, at the earlier development stages, a high share of private expenditure is directed towards cereals and other staples and, later on, as development progresses, towards fruits and vegetables and other food products whose income elasticity is relatively higher.[3] At later stages of development, it is the growing integration of the producing sectors that mainly ensures the capacity of food production to activate the rest of the economy, although the contribution of consumption to the industry multiplier remains sustained through diversification and growth of products with higher income elasticities.

An important feature of agroprocessing industries is that they are a major source of employment and income, thus providing access to food and other necessities to large groups of population. They are, therefore, essential elements in the attainment of food security goals.

Agroprocessing industries (food, beverages and tobacco) typically employ about 10 percent of the total labour force employed in manufacturing in the

---

[3] **The income elasticity of demand refers to the responsiveness of the quantity demanded of a good to changes in the income of consumers. Thus, the higher the income elasticity, the more demand for a good will increase as incomes of consumers grow.**

developed countries and around 20 to 30 percent in the developing countries (Table 6). The highest shares are found in Africa, where they reflect at once the poor development of the other manufacturing sectors and the pioneering role of agroprocessing, and, to a lesser extent, in the Latin American countries in the sample. Table 6 also shows the share of agroprocessing wages and salaries in total wages in manufacturing. By comparing both shares, it appears that, in the developed countries, earnings in agricultural processing were on the whole lower than for other manufacturing activities. For the developing countries, patterns are less distinct, but available data indicate that agroprocessing wages compare favourably with those in most other industrial activities, except those sophisticated activities that generally require more skills and training (such as aircraft, motor vehicles, structural metal production, cement and chemicals).

A factor underscoring the importance of agroprocessing activities as sources of employment and earnings relates to the differences in productivity between, on the one hand, raw material production – where gains have been in many cases spectacular – and, on the other hand, agro-industry. Although intrasectoral comparisons may be misleading (unlike raw materials, volume gains in agro-industrial output may be relatively small per unit of input, but undergo significant quality change), faster progress in labour productivity at the farm level may suggest less ability to create, or retain, employment, than agroprocessing. Further, the share of costs arising from primary products in total processing is in many cases so low as to be of minor significance to the food company. As economic growth and development proceed, the dynamic role of

agroprocessing industries must be appraised in the framework of the increasing complexity of food systems and other agriculture-, fisheries- and forestry-based systems. This growing sophistication is accompanied by shifting relative weights of the value added and employment generated at various stages within these systems. The growth of labour productivity, which is typically faster in agriculture than in other sectors of the economy, contributes to the release of labour force and hence its availability for other sectors, and to the decline of the value of the primary output of agriculture in the value of the final, processed goods. This is particularly noticeable in food products; the share of food in the average consumer's expenditure, in the order of 20 percent in high-income economies and 40 to 60 percent in medium- and low-income countries, compares with shares that are several times lower for the value added of agriculture in GDP. The agroprocessing sectors, as well as the trade and distribution sectors, account for most of this gap. The ability of domestic agroprocessing to capture this economic opportunity and to contribute to progress in the agricultural sector, particularly in the quality dimension, is of great promise for the developing countries. This also underscores the continued significance of agriculture through its role as the basis for economic diversification, at the national as well as at the local level, since much of agroprocessing is taking place and can be developed at a local level, thus contributing to a decentralization of economic and social progress.

The agroprocessing industry and the environment
Despite their important contribution to overall and agricultural development, agroprocessing industries can also give

TABLE 6

Share of agroprocessing employees[1] in total employees in manufacturing, and share of agroprocessing wages in total wages in manufacturing in selected countries, 1992

Countries	Agroprocessing employees out of total employees in manufacturing	Wages to employees in agroprocessing/total wages in manufacturing
	(percentage)	
DEVELOPED		
United States	9.1	7.8
Finland	13.0	12.8
Germany	7.2	5.9
Canada	13.6	12.6
Sweden	9.8	8.8
TRANSITION		
Bulgaria	11.7	13.4
Croatia	15.3	16.7
Kyrgyzstan	12.5	10.8
Russian Federation[2]	11.2	19.6
Lithuania[3]	18.7	23.7
Hungary[3]	20.1	21.5
DEVELOPING		
Africa:		
Cameroon	35.9	38.6
Kenya	32.4	28.4
Botswana	26.1	36.9
Senegal	59.3	55.6
Zimbabwe	17.7	24.4
Asia and the Pacific:		
India	22.8	12.0
Indonesia	20.2	14.5
Korea, Rep.	7.2	6.2
Malaysia	8.4	8.6
Philippines	20.9	22.6
Sri Lanka	20.5	20.3
Latin America and the Caribbean:		
Argentina[2]	27.6	25.2
Brazil	33.0	12.5
Colombia	22.1	22.7
Ecuador	36.1	33.2
Mexico	20.9	17.6
Peru	23.5	25.5

[1] Food, beverages and tobacco.
[2] Data refer to 1993.
[3] Data refer to 1994.

Source: UNIDO. 1997. *Handbook of Industrial Statistics 1997*. Vienna.

BOX 12
TURNING A POLLUTANT INTO A VALUE: THE CASE OF WHEY

Whey, the liquid residual of cheese and casein manufacture, is one of the biggest reservoirs of food protein that still remains outside human consumption channels. Yet a large proportion of total whey supplies is still wasted. Traditionally, whey was considered an undesirable element, of little interest at best, and costly to get rid of at worst. The most common practice was simply to dump it in waterways, a particularly damaging practice from the environmental viewpoint – it is estimated that a cheese factory producing 250 000 litres of whey per day can pollute as much water as does a city of 50 000 inhabitants. A less damaging practice was to feed it to calves or pigs as a supplement to their normal diet. With the development of the cheese industry, it became evident that these traditional solutions were insufficient to cope with the problem of whey disposal. Anti-pollution regulations were introduced and progressively enforced in countries where whey is more abundantly produced, thus obliging cheese manufacturers either to process their whey or to install their own sewage facilities, at a negative unit return. As the former alternative was the lesser of two evils, the industry increased its efforts to develop its existing facilities, particularly for drying, as well as trying to find new uses for whey. Whey-powder production, mainly for feed uses, emerged as the most economic solution and, indeed, this form of industry has expanded considerably over the past decades. At the same time, whey began entering food consumption as an ingredient for a wide variety of products, particularly beverages such as the (originally Swiss Rivella) fruit-flavoured beverages with a high nutritional content, and even "whey champagne" and soft drinks produced on a commercial scale in some Eastern European countries.

Although dumping whey into waterways remains a serious problem in some countries, this practice has been largely reduced, particularly in the industrialized countries, thanks to the tightening of anti-pollution measures. These measures have also contributed to intensifying research into alternative uses of whey, thereby constituting an example of how encouragement and regulation can induce the industries themselves to turn polluting wastage into profit.

rise to undesirable environmental side-effects. Left unchecked, like any other industry, agro-industry can create environmental pollution or hazards in various ways: the discharge of organic or hazardous wastes into water supplies; the emission of dust or gases that affect air quality and produce toxic substances; and the use of dangerous machinery that can put the safety and health of workers at risk. The seriousness of the pollution problems created by agro-industrial activity greatly varies, but it appears that food transformation activities are generally less energy-intensive and release less CO_2 and metal residues than most other industrial activities. In fact, agroprocessing industries, such as sugar mills, can become not only energy self-sufficient through the energy conversion of biomass residues, but also sizeable electricity producers that feed the national grid, thus reducing CO_2 emissions. The risks of pollution are relatively smaller at the initial stages of preservation and transformation, but they may increase with the level of physical and chemical alteration, particularly in the industries using dated equipment and technology (new technologies are less polluting than old ones in terms of wastes and emissions per unit of output). The size of the industry may be an important factor, but not determinant in itself. In fact large, centralized agro-industries can be important sources of punctual pollution, but smaller-scale industries can also generate scattered pollutants with a cumulative effect in a given geographic region. This is especially so since small industries, particularly in low-income countries, lack the financial resources to use modern and clean technologies. The damages and hazards caused by agro-industrial pollution may be all the more serious and immediately perceived since

these industries tend to be concentrated in urban and peri-urban areas. Finally, the incidence of agro-industrial wastage and pollution depends to a very large extent on the efficiency of the legislative setting and regulatory action taken to protect the environment. Anti-pollution regulation can be an important contributor, not only to reducing the release of polluting residues, but also to using them in profitable ways (see Box 12). However, many countries still lack a policy framework that adequately addresses the environmental factor as well as the institutional, legal and monitoring structures to implement pollution control measures effectively.

CHANGING CONDITIONS FOR THE AGROPROCESSING INDUSTRY
Agricultural support and trade regimes and patterns of agro-industrial production

National food and agricultural policies and international trade policies are a major factor determining the international division of labour and the geographical distribution of agricultural and agro-industrial production. Studies of domestic and international market prospects for food and agricultural products are essential to decisions on the set of policies that will enable producers and processors to gain competitiveness and take advantage of market opportunities.

Policies that affect the prices of inputs and outputs to producers, processors and consumers are of critical importance. Therefore, special attention should be given to policies regarding taxation, subsidies, direct price support and tariffs, both in the short and the long term.

The temptation exists for policy-makers to provide incentives or preferential treatment to the industries supplying inputs, or to producers, processors or final consumers of food. These policy interventions are provided in various forms: tax concessions to producers of inputs and products, subsidies on prices of inputs or food, support prices for producers at relatively high levels, protective tariffs or other international trade barriers. The sustainability of such policies must be given careful consideration before adoption, as history is full of examples of the disastrous consequences associated with the abrupt removal of such preferential measures.

It is important that policies applied at all levels of the food production and processing system are compatible and work towards the achievement of the same goal. Whether in the form of a tax,

subsidy, support or tariff, policy interventions must generate net benefits for society. In other words, the loss in fiscal revenue from a reduction in taxes must be more than offset by the increase in jobs and benefits associated with the industry; the cost of a subsidy must be more than offset by gains for the direct and indirect recipients of such a subsidy; relatively high prices must ensure the required increase in production and expansion of the industry concerned, with benefits in terms of employment and income; and the subsidy to final consumers must have net benefits in terms of nutrition and productivity.

An important aspect of agricultural protection policies is the phenomenon that tariffs on processed agricultural products have generally been higher than those on their primary commodities. This tariff wedge between a processed commodity and its corresponding primary commodity is often referred to as tariff escalation. Developing countries have for many years identified tariff escalation as a major issue concerning market access and an important obstacle to their efforts to establish processing industries. However, most of the empirical studies on this process are by now outdated. A recent study by FAO[4] analyses the impact of the Uruguay Round on tariff escalation for agricultural products in the EU, Japan and the United States. The study shows that tariff escalation has been reduced as a result of the Uruguay Round, creating some opportunities for developing countries to diversify their exports into higher-value processed commodities. The

---

[4] FAO. 1997. *The impact of the Uruguay Round on tariff escalation in agricultural products.* ESCP No. 3. Rome.

study concludes, however, that high levels of escalation will still remain after the implementation of the Uruguay Round concessions.

In many developing countries, from colonial times at least until the early 1980s, agriculture tended to be directly or indirectly taxed through a combination of measures involving forced procurement at prices below market prices, taxation of inputs, subsidization of manufactures and overvalued exchange rates. However, this phenomenon presented very diversified situations. On the one hand, for tropical beverages, oils, alcohol and tobacco, often against a backdrop of underpaid or taxed agriculture, huge subsidies were paid to the processing industry, which was either organized in the form of parastatals (as in Africa), or controlled by multinationals (as in Central America and Asia), or again characterized by a tight oligopolistic structure (as in much of Latin America).

On the other hand, the rise of a modern food processing sector has often been delayed or even suppressed by the combination of agricultural taxation and consumption subsidies characteristic of traditional food policy in developing countries. Food distribution systems, in particular, have relied on forced procurement and import subsidies, thus lowering simultaneously the supply of local produce and prices of processed food products. Incentives to develop local manufactures for a variety of food products have thus been artificially depressed, especially in sectors such as dairy products, packed meat and wheat derivatives. On the other hand, in several developing countries the rise of a domestic fruit and vegetable processing industry has been indirectly encouraged by the punitive policies adopted against the production of basic food items. A policy of "benign neglect" or, in some

cases, of open subsidization in favour of irrigated crops has thus favoured the growth of an agro-industrial complex based on fruits and vegetables in such diverse countries as Morocco, Turkey, Mexico and Chile. Similarly, in the case of tropical fruits, many new industrial enterprises have been successful in producing fruit juices, preserves and products for domestic industries as a result of the relatively high profitability of these products, technological advances in the transformation processes and the need to diversify out of sugar and other plantation crops.

An interesting example of a development of the latter type is Brazil, where the production of juices from tropical fruits has increased more than twentyfold in the past ten years. These fruits, produced mostly in the northern and northeastern areas of the country, used to be consumed in processed form only in local markets, mainly because the technology did not allow the production of juices with the amount of chemicophysical stability necessary to maintain the organoleptic characteristics of the product at a commercially acceptable level. This technological barrier has been completely overcome in the course of the 1980s. As a consequence, the Brazilian industry that processes tropical fruits, together with the production of fruits themselves, has greatly expanded and acquired a large share of the export market where, for certain products (e.g. maracujá) it almost has a monopoly.

A special problem of change that concerns both food price policies and the processing industry is the transition to market economies of the former centrally planned economies of Eastern Europe and the CIS. Here the pricing system prior to transition was characterized by extreme subsidies to both food producers and consumers. While roughly two-thirds of agricultural land was in the hands of state or collective farms, virtually all agro-industries were state-owned monopolies. These paid little attention to quality and technological development, even for products that were high-value sources of foreign exchange (such as caviar). The transition process has changed the economic environment by removing or substantially reducing food subsidies, by privatizing agriculture and industry and by deregulating local markets. In the absence of a comprehensive liberalization programme, however, new disequilibria have been created. Higher retail prices for food are often not transmitted to farmers because the processing industry is free to use market power to appropriate monopolistic rents. At the same time local producers are faced with strong competition from imports of higher-quality, Western processed food.

The current trend towards liberalization and increased market-orientation of agricultural policies opens a series of interesting perspectives for agricultural and agro-industrial producers. In an international macroeconomic framework characterized by low inflation and low interest rates in the industrialized countries, international trade should receive a significant impulse, especially in liberalizing agricultural markets. Growth prospects appear favourable, particularly because of the increasing diversity of food consumption, the switch to high income-elasticity goods and the increasing importance of marketing and processing. These phenomena could result in a massive reallocation of agricultural products along new lines of comparative advantage, following both the new market perspectives and the possibilities disclosed by technology and the evolution of tastes.

Moreover, in many developing countries, from the mid-1980s onwards and in the wake of the general move towards increased liberalization and market orientation, there seems to have emerged a new consciousness of the importance of agriculture and related sectors. In many cases this new awareness has coincided with important policy changes such as the privatization of government-owned marketing and processing companies and with the end of the willingness to subsidize private oligopolies in the commodity sector. The stage appears to have been set, therefore, for an endogenous growth of the domestic food industry wherever a comparative advantage can be exploited. Nevertheless, it must be emphasized that, in many cases, discrimination against domestic agrifood industrial activities in developing countries continues, as the discriminatory policies have only attenuated rather than disappeared.

Evolution of technology and food consumption patterns

Additional factors shaping the future of agro-industrial production and trade are developments occurring in technology and food consumption patterns, most noticeably in the industrialized countries. In this respect, technological development in agriculture is going through a transition phase of great interest. On the one hand, improvements in production techniques based on traditional chemical and mechanical innovations have permitted exceptional increases in yields and large improvements in quality, mainly concerning product homogeneity and lack of physical defects. On the other hand, more recent trends in agricultural research and technology point to different models, based mostly on innovations of a biological and biotechnological type as well as on modern processing technologies.

Thus, while, historically, productivity growth and price gains achieved through processing innovations have been paramount in primary agriculture, and have been easily transferred to the agro-industrial sector, product innovations are also beginning to materialize. Although the resulting improved variety and quality of final products do not necessarily go hand in hand with lower costs, the innovations promise to increase efficiency in agro-industry and, through the correspondent increase in demand for agricultural inputs by the processing industry, they can contribute to mitigating the tendency towards price declines facing primary producers.

Parallel to technological development, patterns of food consumption in industrialized countries are evolving (Table 7). Between 1969-71 and 1990-92 the share of cereals, sugar and roots and tubers declined at the world level, while that of livestock products, fish and vegetable oils and fats tended to rise. There were significant variations in the patterns among country groups and regions, however. In the developing regions, for instance, the increased share of animal products was most evident in East and Southwest Asia, followed by South Asia and Latin America and the Caribbean countries, whereas a similar increase did not occur in the Near East and Africa. The variations were equally significant between developed and developing countries. In the example of sugar, the overall reduced share reflected a marked decrease in the developed countries' share, as that of the developing countries increased.

In industrialized countries two different types of force are shaping food consumption patterns, of which the final effects on the quality, composition and geographical allocation of production are difficult to predict. One is represented by an increasing concern for health and fitness. This was one reason for the marked decline in per caput food consumption of sugar. Also, while the consumption of livestock products has increased significantly over the past decades, the relative importance of these products is progressively decreasing, while a premium is put on products such as vegetable products and fruits which, until only recently, were considered complementary in nature and largely of lower value relative to animal products. These trends are expected to continue in future years, as shown by the example of European countries (Table 8).

Fish and other marine and water products, the supply of which is enhanced and enlarged by the growth of aquaculture and other farming techniques, have also become choice foods in the diet of higher-income earners in the developed countries. Another aspect of this tendency is the revaluation of those characteristics of food products that can be traced back to an "original" or "natural" pattern of production. In addition, another biological agriculture, which appeals to environmentalistic attitudes and value judgements of intrinsic characteristics of food, is part of the tendency, as is the trend towards more nutritious products, which also possess other desirable dietary properties. These changes in the dietary patterns of middle-income brackets in developed countries mark a transformation of attitudes which is likely to have profound implications for food production patterns.

On the other hand, modern food production technology tends to multiply the variety of products derived from original, natural products. A proliferation of goods that incorporate innovations in form, colour, organoleptic and

TABLE 7

Share of major food groups in total dietary energy supply (DES), 1969-71 and 1990-92

Food group	World		Developed countries		Developing countries	
	1969-71	1990-92	1969-71	1990-92	1969-71	1990-92
	(percentage)					
VEGETABLE PRODUCTS	84.4	84.3	71.7	70.9	92.3	89.7
Cereals	50.1	51.2	32.6	30.4	60.9	59.6
Sugar	9.1	8.8	13.2	12.8	6.6	7.2
Vegetable oils and fats	5.7	8.2	8.2	11.1	4.1	7.0
Roots and tubers	7.5	5.0	5.0	3.8	9.0	5.4
Vegetables and fruits	4.2	4.3	4.5	4.9	4.5	4.8
Pulses and nuts	4.8	4.0	2.3	2.3	2.3	4.7
Alcoholic beverages	2.7	2.4	5.3	4.9	5.3	1.3
Stimulants and spices	0.4	0.4	0.4	0.6	0.4	0.4
ANIMAL PRODUCTS	15.6	15.7	28.3	29.1	7.7	10.3
Meat and offal	6.4	7.4	11.1	12.8	3.5	5.2
Milk	4.8	4.3	8.9	8.6	2.2	2.6
Animal oils and fats	2.7	2.0	5.4	4.4	1.0	1.1
Eggs	0.8	0.9	1.5	1.8	0.3	0.7
Fish	0.9	1.0	1.4	1.3	0.6	0.7

Source: FAO.

TABLE 8

Growth rate in per caput consumption of selected foods, Western Europe, 1970-90 and 1988-90 to 2010

	1970-90	1988-90 to 2010
	(percentage)	
Cereals and products	0.2	-0.2
Potatoes	-0.4	-0.4
Sugar	-0.5	0.0
Pulses	1.4	0.0
Vegetables and products	1.3	0.5
Fruit and products	0.8	0.8
Vegetable oils	1.3	0.8
Milk and products	0.7	-0.3
Eggs	-0.5	-0.2
Meat and products	0.8	0.4
Population growth rate	0.2	0.1

Source: FAO food balance sheets and projections; FAO. 1995. *World Agriculture: towards 2010.* Edited by N. Alexandratos. Rome, FAO and Chichester, UK, Wiley.

conservation properties is flooding the supermarkets and presenting consumers with alternative choices. The return to "naturalness" and the artisanal nature of original food is thus matched, somewhat paradoxically, by an increase in the artificial nature of these new products, especially the more industrially sophisticated ones. The challenge to the food industry, in this case, is to try to reconcile the two tendencies through processing and product innovation.

An important issue is the extent to which changes in consumption patterns and the growing importance of transformed or processed food in total food consumption may affect consumer safety. In general, the contribution of agrifood industries to raising the quality, variety, nutritional value and safety of food cannot be overstated. However, risks of food infection may arise at all the stages of the food industry – production, transformation, packaging, storing and transport. Also, if inadequately controlled, the growing sophistication of the product, with the addition of preservatives, additives and other substances that may enhance its market value, may be a source of greater risk for consumers. A further factor affecting food quality and safety is the intensification of trade in food products, resulting from the general process of interdependence of agrifood systems (see the section, The internationalization of agrifood systems, p. 250) and factors such as shifts in tastes and preferences towards well-publicized imported products, and greater demand for convenience foods. Intensified trade flows, however, raise the potential of exposing consumers in one part of the world to the food quality and safety problems of other regions. Rapid transport and increased shelf-life technology may allow for contaminated products to reach

their intended destinations more quickly and remain on the market longer, thus affecting greater numbers of consumers. These problems raise the importance of adequate food standards and mechanisms for the rigorous vigilance and monitoring of the quality and safety of processed foods, of both domestic and foreign origin.

Evolution of the agroprocessing industry and developing countries

The developments in international agro-industry discussed here have implications for developing countries and the possibility of developing their agro-industrial sectors. Thus, on the one hand, the gradual process towards increased liberalization of trade and market-orientation of domestic policies in the developed countries will hopefully offer increasing opportunities for developing countries. On the other hand, the need to adapt production to the increasingly sophisticated and demanding requirements of these markets poses challenges to both agriculture and agro-industry in countries wishing to supply these markets. Indeed, the success of a number of developing countries in expanding agro-industrial production and exports has to a large extent depended on their ability to meet the requirements of the developed countries' markets.

Because developed countries practically consume only processed food, as even fresh vegetables are variously cleaned, prepared and packaged when they reach distribution outlets, the development of agro-industries is increasingly becoming one with development of industrial agriculture. Indeed, although most of the so-called new agricultural exporters, such as Chile and Thailand, have expanded their capacity to provide markets with both fresh and processed products (see Box 13), on closer inspection, even "fresh" fruits and vegetables are themselves processed goods undergoing sophisticated operations in collection, quality control, packaging, storage, refrigeration and transport.

Even disregarding some of the more exceptional cases, agro-industry has been an important growth component in a great number of the better performing economies of the developing world. Econometric studies show that this new and integrated form of agricultural development is invariably based on productivity growth and technological development that are as rapid and spectacular as those occurring in the manufacturing sector. Many studies report higher growth rates of total factor productivity in the agricultural sector than in other sectors.[5] Just as important for many countries is the drive towards diversification, as this allows them to end their dependence on primary goods, which often constitute a crucial obstacle to self-sustained growth. The economy-wide drive towards diversification can be accompanied by a tendency to diversify within the sector, with recourse to an increasing number of processing technologies that expand value added and productivity for agricultural products beyond the boundaries of traditional agriculture.

One characteristic of the new agro-industrial development is the increasing importance of processing and marketing activities. That this is a key to acquiring stable shares of international markets had been realized by Israel, which represents the success story of the 1970s and was the model for similar experiences in other countries. The extraordinary export growth achieved in the 1980s and 1990s by some countries has depended on the thorough planning of all product transformation phases, from the original producers to the final consumers. For off-season fruits and vegetables, for example, which have been one major expanding export of Chile, careful time planning has been used to ensure that they arrive on the European markets precisely in the intraseasonal intervals when local products, including off-season produce, are not available.

[5] D. Evans. 1987. The long-run determinants of North-South terms of trade and some recent empirical evidence. *World Development*, 15(5): 657-671; D. Jorgenson, F. Gollop and B. Fraumeni. 1987. *Productivity and US economic growth.* Harvard University Press, Cambridge, Mass., USA; P. Lewis, W. Martin and C. Savage. 1988. Capital investment in the agricultural economy. *Quarterly Review of the Rural Economy*, 10(1): 48-53.

BOX 13
SUCCESS STORIES IN EXPORT-ORIENTED AGRO-INDUSTRY

Up to ten years ago, Chile had a tradition of producing high-quality fresh fruits. The development of its capacity to export against the established producers of Europe, North America and Mexico was based on careful studies of potential competitive advantage, including cost, quality and marketing characteristics such as off-seasonality and timeliness of delivery. This effort, sustained over a trial period of three to five years, brought about an expansion of exports of unprecedented magnitude, not only for Chile's fresh fruit, but also for many of its agro-industrial products such as wine and food preserves. Timeliness in harvesting, processing and transport depend on an industrial marketing structure that coordinates sales contracts, temporary storage and quality controls in all phases of the product cycle. Reliability in terms of quality, timeliness of delivery and other contractual conditions (composition, prices, packaging, etc.) have gradually contributed to earning Chilean products a reputation that ensures them a stable share of the international markets.

In addition to product choices, seasonality and careful planning of other market characteristics, a more detailed analysis of the Chilean case reveals other key factors for success. Chilean agriculture took off in the 1970s, when a series of market-friendly reforms removed earlier restrictions and ended longstanding import substitution policies. In the growth of the agricultural sector, moreover,

THE INTERNATIONALIZATION OF AGRIFOOD SYSTEMS
Agrifood trade and interdependence of national agrifood systems

In 1994 world agrifood trade was valued at about $390 billion, about 10 percent of total world trade. A predominant role was played by Europe, which accounted for almost 50 percent of all imports and 45 percent of all exports. As highlighted in Figure 17, p. 254, Asia is also an important economic area with the Japanese market playing a major role.

Latin America and the Caribbean has gained a significant market share in the past 20 years by virtue of high diversification of agricultural production and dynamic growth of primary processing industries as well as progressive trade liberalization, factors a major role has been played by transnational agro-industrial companies, which have planned the development of fruit production in a vertically integrated mode, according to modern industrial standards and by exploiting their experience of export markets.

Chilean agriculture also constitutes a good example of the sector's importance as an engine of aggregate growth of an economy. The process of diversification and integration of the agricultural sector has coincided with analogous diversification processes of the economy which, in the early 1970s, was still heavily dependent on the exports of copper (which represented more than 70 percent of export earnings). Industrial development and a widening of the production base, accomplished in the 1980s and the 1990s, have gone hand in hand with the development of a modern agro-industrial sector, at the bottom of which industrialized agriculture has shown productivity growth comparable with that of the most advanced manufacturing activities.

Another interesting success story is that of Thailand, which was among the world's top export performers in the 1980s when its exports expanded by an annual average of 13.2 percent in real terms, accounting for as much as 38 percent of GDP in 1990. Exports continued expanding dramatically during the first half of the 1990s, doubling in value between 1990 and 1995. Agro-industrial products, which were responsible for more than 65 percent of total exports, were developed by ensuring a market-friendly economic environment and providing adequate financial and support services. Some elements of this success story also give an idea of the potential of agro-industry as a leading sector. Indeed, the number of manufacturing jobs in Thailand doubled between 1978 and 1991, with agro-industry accounting for 60 percent of all workers in manufacturing industries by 1990, and for 15.4 percent of GDP (up from 9.7 percent in 1960). Agro-industry grew at a rate exceeding 8 percent per year from 1980 to 1990 and, by 1990, numbered 32 000 private enterprises or 62 percent of the total number of establishments in the manufacturing industry.

which have allowed this region to integrate remarkably well in international markets. On the other hand, Africa's presence in agrifood markets has remained modest, while the small market share of countries in Central and Eastern Europe and the CIS bear witness to the difficult integration of these countries in world markets.

International capital activities in agro-industry have reached a very high level: out of a total of about $300 billion of foreign direct investment (FDI) in 1995, an estimated $25 billion went to the agrifood industry (see Box 15).

Underlying the growing importance of international trade and capital flows in agro-industry has been a process of internationalization, which has increased in intensity over the past decades and has manifested itself in:

BOX 14
VERTICAL INTEGRATION

Despite growth and diversification in agro-industry, vertical integration and vertical coordination activities appear to be increasing in the sector. This can be seen in the progressive incorporation of large agricultural estates into food multinationals and in the rapid increase of preproduction contracts between farmers and industry. In the United States, for example, where these phenomena are more evident and tend to precede similar developments in other countries, in 1996 more than 50 percent of broiler and almost 16 percent of fruit and vegetable production were regulated through preproduction contracts. The objective of reducing transaction costs accounts for much of the growth of vertically integrated companies, and explains some of the attempts to coordinate agricultural supply with industry needs. An integrated firm may save resources by consolidating the many contracts that pertain to sales of agricultural goods into a single line of business. Cost reductions may also derive from the consolidation of upstream contracts with labour, land and other inputs of agricultural production.

A second cause of vertical integration lies in the need for agro-industrial production to meet the quality standards required by an increasingly specific and diversified consumer demand. Because of the extra costs associated with enforcing these standards in the field, there is an incentive for individual agricultural enterprises to free-ride on quality levels already achieved. Vertical integration may also be a way of dealing with this type of problem.

- an increasing interdependence and integration of the different national economies and agricultural systems, favoured in particular by the liberalization and external opening of domestic markets and the establishment of international zones of free exchange;
- a rapid progress and diffusion of technological innovation;
- a trend towards more homogeneous consumer products with standard characteristics at the international level – this is interrelated with the apparently contrasting process of market segmentation, whereby market segments are multiplying much faster than in the past and, rather than being limited to a single country, are extending to the international level (see Box 16).

Multinationals in the internationalization process
An important aspect of the internationalization process is the

BOX 15
FOREIGN DIRECT INVESTMENT IN AGRO-INDUSTRY

An important aspect of the economic internationalization process has been the dramatic increase in foreign direct investment (FDI), generally and in agro-industry, in the 1980s and 1990s.

According to the World Bank Debtor Reporting System, total net flows of FDI to developing countries rose from $24.5 billion in 1990 to $95.5 in 1995, while preliminary estimates for 1996 indicate a further increase to $109.5 billion in 1996.[1] Multinational enterprises in the industrialized countries are the main source of FDI, accounting for more than 90 percent of flows in recent years.

The sectoral composition of investment flows towards developing countries is not so well documented. However, according to statistics[2] on total flows of FDI from OECD countries to all destinations, the share going towards the food, beverages and tobacco manufacturing subsector was quite significant for a number of the major providers. Based on data for 1993 the share of FDI flows to this subsector amounted to 9.9 percent for the United States, 5.7 percent for the United Kingdom, 2.5 percent for Japan, 4.2 percent for France, 35.9 percent for the Netherlands and 13.5 percent for Switzerland, but only 0.5 percent in the case of Germany.

[1] See Box 1, External debt and financial flows to developing countries, p. 41.

[2] OECD. 1995. *International Direct Investment Statistical Yearboook 1995*. Paris.

increased role of multinational corporations in the agro-industrial sector of numerous countries. The creation of a multinational as an organizational entity may in many cases represent the final leap in the process of internationalizing the enterprise, a process which generally begins with the export phase.

In the current environment of increasing competition in international markets the main strategies adopted by the agrifood enterprises have been those of obtaining, through acquisitions of other enterprises operating on foreign markets, a level of competitiveness which would otherwise have been more costly or risky to achieve. Indeed, the food industry has been affected since the early 1980s by major acquisitions, mergers and agreements, the main product of which has been a strong market concentration in numerous sectors. According to data from UNCTAD,[6] over the period 1990-95,

[6] See UNCTAD. 1996. *World Investment Report 1996*. Geneva, UN.

254

Figure 17

Source: GATT

BOX 16
MARKET FRAGMENTATION

The evolution of the food industry in the past 15 years may be considered as a case-study of a fragmented market that is becoming increasingly global under the effect of two powerful forces: the evolving patterns of consumption and technological progress. In the 1970s the food industry was characterized by:
i) a large number of local producers, generally specialized in the production of a single good or in a set of closely related products; ii) a small number of national or international producers also specializing in a single core business; iii) an even smaller number of multinational firms, which were either extremely diversified (Unilever, Nestlé) or strictly specialized (Coca Cola).

The fragmented nature of the market was the result of both natural and policy-induced constraints. Natural constraints mainly comprised, for local products, tastes, local equipment, brand loyalty and consumer information. Policy-induced constraints resulted mainly from non-tariff barriers associated with health and hygiene regulations and from discriminatory policies of local traders and retail shops. Because their

products could not be replicated in a standard form by the larger producers, local manufacturers enjoyed the double advantage of higher prices and lower transport costs. Their traditional equipment and the local brands also proved to be a very effective means of discouraging national producers from trying to penetrate local markets, except with products that did not compete directly with local ones.

Starting in the mid-1980s, however, the larger producers in Europe and the United States gradually took over local markets by developing a high-growth strategy based on three tenets: i) covering the market to achieve dominance of a few standard products; ii) increasing the degree of differentiation by acquiring or by directly challenging the local leaders; and iii) introducing new products that could embody some of the characteristics of local products without trying to replicate them. This strategy not only required rapid growth, but also an expansionary policy of horizontal acquisitions and aggressive control of marketing activities, such as

advertising, retailing and investment in research and development for product innovation. The present trends, which constitute a continuation of the expansion at the national level, are mostly characterized by national producers' attempts to upgrade their traditional leadership to an international level.

BOX 17
BENEFITS OF FOREIGN DIRECT INVESTMENT

In its 1996 annual report,[1] WTO discusses several aspects of FDI. The report contains a review and discussion of some of the benefits and costs of FDI to the host country, a question which has been the object of strong debate between supporters and critics of this type of investment. Although the discussion relates to all forms of FDI, it is of obvious relevance to the debates on the role of FDI in the agro-industrial sector and on the agrifood multinationals. Following are some of the main points that emerge from the WTO report.

According to the proponents of FDI, in general

terms the benefits accruing to the host country are represented by an increase in national output and income exceeding the gain to the investor. These benefits can accrue either to domestic labour (in the form of expanded real wages), domestic consumers (through lower prices and/or improved product quality) or government (as increased revenues).

Much criticism has, however, been voiced against FDI and the role of multinational corporations. Critics point to potential negative balance-of-payments effects in the medium term, as the multinational corporations increase imports of intermediate goods and start repatriation of profits. Other points of criticism or concern are the potential

---

[1] WTO. 1996. *Annual Report 1996.* Geneva.

---

cross-border mergers and acquisitions in the food, beverages and tobacco manufacturing subsectors amounted to an annual average of $12.2 billion, representing 7.7 percent of total cross-border mergers and acquisitions over the period.

Within the framework of the increasing market concentration, the multinationals have played a role of primary importance, strengthening their position in the

majority of the world agrifood sectors and basing their competitive strength on high degrees of diversification (Table 9).

The majority of the top 100 agrifood multinationals are located in Europe. Over the past 20 years the multinationals of European and Japanese origin have increased their share of the top ranking as compared with the Americans who, in 1974, occupied 50 positions out of 100

market power of multinational corporations on the domestic market of the host country, which would allow them to engage in various restrictive practices that reduce competition, and the possible vulnerability of the host country governments to political pressures. In general, WTO does not believe that these concerns can constitute a sufficient case against FDI as such. As for the potential negative balance-of-payments effect, it is pointed out that FDI in countries with high levels of import protection tends to be less export-oriented than in countries with low protection levels and also that any balance-of-payments effect will depend on the exchange rate regime of the country. In any case, it does not appear that the potential costs associated

with FDI outweigh the benefits deriving from it. Also, it is the belief of WTO that some of the problems and concerns associated with FDI could be adequately dealt with in the framework of a multilateral agreement on FDI.

On the positive side, FDI has considerable importance as a vehicle for technology transfer. This transfer can of course take place directly to the firms affected, but there may also be important effects of indirect diffusion of technology in the host country. Such diffusion may be deliberate, for example through the upgrading of technologies in other domestic firms doing business with the foreign affiliate, or in the form of spillover effects, such as when technology is copied by other firms. Other

important positive effects in the host country could be the pressure on domestic producers to upgrade and improve efficiency. According to WTO, the empirical evidence tends to support the view that FDI is the most potent vehicle for technology transfer and that FDI leads to higher productivity in locally owned firms.

FDI also has important effects on employment The view that multinational corporations may have little impact on the development of local skills is rejected by the empirical evidence; rather, evidence tends to support the view that multinational corporations can fill critical management gaps, facilitate employment of local labour and transfer skills to local managers and entrepreneurs.

(Table 10). Out of a total business volume of $599 billion in 1990, the top ten multinational groups operating in the agrifood sector accounted for 32 percent, and the market is becoming even more concentrated in the hands of a few multinationals.

The geographical distribution of the industry is subject to rapid change. The United States, which was the leading

producer at the beginning of the 1980s, lost ground in the course of the 1980s and the early 1990s, to the point where the EU is now the main world producer, with a turnover of more than $600 billion, corresponding to more than 35 percent of the value of total production. The reduction in the United States' supremacy, however, is less accentuated in terms of the largest holdings, with Cargill, Kraft,

TABLE 9

The top 20 multinationals of the agrifood industry, 1994

Group	Country	Main sector of activity	Agrifood business volume (million $)
Philip Morris	United States	Multiproduct	53 288
Cargill	United States	Cereal transformation	50 000
Nestlé	Switzerland	Multiproduct	40 247
Pepsico	United States	Beverages and soft drinks	28 472
Unilever	Netherlands	Multiproduct	26 150
Coca Cola	United States	Beverages and soft drinks	23 828
Conagra	United States	Multiproduct	23 512
RJB Nabisco	United States	Multiproduct	15 366
Danone (BSN)	France	Multiproduct	12 843
Anheuser Bush	United States	Beer	11 364
Grand Metropolitan	United Kingdom	Multiproduct	11 300
Snow Brand Milk Products	Japan	Dairy products	10 600
Archer Daniels Midland	United States	Oils and vegetable fats	10 344
Bunge y Born	Argentina	Cereal transformation	9 500
Maruha (Taiyo Fishery)	Japan	Fish	9 221
Eridania/Beghin-Say	Italy	Oils and vegetable fats	9 157
Kirin Brewery	Japan	Beer	9 020
George Weston Ltd	Canada	Food distribution	8 939
General Mills	United States	Multiproduct	8 517
Allied Domecq Plc	United Kingdom	Wines and liquors	8 375

Source: Agrodata.

TABLE 10

Division by zone of origin of the top 100 agrifood multinationals

Countries	Number 1974	1994
United States	50	28
Western Europe	37	43
Japan	7	20
Others	6	9

Source: Agrodata.

BOX 18
UNILEVER

Perhaps no other company may be taken to represent the worldwide food business as Unilever. Founded in the early nineteenth century through the merger of two successful "colonial" companies, respectively the property of the English and the Dutch crown, Unilever has grown to become perhaps the single largest producer of processed food in the world. With 1 700 subsidiaries in all countries of the world, Unilever's profits place it twenty-first in *Fortune*'s 500 top-ranking companies. Fully 50 percent of its business is from food, with a portfolio of a balanced mix of local, regional and international brands which take into account the differences as well as the similarities in consumer demand.

Unilever describes itself as "international", not "global", because it does not attempt to enter all markets with the same product. Rather, it takes the view that successful food business must be based on local tastes. As a multinational conglomerate, however, Unilever can hardly be said to be local, except for its intense involvement with the food business of a great many countries, with special attention for developing ones. Recent business expansions, for example, concern Malaysia, Thailand,

Pakistan, Bangladesh, the United Republic of Tanzania and Mozambique. Older, better established and rather successful ventures can be counted in Mexico, Brazil, India and several other middle-income countries.

According to the official company account: "Generating growth in emerging markets is a key business priority for Unilever. These markets are set to overtake the advanced industrial countries in their share of world output by the year 2000. Unilever already has a strong presence in emerging markets."

Rationalizing its strategy as one of diversification and market winning, the company statement goes on by describing its product innovation philosophy: "A 'broad product base' is more than an expression of size. It conveys strategic flexibility. Unilever can enter a market through the product category which is most relevant: it may be laundry soap (Brazil), margarine (Hungary), tea (Arabia) or detergents (Thailand). It can then gradually build its business by introducing other categories."

Pepsico and Coca Cola still at the top of the industry, respectively in first, third, fifth and sixth place in the worldwide ranking by turnover, while the Swiss Nestlé and the Dutch-English Unilever occupy second and fourth position.

The need to control the supply of raw materials and the increasing concentration of the industry has resulted in a process of expansion based on foreign subsidiaries. On average, the first 100 companies control 15 subsidiaries abroad, but this number reaches 42 for the 13 more internationalized companies. This process of expansion by subsidiaries has slowed down in the course of the last 15 years for the United States-based companies, while it has accelerated for the European ones. At the same time, the subsidiaries located in developing countries have increased in number and size, while the opposite has occurred for those located in the United States, Canada and continental Europe.

A POLICY ENVIRONMENT FOR AGRO-INDUSTRIAL DEVELOPMENT

Importance of economy-wide policies

To a very large extent promoting agro-industrial development and ensuring that agro-industry provides the optimal contribution to economic development depend on appropriate economic and other policies throughout the economy, more than on sector-specific policies and interventions. Worldwide experience has shown that competitive markets are the best way yet found for efficiently organizing the production and distribution of goods and services. Domestic and external competition provides the incentives that unleash entrepreneurship and technological progress. However, markets cannot operate in a vacuum – they require a legal and regulatory framework that only governments can provide. Also, there are many other tasks in which markets sometimes prove inadequate or fail altogether. That is why governments must, for example, invest in infrastructure and provide essential services for the poor. It is not a question of state or market: each has a large and irreplaceable role.

The consensus that has been gradually forming emphasizes the role of government in creating an enabling environment conducive to private sector investment, principally by providing a stable macroeconomic foundation and removing market distortions and rigidities through policy reforms. Without going into the components of such an economy-wide enabling environment,[7] the most general

aspect would be the need to establish a stable macroeconomic framework through sound monetary and fiscal policies that control inflation, limit budgetary deficits and public sector borrowing requirements and maintain realistic exchange rates. Other important elements would be open trade policies, an efficient financial system and liberal financial markets, together with free international capital movements. A favourable business environment also depends on the absence of legal and regulatory constraints to enterprise, such as price controls, investment licensing, etc. as well as the existence of modern business legislation, a reliable judicial system and liberal labour codes and landownership laws. Further elements in a favourable general economic environment would be efficient and non-distorting systems of taxation and the reduction of the public sector's role in productive activities, among other things, to avoid the diversion of allocations from important support services (such as infrastructure and education) required by the private sector.

Taking for granted the fundamental importance of an appropriate economy-wide enabling environment, the following section briefly identifies some of the key policy issues that are of particular importance for development of agro-industrial potential in developing countries. The discussion does not claim to introduce elements of originality, but can be said largely to reflect lessons of experience as well as the current consensus.

Promoting domestic agriculture

The specificity of agro-industry *vis-à-vis* other industrial sectors lies in the agricultural origin of a large part of its inputs. In most cases, for developing countries it is domestic agriculture which is, or would be, the main supplier of raw materials to agro-industry, just as the

---

[7] See FAO. 1995. *World agriculture: towards 2010*, Chap. 7, p. 257-293. Edited by N. Alexandratos. Rome, FAO and Chichester, UK, Wiley; and FAO. 1996. Socio-political and economic environment for food security. *World Food Summit technical background documents*, Vol. 1. Rome.

potential for agro-industrial development in developing countries is largely linked to the actual or potential availability of such agricultural inputs to the processing industries. For this reason, increasing the efficiency of domestic agriculture is an important aspect of promoting agro-industrial development. At the same time agro-industrial processing activities can themselves have a positive impact on efficiency in primary agriculture by promoting technological innovation and stimulating competition within the sector.[8]

Investment and technology policies

Governments have often sought to promote agro-industry by investing directly in state-owned enterprises, but have lacked sufficient familiarity with technical and market requirements to prepare adequate feasibility studies and make appropriate technological choices. Public investment projects designed by foreign consultants and funded by aid have too often turned out to be white elephants because the sponsors have lacked personal stakes in, or a long-term commitment to, the commercial viability of the project. Technical and managerial resources to run state-owned enterprises efficiently are generally scarce and, in any case, budgetary constraints are requiring governments to look increasingly to the private sector as the main source of investment in agro-industry.

Ways of raising technology levels in national agro-industry in the absence of direct government involvement in the sector include the tapping of the research and development capacities of multinational corporations by encouraging direct investment, promoting joint ventures and licensing and franchising arrangements and encouraging the secondment of their staff. Foreign manufacturers of agro-industrial machinery and equipment can be encouraged to establish plants or partnerships in developing countries to develop technology that is better adapted than much imported technology to the available raw materials, scales of production, worker skills and consumer requirements of the domestic markets in those countries. Also, freedom of entry should be granted to foreign and domestic suppliers of services to agro-industry, including accountants, technical consultants, suppliers of raw materials, intermediate inputs and equipment.

FDI can provide an important contribution to economic development in general, and to agro-industrial development in particular. The benefits of direct investment lie not only in attracting additional capital and skills but also in expediting the transfer and assimilation of technology and managerial expertise as well as in a readier access to international markets. An essential condition for attracting such investment is the existence of a generally favourable business environment, as discussed above. But other more specific measures aimed at encouraging direct investments would be the lifting of restrictions on entry by foreign firms as well as on their access to foreign exchange and on dividend and profit remittances, on foreign ownership of land and financial assets; and on the employment of expatriates.[9]

---

[8] The various technical, institutional and financial aspects involved in agricultural efficiency and development are discussed in FAO. 1996. *World Food Summit technical background documents*, Vol. 3. Rome.

---

[9] For a more detailed discussion of specific incentives to FDI, see WTO. 1996. *Annual Report 1996*. Geneva.

Protecting the environment

In order to minimize the impact of agro-industrial residues on the environment, administrative tools to limit such releases must be developed. The most direct is enforced legislation prohibiting the discharge of residues into the environment. This can be coupled with incentives such as soft loans to invest in control measures. Legislation can also be accompanied by economic disincentives that penalize polluting industries. Other measures, applicable according to the circumstances, may be pollution entitlement shares and permissible limits (including trade permits); taxes on inputs or resource use (e.g. on water) rather than on the level of pollutants; subsidies to invest in environmentally friendly technologies; fees to cover the costs of removing pollutants, etc. It is important in any case that standards and regulations be realistic, enforceable and consistent with the overall policy environment.

In many cases, prohibiting the release of residuals results in a more profitable use of raw materials.[10] The case of whey, discussed above, is an example. Others are the recovery of blood from slaughter operations and mill stream offals from cereals which can be converted into feeds, and the recovery of fish processing waste for food and feed products. Residues from the sugar and starch processing industries can be easily converted into fuel alcohol through fermentation. This would provide the double advantage of utilizing a processing residue and at the same time producing

an energy source that is less polluting than conventional fossil fuels.

Although technological means of improving the environmental performance of many industrial activities already exist, their mere existence does not guarantee that they will be adopted, especially by small firms. One effective way to influence small firms is through extension and advisory services for industries. For example, the Pollution Control Cell of the National Productivity Council in India's Ministry of Labour works to devise solutions that both reduce pollution and improve profits.

Generally, building pollution prevention into new agrifood investments is cheaper than adding it on later. Hence the importance of undertaking environmental impact assessments for proposed new large-scale investments. Developing countries with open markets will be able to gain from importing clean technologies already in use in industrial countries.

Protecting the consumer

For agro-industrial development to go ahead, it is important for countries to introduce and update national food legislation. Without up-to-date food laws, modern approaches to food control cannot be implemented, thus often preventing the efficient use of precious resources and impeding the government's authority and ability to regulate the food industry. With a properly administered modern food law, consumers and traders are provided the necessary assurances that build the type of confidence required for food products to be accepted as being of suitable quality and safety for both domestic consumption and trading in international markets. There is little doubt that trade at all levels has played a significant role in improving social, political and economic conditions

---

[10] See *Farming, processing and marketing systems for SARD*. FAO/Netherlands background document No. 4, Den Bosch Conference on Agriculture and the Environment, the Netherlands, 15-19 April 1991.

worldwide. Countries that increase their trade prospects by assuring safe and high-quality food products for international markets will benefit at the expense of those who do not.

FAO/WHO guidelines for developing food control systems lay down basic principles based on national practice and experience. They suggest that food law be kept simple with detailed specification about food processing, food standards, hygienic practices, packaging and labelling and food additives to be incorporated in a body of food regulations, rather than the food law. Prompt revisions of regulations may become necessary because of new scientific knowledge, changes in food processing technology or emergencies requiring quick action to protect public health. Such revisions can be made more expeditiously by executive agencies than by legislative bodies. Regulations must be written in clear, concise language and a regulation should be promulgated only when there is a recognized need for it. When a regulation is developed as a result of a recognized need, it is more likely to be practicable and acceptable to the regulated sector. Regulations that are prepared by the government with the participation of the affected industries, consumers and other interested parties hold the best chance of acceptability because the stakeholders have had a part in their development and recognized their need.

The national food control system should include appropriately organized, multidisciplinary and multipurpose functional units that collectively contribute to the overall official food control effort. This can be achieved through specialized government agencies in public health, agriculture or trade, or, in some cases, through a single food control agency with multidisciplinary subdivisions. A national food control system should include inspectional, investigational, analytical and compliance (regulatory or voluntary) functions; provide technical, advisory and educational services; and be oriented towards public service in terms of industry, media and the public. Decisions made by food control officials should be based on up-to-date scientific information, carried out in a transparent manner and represent a fair balance of the sometimes competing interests of consumer protection, industry and trade development.

The production and handling of food throughout the chain (from farm to table) must be carried out under appropriate conditions in compliance with established principles that are consistent, transparent and scientifically supported. Such principles should be an integral part of any national set of food standards and regulations, established under the authority of an up-to-date food law to protect public health and facilitate trade in food. Many of these principles already exist and were established by the Codex Alimentarius Commission (CAC) in a harmonized manner using hazard analysis and risk assessment methods. They include more than 40 different commodity-related codes of practice; the General Principles of Food Hygiene; a system of food safety based on the Guidelines on the Application of Hazard Analysis and Critical Control Point (HACCP); and Good Manufacturing Practices.

In addition, 237 standards for foods considered to be most important to international trade have been promulgated by CAC for adoption by the Member Governments of FAO and WHO. CAC has also evaluated the use of 185 different pesticides; set safe residue levels for 3 274 pesticides; established guidelines for the maximum levels of 25 environmental and industrial food contaminants; established acceptable daily intake levels of over 780 chemical additives to foods; and evaluated the use of 54 different veterinary drugs used in animal husbandry. These guidelines and standards should serve as a benchmark for national governments in the regulation of their food industry. National governments which meet the requirements of Codex standards are also presumed to meet the international requirements expressed in WTO's Agreement on the Application of Sanitary and Phytosanitary Measures for food safety in international trade, providing a competitive advantage and assurance of acceptability for traders worldwide. Compliance with these standards is essential for the protection of public health and for successful trade in both international and domestic markets.

ANNEX TABLE

Countries and territories used for statistical purposes

	Developed countries	Countries in transition	Developing countries	Developing regions			
				Sub-Saharan Africa	Asia and the Pacific	Latin America and the Caribbean	Near East and North Africa
Afghanistan			x				x
Albania	x	x					
Algeria			x				x
American Samoa			x		x		
Andorra	x						
Angola			x	x			
Anguilla			x			x	
Antigua and Barbuda			x			x	
Argentina			x			x	
Armenia	x	x					
Aruba			x			x	
Australia	x						
Austria	x						
Azerbaijan	x	x					
Bahamas			x			x	
Bahrain			x				x
Bangladesh			x		x		
Barbados			x			x	
Belarus	x	x					
Belgium/Luxembourg	x						
Belize			x			x	
Benin			x	x			
Bermuda			x			x	
Bhutan			x		x		
Bolivia			x			x	
Bosnia and Herzegovina	x	x					
Botswana			x	x			
Brazil			x			x	
British Virgin Islands			x		x		

(continued)

	Developed countries	Countries in transition	Developing countries	Developing regions			
				Sub-Saharan Africa	Asia and the Pacific	Latin America and the Caribbean	Near East and North Africa
Brunei Darussalam			x		x		
Bulgaria	x	x					
Burkina Faso			x	x			
Burundi			x	x			
Cambodia			x		x		
Cameroon			x	x			
Canada	x						
Cape Verde			x	x			
Cayman Islands			x			x	
Central African Rep.			x	x			
Chad			x	x			
Chile			x			x	
China			x		x		
Cocos Islands			x		x		
Colombia			x			x	
Comoros			x	x			
Congo, Rep.			x	x			
Cook Islands			x		x		
Costa Rica			x			x	
Côte d'Ivoire			x	x			
Croatia	x	x					
Cuba			x			x	
Cyprus			x				x
Czech Republic	x	x					
Democratic Republic of the Congo			x	x			
Denmark	x						
Djibouti			x	x			
Dominica			x			x	
Dominican Republic			x			x	
East Timor			x		x		
Ecuador			x			x	
Egypt			x				x

(continued)

	Developed countries	Countries in transition	Developing countries	Developing regions			
				Sub-Saharan Africa	Asia and the Pacific	Latin America and the Caribbean	Near East and North Africa
El Salvador			x			x	
Equatorial Guinea			x	x			
Eritrea			x	x			
Estonia	x	x					
Ethiopia			x	x			
Faeroe Islands	x						
Falkland Islands (Malvinas)			x			x	
Fiji			x		x		
Finland	x						
France	x						
French Guiana			x			x	
French Polynesia			x		x		
Gabon			x	x			
Gambia			x	x			
Gaza Strip			x				x
Georgia	x	x					
Germany	x						
Ghana			x	x			
Gibraltar	x						
Greece	x						
Greenland			x				
Grenada			x			x	
Guadeloupe			x			x	
Guam			x		x		
Guatemala			x			x	
Guinea			x	x			
Guinea-Bissau			x	x			
Guyana			x			x	
Haiti			x			x	
Honduras			x			x	
Hungary	x	x					
Iceland	x						
India			x		x		

(continued)

	Developed countries	Countries in transition	Developing countries	Developing regions			
				Sub-Saharan Africa	Asia and the Pacific	Latin America and the Caribbean	Near East and North Africa
Indonesia			x		x		
Iran, Islamic Rep.			x				
Iraq			x				x
Ireland	x						
Israel	x						
Italy	x						
Jamaica			x			x	
Japan	x						
Jordan			x				x
Kazakstan	x	x					
Kenya			x	x			
Kiribati			x		x		
Korea, Dem. People's Rep.			x		x		
Korea, Rep.			x		x		
Kuwait			x				x
Kyrgyzstan	x	x					
Laos			x		x		
Latvia	x	x					
Lebanon			x				x
Lesotho			x	x			
Liberia			x	x			
Libyan Arab Jamahiriya			x				x
Liechtenstein	x						
Lithuania	x	x					
Macau			x		x		
Madagascar			x	x			
Malawi			x	x			
Malaysia			x		x		
Maldives			x		x		
Mali			x	x			
Malta	x						
Marshall Islands			x		x		
Martinique			x			x	

(continued)

	Developed countries	Countries in transition	Developing countries	Developing regions			
				Sub-Saharan Africa	Asia and the Pacific	Latin America and the Caribbean	Near East and North Africa
Mauritania			x	x			
Mauritius			x	x			
Mexico			x			x	
Micronesia, Fed. States			x		x		
Monaco	x						
Mongolia			x		x		
Montserrat			x			x	
Morocco			x				x
Mozambique			x	x			
Myanmar			x		x		
Namibia			x	x			
Nauru			x		x		
Nepal			x		x		
Netherlands	x						
Netherlands Antilles			x			x	
New Caledonia			x		x		
New Zealand	x						
Nicaragua			x			x	
Niger			x	x			
Nigeria			x	x			
Niue			x		x		
Norfolk Islands			x		x		
Northern Mariana Islands			x		x		
Norway	x						
Oman			x				x
Pakistan			x		x		
Palau			x		x		
Panama			x			x	
Papua New Guinea			x		x		
Paraguay			x			x	
Peru			x			x	
Philippines			x		x		
Poland	x	x					

(continued)

	Developed countries	Countries in transition	Developing countries	Developing regions			
				Sub-Saharan Africa	Asia and the Pacific	Latin America and the Caribbean	Near East and North Africa
Portugal	x						
Puerto Rico			x			x	
Qatar			x				x
Republic of Moldova	x	x					
Réunion			x	x			
Romania	x	x					
Russian Federation	x	x					
Rwanda			x	x			
Saint Helena			x	x			
Saint Kitts and Nevis			x			x	
Saint Lucia			x			x	
Saint Pierre and Miquelon			x				
Saint Vincent and the Grenadines			x			x	
Samoa			x		x		
San Marino	x						
Sao Tome and Principe			x	x			
Saudi Arabia			x				x
Senegal			x	x			
Seychelles			x	x			
Sierra Leone			x	x			
Singapore			x		x		
Slovakia	x	x					
Slovenia	x	x					
Solomon Islands			x		x		
Somalia			x	x			
South Africa	x						
Spain	x						
Sri Lanka			x		x		
Sudan			x	x			x
Suriname			x			x	
Swaziland			x	x			
Sweden	x						
Switzerland	x						

(continued)

	Developed countries	Countries in transition	Developing countries	Developing regions			
				Sub-Saharan Africa	Asia and the Pacific	Latin America and the Caribbean	Near East and North Africa
Syrian Arab Republic			x				x
Taiwan Province of China			x		x		
Tajikistan	x	x					
Tanzania, United Rep.			x	x			
Thailand			x		x		
The Former Yugoslav Republic of Macedonia	x	x					
Togo			x	x			
Tokelau			x		x		
Tonga			x		x		
Trinidad and Tobago			x			x	
Tunisia			x				x
Turkey			x				x
Turkmenistan	x	x					
Turks and Caicos Islands			x			x	
Tuvalu			x		x		
Uganda			x	x			
Ukraine	x	x					
United Arab Emirates			x				x
United Kingdom	x						
United States	x						
United States Virgin Islands			x			x	
Uruguay			x			x	
Uzbekistan	x	x					
Vanuatu			x		x		
Venezuela			x			x	
Viet Nam			x		x		
Wallis and Futuna Islands			x		x		
West Bank			x				x
Yemen			x				x
Yugoslavia	x	x					
Zambia			x	x			
Zimbabwe			x	x			

Special chapters

In addition to the usual review of the recent world food and agricultural situation, each issue of this report since 1957 has included one or more special studies on problems of longer-term interest. Special chapters in earlier issues have covered the following subjects:

1957
Factors influencing the trend of food consumption
Postwar changes in some institutional factors affecting agriculture

1958
Food and agricultural developments in Africa south of the Sahara
The growth of forest industries and their impact on the world's forests

1959
Agricultural incomes and levels of living in countries at different stages of economic development
Some general problems of agricultural development in less-developed countries in the light of postwar experience

1960
Programming for agricultural development

1961
Land reform and institutional change
Agricultural extension, education and research in Africa, Asia and Latin America

1962
The role of forest industries in the attack on economic underdevelopment
The livestock industry in less-developed countries

1963
Basic factors affecting the growth of productivity in agriculture
Fertilizer use: spearhead of agricultural development

1964
Protein nutrition: needs and prospects
Synthetics and their effects on agricultural trade

1966
Agriculture and industrialization
Rice in the world food economy

1967
Incentives and disincentives for farmers in developing countries
The management of fishery resources

1968
Raising agricultural productivity in developing countries through technological improvement
Improved storage and its contribution to world food supplies

1969
Agricultural marketing improvement programmes: some lessons from recent experience
Modernizing institutions to promote forestry development

1970
Agriculture at the threshold of the Second Development Decade

1971
Water pollution and its effects on living aquatic resources and fisheries

1972
Education and training for development
Accelerating agricultural research in the developing countries

1973
Agricultural employment in developing countries

1974
Population, food supply and agricultural development

1975
The Second United Nations Development Decade: mid-term review and appraisal

1976
Energy and agriculture

1977
The state of natural resources and the human environment for food and agriculture

1978
Problems and strategies in developing regions

1979
Forestry and rural development

1980
Marine fisheries in the new era of national jurisdiction

1981
Rural poverty in developing countries and means of poverty alleviation

1982
Livestock production: a world perspective

1983
Women in developing agriculture

1984
Urbanization, agriculture and food systems

1985
Energy use in agricultural production
Environmental trends in food and agriculture
Agricultural marketing and development

1986
Financing agricultural development

1987-88
Changing priorities for agricultural science and technology in developing countries

1989
Sustainable development and natural resource management

1990
Structural adjustment and agriculture

1991
Agricultural policies and issues: lessons from the 1980s and prospects for the 1990s

1992
Marine fisheries and the law of the sea: a decade of change

1993
Water policies and agriculture

1994
Forest development and policy dilemmas

1995
Agricultural trade: entering a new era?

1996
Food security: some macroeconomic dimensions

FAO Economic and Social Development Papers

ENVIRONMENT AND SUSTAINABLE DEVELOPMENT STUDIES

107 Land reform and structural adjustment in sub-Saharan Africa: controversies and guidelines (J.-Ph. Platteau, 1992). French version: Réforme agraire et ajustement structurel en Afrique subsaharienne: controverses et orientations

110 Agricultural sustainability: definition and implications for agricultural and trade policy (T. Young, 1992)

121 Policies for sustainable development: four essays (A. Markandya, 1994)

132 The economics of international agreements for the protection of environmental and agricultural services (S. Barrett, 1996)

138 Economic development and environmental policy (S. Barrett, 1997)

139 Population pressure and management of natural resources. An economic analysis of traditional management of small-scale fishing (J.M. Baland and J.P. Platteau, 1996)

- Halting degradation of natural resources. Is there a role for rural communities? (J.-M. Baland and J.-Ph. Platteau, 1996). Published by Oxford University Press

In preparation

- The implications of regional trading arrangements for agricultural trade (T. Josling)
- Temporary trade shocks and structural adjustment in sub-Saharan Africa (J. Harrigan)
- Growth and trade: an investigative survey (P.L. Scandizzo and M. Spinedi)
- Elasticity of supply response by farmers in developing countries: the role of institutional constraints (A. de Janvry and E. Sadoulet)
- The role of group size and homogeneity in collective action, with special reference to common property resource arrangements (J.-Ph. Platteau and J.-M. Baland)

To acquire ESD papers please write to:
Sales and Marketing Group
Food and Agriculture Organization of the United Nations
Viale delle Terme di Caracalla
00100 Rome
Italy

TIME SERIES FOR SOFA'97 DISKETTE
Instructions for use

As in past years, *The State of Food and Agriculture 1997* includes a computer diskette containing time series data for about 150 countries and the necessary software, FAOSTAT TS, to access and display these time series.

FAOSTAT TS

FAOSTAT TS software provides quick and easy access to structured annual time series databases. Even inexperienced computer users can use FAOSTAT TS, which does not require spreadsheet, graphics or database programs. FAOSTAT TS is fully menu-driven, so there are no commands to learn. Users can browse through and print graphs and tables, plot multiple-line graphs, fit trend lines and export data for use in other programs. FAOSTAT TS is trilingual (English, French, Spanish) and uses a standard menu format.

FAOSTAT TS software is in the public domain and may be freely distributed. The data files accompanying the software, however, are under FAO copyright, and users must attribute FAO as the source. FAO may provide only very limited support to users of this software and the accompanying data and cannot assist users who modify the software or data files. FAO disclaims all warrants of fitness for the software or data for a particular use.

Technical requirements

FAOSTAT TS software requires an IBM or compatible PC with a hard disk, DOS 3.0 or later version, 300 KB of available RAM and graphics capability. Graphics support is provided for all common graphics adaptors (VGA, EGA, MCGA, CGA and Hercules monochrome).

FAOSTAT TS will print graphs on Epson dot matrix, Hewlett-Packard and compatible laser printers. To use FAOSTAT TS with other printers, users can enable their own graphics printing utility before starting the program. One such utility is GRAPHICS.COM in DOS 2.0 or later version.

Because of its use of DOS graphics modes, if FAOSTAT TS is run under MS-Windows or OS/2, it should be set to run in a full-screen DOS session.

Installation

Before running FAOSTAT TS you must install the software and data files on your hard disk. Installation is automated through the INSTALL.BAT utility on the diskette.
- To install from drive A: to drive C:
Insert the diskette in drive A:
  - Type **A:** and press **ENTER.**
  - Type **INSTALL C:** and press **ENTER.**
  - Press any key.

A C:\SOFA97 directory is created and, after installation, you will already be in this directory.

Entering FAOSTAT TS

- To start the FAOSTAT TS software, if you are not already in the C:\SOFA97 directory (as after installation):
  - Change to this directory by typing **CD\SOFA97** and pressing **ENTER.**
  - From the command prompt in the SOFA97 directory, type **SOFA97** and press **ENTER.**

A graphics title screen will be displayed, followed by the main menu screen.

If FAOSTAT TS does not start, graphs do not display correctly or the menus are difficult to read, your computer may not be compatible with the default functions of FAOSTAT TS. The use of a command-line option may help. You may try to start FAOSTAT TS with the -E parameter (by typing **SOFA97-E**) to disable its use of expanded memory. You may also force the use of a particular graphics or text mode by typing its name as a parameter (e.g. -EGA would force the use of EGA mode graphics).

Language choices

The initial default language for FAOSTAT TS is English. To change the default language to French or Spanish:
- Go to the **FILE** menu.
- Select **LANGUAGE** using the **ARROW** key (↓) and pressing **ENTER.**
- Select your choice of language and press **ENTER**.

The language selected will remain the default language until another is selected.

Navigating the menus

The main menu bar consists of FILE, DATA, GRAPH, TABLE and HELP menus. Most menu options are disabled until you open a data file. Navigate the menus by using the **ARROW** keys (↑↓↔) and make a selection by highlighting an item and pressing **ENTER**. To back out of a selection, press the **ESC** key.

• If you have a mouse, menu items can be selected with the mouse cursor. The left mouse button selects an item and the right mouse button acts as the ESC key.

After you have made a menu selection, the menu will redraw and highlight a possible next choice.

• Several shortcut keys are available throughout the program:

Key	Action
F1	- HELP: displays context-sensitive help text.
ESC	- ESCAPE: backs out of the current menu choice or exits the current graph or table.
ALT+N	- NOTES: displays text notes associated with the current data file, if the text file is available. This text may be edited. Notes will not appear while a graph is displayed.
ALT+X, ALT+Q	- Exit: exits FAOSTAT TS immediately, without prompting.

Help

• You will see context-sensitive help displayed at the bottom of each screen. Press **F1** for more extensive help on a highlighted option.

• Select **HELP** from the main menu to access the help information. Introductory information on the software, help topics and an "About" summary screen are available from the **HELP** menu.

•The **HELP** menu options call up the same windows obtained by pressing the **F1** key at any of the menu screens:
- FAOSTAT TS displays the top-level help page.
- TOPICS lists the help contents.
- ABOUT shows summary program information.

Opening a data file

• To display a list of FAOSTAT TS data files:
- Go to the **FILE** menu.
- Select **OPEN**.

All of the FAOSTAT TS data files in the current directory are displayed. Initially, only SOFA97 will be present. Other FAOSTAT PC data files, version 3.0, can be used with FAOSTAT TS.

• Use the **ARROW** keys to highlight the file you wish to view and press **ENTER** to select it. Files are shown with the date of their last revision. You can also highlight your choice by typing the first letters of the filename. The current search string will appear in the lower left corner of the list.

• You can change the default data drive and directory from the file list by selecting the directory or drive of your choice.

If a current data file is open, loading in a new file will return FAOSTAT TS to its defaults (time trend, no trend line, no user-specified units or scalar). Only one file can be loaded at a time.

Once you have made a file selection, all the menu selections are activated.

Selecting a data series

• Use the **DATA** menu to select or modify a data series or to fit a statistical trend.

• Select a data series by choosing the name of a country and a data element from scrolling menus. The first entry displays a list of country names, the second entry displays a list of data item names and the third displays a list of data element names.

If you type the first letters of a name in a list, the menu selection bar will jump to the matching name. For example:

- Type **NEW** to skip to New Zealand.
- Press **ENTER** to select the highlighted name.

Displaying graphs and graph options

The **GRAPH** menu allows you to view the data in chart form. You can display time trends and table or column profiles. Options under the **GRAPH** menu change the data series shown as well as its display.

For example, to show a plot of the data selected:

- Go to the **GRAPH** menu.
- Select **DISPLAY**.

Many options to modify, save or print a graph are available only while the graph is on-screen. Remember to use the F1 help key for a reminder of your options.

Graph action keys. You have several options when a graph is displayed:

- Press **ESC** to exit the graph and return to the main menu.
- Press **F1** for help on the graph action keys. The help box lists the choices available while a graph is on-screen. You must exit the help box before making a selection.
- Press the **ARROW** (↑↓) and **PAGEUP**, **PAGEDOWN** keys to change the series displayed.
- The plus key (**+**) allows you to add from one to three additional series to the one displayed. Press the **MINUS** key (**-**) to remove a series. To create a multiline chart:
  - Display an initial series.
  - Press the **+** key to add subsequent series to the chart.
- Press **A** to display a table of the axis data with statistics. Press **T** to show a table of the fitted trend data, the residuals and fit statistics (if a trend line is selected, see below).
- The **INS** key permits you to insert text directly on the graph. While inserting text, press **F1** for help on your text options. You can type small or large, horizontal or vertical text.

- To print a graph, press **P** and select your choice of printer from the menu. The print output is only a screen dump of the display, so the quality is limited.
- To save a graph for later printing or viewing, press **S**. The graph image will be saved in the common PCX bitmap format. You can use the PRINTPCX program or other software to view or print multiple images later. PRINTPCX also permits you to convert colour PCX images into black and white images suitable for inclusion in a word processing document.

Fitting trend lines

- To fit a statistical function to a data series, select **FIT** from the **DATA** menu. The options under **FIT** allow you to select the type of function, data year limits to include in the fit and a final projection year for a statistical forecast.
- By fitting a trend line (selecting the option under **FIT**) with a projection (selecting **PROJECTION** under **FIT**), a statistical forecast can be plotted. Use the **+** key to add a new data series to the graph, which can be made with only a few key strokes.

Charting profiles

The options under the **GRAPH** menu allow you to change the year span or style of the graph display (options **LIMITS** and **STYLE**, respectively), or to switch from a time trend to a table or column data profile (**VIEWPOINT**). The **VIEWPOINT** option is an easy means to compare data for a particular year.

Viewpoint

- If you want to change from a time series display to a country or item profile display for a given year, select **VIEWPOINT** from the **GRAPH** menu. Select **DISPLAY** from the **GRAPH** menu, and the profile will be drawn. The initial profile display is for the last year of historical data. To change the year, use the **ARROW** (↑↓) keys. Press **F1** for help.
- For a tables profile (profile of data across countries), you can either choose the tables to be displayed or let FAOSTAT TS select the top members and array them in order.

A limit of 50 items can appear in one profile. By selecting **TOP MEMBERS** instead of **SELECTED MEMBERS**, FAOSTAT TS will sort the values in the file and display a ranking of table or column values.

Viewing tables

• The **TABLE** menu allows you to look at data in a tabular format and to define subset tables that may be saved and imported into other software packages.
 - Go to the **TABLE** menu.
 - Select **BROWSE DATA** to view individual data tables from the current file.

• When viewing tables, a help bar appears at the bottom of the screen. Press **PAGEUP** or **PAGEDOWN** to change the table displayed or press **ALT+1** or **ALT+2** to choose from a list of tables. Use the **ARROW** keys ($\uparrow\downarrow\leftrightarrow$) to scroll the columns and rows.

Series data

• The I **SERIES DATA** option under the **TABLE** menu displays the last data series selected, including summary statistics. This is the series used to plot a graph. To change the series, you must make a new choice from the **DATA** menu.

• The **SERIES DATA** screen can also be displayed while you are in a graph by pressing the letter **A**. If more than one series has been plotted, only the last series is shown. The range of years used for the series and statistics can be adjusted through the **LIMITS** option under the **GRAPH** menu.

• To view country or item profile lists and statistics, select **VIEWPOINT** from the **GRAPH** menu. You can quickly see a list of the tables with the greatest values (for example, countries with the highest commodity consumption) by choosing a table profile from **VIEWPOINT** and selecting the **TOP MEMBERS** option. Then select **SERIES DATA** from the **TABLE** menu to view the list or select **DISPLAY** from the **GRAPH** menu to plot a chart.

Trend data

• If the **FIT** option has been selected (from the

DATA menu) for a time trend, then the values composing the trend can be displayed with the **TREND DATA** option. Summary statistics for the original series and for the trend as well as residual values are included. The list scrolls with the **ARROW** keys, and you can toggle between the axis and trend data with the **A** and **T** keys.

Exporting data

• The **EXPORT** option under the **FILE** menu allows you to export FAOSTAT TS data into other file formats or to create custom tables for viewing or printing. By selecting **EXPORT**, you will jump into another set of menus.

• To select the tables and columns you want to view or save, go to the **DATA** menu. You must mark your choice of options with the + key. To undo all your selections quickly, select **RESET MARKS**.

• To arrange, view, save or print data, go to the options under **EXPORT** (in the **FILE** menu):
 - **FAO TABLE** creates a table with data from the last four available years.
 - **VIEW** displays a temporary text file of the data selected. It is a convenient way to view a subset of the tables and columns in a FAOSTAT TS file and can also be used to see the effects of the **ORIENTATION** or **LAYOUT** selections before using the **SAVE** or **PRINT** option.
 - **SAVE** displays a list of file formats to let you save your data choices in a file. You will be prompted for a file name. If you need to export FAOSTAT TS data for use with other software, use this menu item. The WK1 and DBF file format selections are not affected by the **LAYOUT** options (see below).
 - **PRINT** prints your current table and column selections. Many printers cannot print more than five columns of FAOSTAT TS data. Select **VIEW** to check the table width before printing.
 - **LAYOUT** allows you to display years across rows or down columns. The default direction is down columns.

• To get back to the main FAOSTAT TS menu or to clear your selections and create more tables, go to the **RETURN** option.

Making notes

• To read or edit textual information on the current data file, select **NOTES** from the **FILE** menu. You also can call up the Notes box by pressing **ALT+N** at any of the menus. The option **NOTES** allows you to read or edit text associated with the data file.

DOS shell and exit

The **DOS SHELL** option under the **FILE** menu returns you to the DOS prompt temporarily but keeps FAOSTAT TS in memory. This is not the normal way to exit the program. It is useful if you need to execute a DOS command and would like to return to the same data file. The data file itself is dropped from memory and reloaded on return, so default values will be in effect.

Exiting FAOSTAT TS

• To exit FAOSTAT TS:
  - Go to the **FILE** menu.
  - Select **EXIT**.
The Alt+X or Alt+Q key combinations are short-cuts to exit the program from almost any screen.

• ANGOLA
Empresa Nacional do Disco e de
Publicações, ENDIPU-U.E.E.
Rua Cirilo da Conceição Silva, Nº 7
C.P. Nº 1314-C
Luanda

• ARGENTINA
Librería Agropecuaria
Pasteur 743
1028 Buenos Aires
Oficina del Libro Internacional
Av. Córdoba 1877
1120 Buenos Aires

• AUSTRALIA
Hunter Publications
P.O. Box 404
Abbotsford, Vic. 3067

• AUSTRIA
Gerold Buch & Co.
Weihburggasse 26
1010 Vienna

• BANGLADESH
Association of Development
Agencies in Bangladesh
House No. 1/3, Block F,
Lalmatia
Dhaka 1207

• BELGIQUE
M.J. De Lannoy
202, avenue du Roi
1060 Bruxelles
CCP 000-0808993-13
E-mail: jean.de.lannoy@infoboard.be

• BOLIVIA
Los Amigos del Libro
Av. Heroínas 311, Casilla 450
Cochabamba;
Mercado 1315
La Paz

• BOTSWANA
Botsalo Books (Pty) Ltd
P.O. Box 1532
Gaborone

• BRAZIL
Book Master Livraria
Rua do Catete 311 lj. 118/119
22220-001 Catete
Rio de Janeiro
Editora da Universidade Federal
do Rio Grande do Sul
Av. João Pessoa 415
Bairro Cidade Baixa 90
040-000 Porto Alegre/RS
Fundação Getúlio Vargas
Praia do Botafogo 190, C.P. 9052
Rio de Janeiro
E-mail: valeria@sede.fgvrj.br
Núcleo Editora da Universidade
Federal Fluminense
Rua Miguel de Frias 9
Icaraí-Niterói 24
220-000 Rio de Janeiro
Fundação da Universidade
Federal do Paraná - FUNPAR
Rua Alfredo Bufrem 140, 30º andar
80020-240 Curitiba

• CANADA
BERNAN Associates (ex UNIPUB)
4611/F Assembly Drive
Lanham, MD 20706-4391
Toll-free 800 274-4888
Fax 301-459-0056
Website: www.bernan.com
E-mail: info@bernan.com
Guérin - Editeur
4501, rue Drolet
Montréal, Québec H2T 2G2
Tel. (514) 842-3481
Fax (514) 842-4923

Renouf Publishing
5369 chemin Canotek Road, Unit 1
Ottawa, Ontario K1J 9J3
Tel. (613) 745-2665
Fax (613) 745 7660
Website: www.renoufbooks.com
E-mail: renouf@fox.nstn.ca

• CHILE
Librería - Oficina Regional FAO
Calle Bandera 150, 8º Piso
Casilla 10095, Santiago-Centro
Tel. 699 1005
Fax 696 1121/696 1124
E-mail: german.rojas@field.fao.org
Universitaria Textolibros Ltda.
Avda. L. Bernardo O'Higgins 1050
Santiago

• CHINA
China National Publications
Import & Export Corporation
16 Gongti East Road
Beijing 100020
Tel. 6506 30 70
Fax 6506 3101
E-mail: cnpiec@public.3.bta.net.cn

• COLOMBIA
Banco Ganadero
Vicepresidencia de Fomento
Carrera 9ª Nº 72-21, Piso 5
Bogotá D.E.
Tel. 217 0100

• CONGO
Office national des librairies
populaires
B.P. 577
Brazzaville

• COSTA RICA
Librería Lehmann S.A.
Av. Central, Apartado 10011
1000 San José

• CÔTE D'IVOIRE
CEDA
04 B.P. 541
Abidjan 04

• CUBA
Ediciones Cubanas
Empresa de Comercio Exterior
de Publicaciones
Obispo 461, Apartado 605
La Habana

• CZECH REPUBLIC
Artia Pegas Press Ltd
Import of Periodicals
Palác Metro, P.O. Box 825
Národní 25
111 21 Praha 1

• DENMARK
Munksgaard, Book and
Subscription Service
P.O. Box 2148
DK 1016 Copenhagen K.
Tel. 4533128570
Fax 4533129387
Website: www.munksgaard.dk; E-mail:
subscription.service@mail.munksgaard.dk

• DOMINICAN REPUBLIC
CUESTA - Centro del libro
Av. 27 de Febrero, esq. A. Lincoln
Centro Comercial Nacional
Apartado 1241
Santo Domingo

• ECUADOR
Libri Mundi, Librería Internacional
Juan León Mera 851
Apartado Postal 3029
Quito
E-mail: librimul@librimundi.com.ec

Universidad agraria del Ecuador
Centro de Información Agraria
Av. 23 de Julio, Apdo 09-01-1248
Guayaquil
Librería Española
Murgeón 364 y Ulloa
Quito

• EGYPT
The Middle East Observer
41 Sherif Street, Cairo
E-mail: fouda@soficom.com.eg

• ESPAÑA
Librería Agrícola
Fernando VI 2
28004 Madrid
Librería de la Generalitat de
Catalunya
Rambla dels Estudis 118 (Palau Moja)
08002 Barcelona
Tel. (93) 302 6462
Fax (93) 302 1299
Mundi Prensa Libros S.A.
Castelló 37
28001 Madrid
Tel. 431 3399
Fax 575 3998
Website: www.tsai.es/MPRENSA
E-mail: mundiprensa@tsai.es
Mundi Prensa - Barcelona
Consejo de Ciento 391
08009 Barcelona
Tel. 301 8615
Fax 317 0141

• FINLAND
Akateeminen Kirjakauppa
Subscription Services
P.O. Box 23
FIN-00371 Helsinki

• FRANCE
Editions A. Pedone
13, rue Soufflot
75005 Paris
Lavoisier Tec & Doc
14, rue de Provigny
94236 Cachan Cedex
Website: www.lavoisier.fr
E-mail: livres@lavoisier.fr
Librairie du Commerce
International
10, avenue d'Iéna
75783 Paris Cedex 16
E-mail: pl@net-export.fr
Website: www.cfce.fr

• GERMANY
Alexander Horn Internationale
Buchhandlung
Friedrichstrasse 34
D-65185 Wiesbaden
S. Toeche-Mittler GmbH
Versandbuchhandlung
Hindenburgstrasse 33
D-64295 Darmstadt
Uno Verlag
Poppelsdorfer Allee 55
D-53115 Bonn 1

• GHANA
SEDCO Publishing Ltd
Sedco House, Tabon Street
Off Ring Road Central, North Ridge
P.O. Box 2051, Accra

• GREECE
Papasotiriou S.A.
35 Stournara Str., 10682 Athens
Tel. +301 3302 980
Fax +301 3648254

• GUYANA
Guyana National Trading
Corporation Ltd
45-47 Water Street, P.O. Box 308
Georgetown

• HAÏTI
Librairie «A la Caravelle»
26, rue Bonne Foi
B.P. 111
Port-au-Prince

• HONDURAS
Escuela Agrícola Panamericana
Librería RTAC
El Zamorano, Apartado 93
Tegucigalpa
Oficina de la Escuela Agrícola
Panamericana en Tegucigalpa
Blvd. Morazán, Apts. Glapson
Apartado 93
Tegucigalpa

• HUNGARY
Librotrade Kft.
P.O. Box 126
H-1656 Budapest

• INDIA
EWP Affiliated East-West
Press PVT, Ltd
G-I/16, Ansari Road, Darya Gany
New Delhi 110 002
Oxford Book and Stationery Co.
Scindia House
New Delhi 110 001;
17 Park Street
Calcutta 700 016
Oxford Subscription Agency
Institute for Development Education
1 Anasuya Ave, Kilpauk
Madras 600 010
Periodical Expert Book Agency
G-56, 2nd Floor, Laxmi Nagar
Vikas Marg, Delhi 110092

• IRAN
The FAO Bureau, International
and Regional Specialized
Organizations Affairs
Ministry of Agriculture of the Islamic
Republic of Iran
Keshavarz Bld, M.O.A., 17th floor
Teheran

• IRELAND
Publications Section
Government Stationery Office
4-5 Harcourt Road
Dublin 2

• ISRAEL
R.O.Y. International
P.O. Box 13056
Tel Aviv 61130
E-mail: royil@netvision.net.il

• ITALY
FAO Bookshop
Viale delle Terme di Caracalla
00100 Roma
Tel. 5225 5688
Fax 5225 5155
E-mail: publications-sales@fao.org
Libreria Commissionaria Sansoni
S.p.A. - Licosa
Via Duca di Calabria 1/1
50125 Firenze
E-mail: licosa@ftbcc.it
Libreria Scientifica Dott. Lucio de
Biasio "Aeiou"
Via Coronelli 6
20146 Milano

• JAPAN
Far Eastern Booksellers
(Kyokuto Shoten Ltd)
12 Kanda-Jimbocho 2 chome
Chiyoda-ku - P.O. Box 72
Tokyo 101-91
Maruzen Company Ltd
P.O. Box 5050
Tokyo International 100-31
E-mail: h_sugiyama@maruzen.co.jp

WHERE TO PURCHASE FAO PUBLICATIONS LOCALLY
POINTS DE VENTE DES PUBLICATIONS DE LA FAO
PUNTOS DE VENTA DE PUBLICACIONES DE LA FAO

6/97

KENYA
Text Book Centre Ltd
Kijabe Street
P.O. Box 47540
Nairobi

LUXEMBOURG
M.J. De Lannoy
202, avenue du Roi
1060 Bruxelles (Belgique)
E-mail: jean.de.lannoy@infoboard.be

MADAGASCAR
Centre d'Information et de
Documentation Scientifique et
Technique
Ministère de la recherche appliquée
au développement
BP 6224 Tsimbazaza
Antananarivo

MALAYSIA
Electronic products only:
Southbound
Sendirian Berhad Publishers
College Square
250 Penang

MALI
Librairie Traore
Rue Soundiata Keita X 115
B.P. 3243
Bamako

MAROC
La Librairie Internationale
70 Rue T'ssoule
B.P. 302 (RP)
Rabat
Tel. (07) 75-86-61

MEXICO
Librería, Universidad Autónoma de
Chapingo
56230 Chapingo
Libros y Editoriales S.A.
Av. Progreso Nº 202-1º Piso A
Apdo. Postal 18922
Col. Escandón
11800 México D.F.

NETHERLANDS
Roodveldt Import b.v.
Brouwersgracht 288
1013 HG Amsterdam
E-mail: roodboek@euronet.nl
Swets & Zeitlinger b.v.
P.O. Box 830, 2160 Lisse
Heereweg 347 B, 2161 CA Lisse

NEW ZEALAND
Legislation Services
P.O. Box 12418
Thorndon, Wellington
E-mail: gppmjxf@gp.co.nz

NICARAGUA
Librería HISPAMER
Costado Este Univ. Centroamericana
Apdo. Postal A-221
Managua
Universidad centroamericana
Apartado 69
Managua

NIGERIA
University Bookshop (Nigeria) Ltd
University of Ibadan
Ibadan

NORWAY
NIC Info A/S
Bertrand Narvesens vei 2
P.O. Box 6512, Etterstad
0606 Oslo 6
Tel. (+47) 22-57-33-00
Fax (+47) 22-68-19-01

● **PAKISTAN**
Mirza Book Agency
65 Shahrah-e-Quaid-e-Azam
P.O. Box 729, Lahore 3

● **PARAGUAY**
Librería Intercontinental
Editora e Impresora S.R.L.
Caballero 270 c/Mcal Estigarribia
Asunción

● **PERU**
INDEAR
Jirón Apurimac 375, Casilla 4937
Lima 1
Peruvian Book Central S.r.l.
Jr. Los Lirios 520 - A.P. 733
Lima
Universidad Nacional "Pedro Ruiz
Gallo"
Facultad de Agronomía, A.P. 795
Lambayeque (Chiclayo)

● **PHILIPPINES**
International Booksource Center,
Inc.
Room 720, Cityland 10 Tower 2
H.V. de la Costa, Cor. Valero St
Makati, Metro Manila

● **POLAND**
Ars Polona
Krakowskie Przedmiescie 7
00-950 Warsaw

● **PORTUGAL**
Livraria Portugal, Dias e Andrade
Ltda.
Rua do Carmo 70-74
Apartado 2681
1200 Lisboa Codex

● **SINGAPORE**
Select Books Pte Ltd
03-15 Tanglin Shopping Centre
19 Tanglin Road
Singapore 1024

● **SLOVAK REPUBLIC**
Institute of Scientific and
Technical
Information for Agriculture
Samova 9
950 10 Nitra
Tel. +42 87 522 185
Fax +42 87 525 275
E-mail: uvtip@nr.sanet.sk

● **SOMALIA**
Samater
P.O. Box 936, Mogadishu

● **SOUTH AFRICA**
David Philip Publishers (Pty) Ltd
P.O. Box 23408
Claremont 7735
Tel. Cape Town (021) 64-4136
Fax Cape Town (021) 64-3358

● **SRI LANKA**
M.D. Gunasena & Co. Ltd
217 Olcott Mawatha, P.O. Box 246
Colombo 11

● **SUISSE**
Buchhandlung und Antiquariat
Heinimann & Co.
Kirchgasse 17
8001 Zurich
UN Bookshop
Palais des Nations
CH-1211 Genève 1
Website: www.un.org
Van Diermen Editions Techniques
ADECO
41 Lacuez
CH-1807 Blonzy

● **SURINAME**
Vaco n.v. in Suriname
Domineestraat 26, P.O. Box 1841
Paramaribo

● **SWEDEN**
Books and documents:
C.E. Fritzes
P.O. Box 16356
103 27 Stockholm
Subscriptions:
Information Services AB
P.O. Box 1305
171 25 Solna

● **THAILAND**
Suksapan Panit
Mansion 9, Rajdamnern Avenue
Bangkok

● **TOGO**
Librairie du Bon Pasteur
B.P. 1164, Lomé

● **TUNISIE**
Société tunisienne de diffusion
5, avenue de Carthage
Tunis

● **TURKEY**
Kultur Yayiniari is - Turk Ltd Sti.
Ataturk Bulvari Nº 191, Kat. 21
Ankara
Bookshops in Istanbul and Izmir
DUNYA INFOTEL
Basin Yayin Haberlesme
Istikal Cad. Nº 649
80050 Tunel, Istanbul
Tel. 0212 251 9196
Fax 0212 251 9197

● **UNITED KINGDOM**
The Stationery Office
51 Nine Elms Lane
London SW8 5DR
Tel. (0171) 873 9090 (orders)
(0171) 873 0011 (inquiries)
Fax (0171) 873 8463
and through The Stationery Office
Bookshops
Website: www.the-stationery-office.co.uk
Electronic products only:
Microinfo Ltd
P.O. Box 3, Omega Road
Alton, Hampshire GU34 2PG
Tel. (01420) 86848
Fax (01420) 89889
Website: www.microinfo.co.uk
E-mail: emedia@microinfo.co.uk

● **URUGUAY**
Librería Agropecuaria S.R.L.
Buenos Aires 335, Casilla 1755
Montevideo C.P. 11000

● **UNITED STATES**
Publications:
BERNAN Associates (ex UNIPUB)
4611/F Assembly Drive
Lanham, MD 20706-4391
Toll-free 1-800-274-4447
Fax 301-459-0056
Website: www.bernan.com
E-mail: info@bernan.com
Periodicals:
Ebsco Subscription Services
P.O. Box 1943
Birmingham, AL 35201-1943
Tel. (205) 991-6600
Telex 78-2661
Fax (205) 991-1449
The Faxon Company Inc.
15 Southwest Park
Westwood, MA 02090
Tel. 6117-329-3350
Telex 95-1980
Cable FW Faxon Wood

● **VENEZUELA**
Fundación La Era Agrícola
Calle 31 Junín Qta Coromoto 5-49
Apartado 456
Mérida
Fundación para la Investigación
Agrícola
San Javier
Estado Yaracuy
Apartado Postal 182
San Felipe
Fax 054 44210
E-mail: damac@diero.conicit.ve
Fudeco, Librería
Avenida Libertador-Este
Ed. Fudeco, Apartado 254
Barquisimeto C.P. 3002, Ed. Lara
Tel. (051) 538 022
Fax (051) 544 394
Telex (051) 513 14 FUDEC VC
Librería FAGRO
Universidad Central de Venezuela
(UCV)
Maracay
Librería Universitaria, C.A.
Av. 3, entre 29 y 30 Nº 29-25
Edif. EVA
Mérida
Fax 074 52 09 56
Tamanaco Libros Técnicos S.R.L.
Centro Comercial Ciudad Tamanaco
Nivel C-2
Caracas
Tel. 261 3344/261 3335/959 0016
Tecni-Ciencia Libros S.A.
Torre Phelps-Mezzanina
Plaza Venezuela
Apartado Postal 20.315
1020 Caracas
Tel. 782 8697/781 9945/781 9954
E-mail: tchlibros@ibm.net
Tecni-Ciencia Libros, S.A.
Centro Comercial
Av. Andrés Eloy, Urb. El Prebo
Valencia, Ed. Carabobo
Tel. 222 724

● **ZIMBABWE**
Grassroots Books
100 Jason Moyo Avenue
P.O. Box A 267, Avondale
Harare;
61a Fort Street
Bulawayo

● **Other countries/Autres pays/
Otros países**
Sales and Marketing Group
Information Division, FAO
Viale delle Terme di Caracalla
00100 Rome, Italy
Tel. (39-6) 57051
Fax (39-6) 5705 3360
Telex 625852/625853/610181 FAO I
E-mail: publications-sales@fao.org